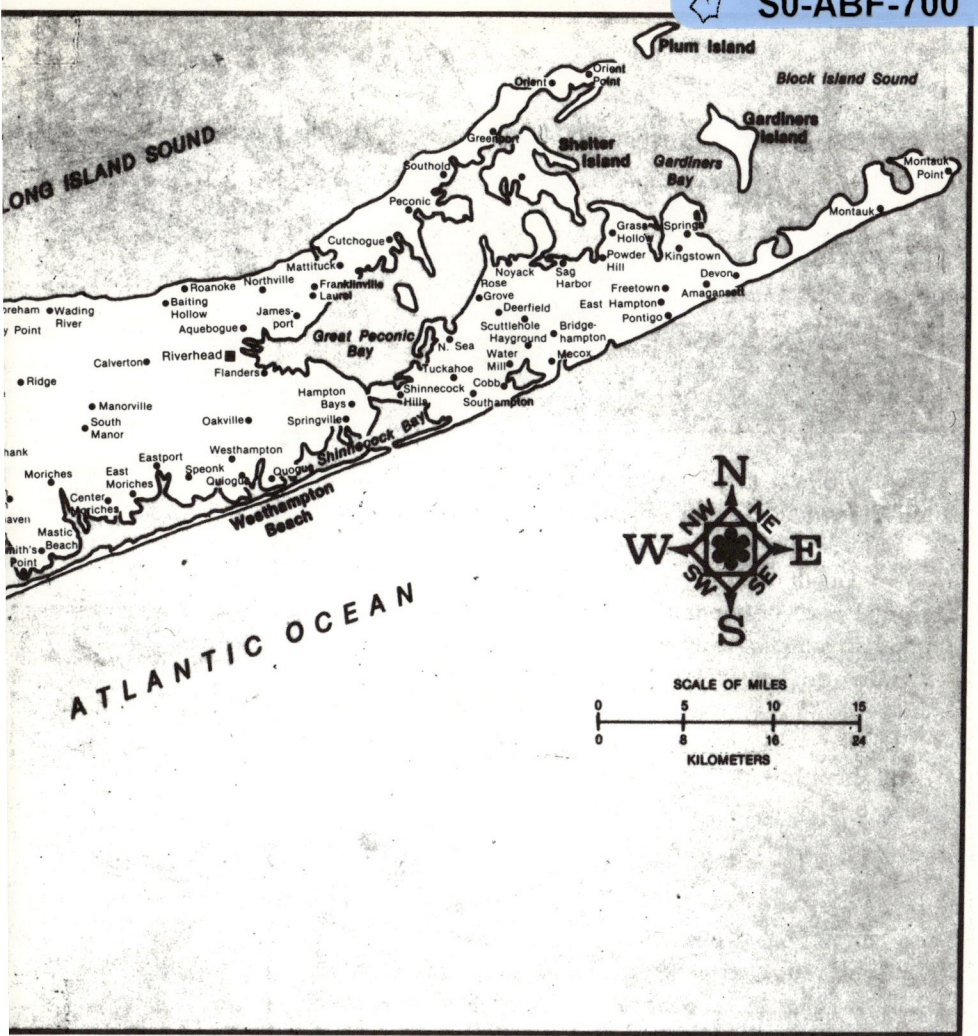

<u>Deer Park</u>: With 41.6 percent of the community of Italian ancestry, it is one of the Island's largest center of Italian American population.

<u>North Lindenhurst</u>: 40.1 percent of the population is of Italian extraction.

<u>Shirley</u>: One of the more recent centers of Italian American population, 40.1 percent of the people are of Italian background.

<u>Rocky Point</u>: Boasts of an Italian American population of 37.6 percent.

<u>North Babylon</u>: Houses a population of which 38.2 percent are of Italian background.

<u>Valley Stream</u>: 38 percent of the community is of Italian heritage.

<u>Selden</u>: 38.6 percent of the community is of Italian heritage.

<u>West Babylon</u>: 37.4 percent of the community is of Italian heritage.

FROM STEERAGE TO SUBURB:
LONG ISLAND ITALIANS

To Tony,

who appreciates his ethnic heritage

Auguri

Salvatore J. LaGumina

FROM STEERAGE TO SUBURB
LONG ISLAND ITALIANS

By
SALVATORE J. LAGUMINA

**1988
Center for Migration Studies
New York**

The Center for Migration Studies is an educational non-profit institute founded in New York in 1964 to encourage and facilitate the study of sociodemographic, economic, political, historical and legislative aspects of human migration and refugee movements. The opinions expressed in this work are those of the author.

FROM STEERAGE TO SUBURB
LONG ISLAND ITALIANS

First Edition

Copyright @ 1988 by

The Center for Migration Studies of New York, Inc.
209 Flagg Place
Staten Island, New York 10304-1199

Library of Congress Cataloging-in-Publication Data

```
LaGumina, Salvatore John, 1928-
    Immigrants in suburbia.

    Includes index.
    1. Italian Americans--New York (State)--Long Island--History.
2. Long Island (N.Y.)--History.  I. Title.
F127.L8L34   1987              974.7'2100451              87-20842
ISBN 0-934733-33-3  (Hardcover)          0-934733-28-7 (Paperback)
```

TABLE OF CONTENTS

xi
ACKNOWLEDGMENTS

1
CHAPTER ONE
FROM STEERAGE TO SUBURBS
Immigrants in Suburbia: Long Island's Italians

6
CHAPTER TWO
EARLY ITALIAN IMMIGRANTS
How This Garden Grew • Settlement Intermediaries • Port Washington Settlement Patterns • Glen Cove Settlement Patterns • Inwood Settlement Patterns • Patchogue and Vicinity Settlement Patterns • Copiague and Marconiville

25
CHAPTER THREE
SETTLEMENT
The Boarding House • The Marinos: Port Washington Leaders • Settlers from Sturno • Immigrant Labor on the Estates • Constantino Posillico: Estate Owner • Scrub Oak Settlement in Patchogue • Promoting Marconiville • John Campagnoli

40
CHAPTER FOUR
UNITY FOR EMPLOYMENT
Hicks Nursery • Long Island Railroad • Small Factories • Construction Workers Activity • Sand Mine Workers • Workers of the Soil • Small Industries • Organizing Lace Mill Workers

56
CHAPTER FIVE
CRIME AND VIOLENCE
The Black Hand • Crime and Melodramatic Journalism • Law Enforcement

66
CHAPTER SIX
PREJUDICE
Negative Climate • Prejudice in Copiague • Americanization Pressures • Prejudice in the Fire Department • The Ku Klux Klan and Anti-Italianism • The Irony of Discrimination • World War II Leads to Discrimination • Loyalty in the Face of Discrimination • Post-War Discrimination

80
CHAPTER SEVEN
ESTABLISHING ROOTS
The Orchard • Old World Traditions in Glen Cove • Growth of Glen Cove's Little Italy • Family Profile • Alarm Over Health Dangers • The Emergence of Westbury's Little Italy • The Family: A Flexible Institution • Early Organization Life: Mutual Aid Societies • St. Rocco Society • Dell'Assunta Society • Fraternal Organizations • Sons of Italy Lodge • Labor Organizations • Band Organizations • Foresters of America • Italian Welfare Club • Italian Political Club • Civic Associations

99
CHAPTER EIGHT
THE FIRST WORLD WAR
To Fight for the Fatherland • War Casualties • Persistent Loyalty • Marconiville Participants • Inwood Community Support • War's Impact on Community

108
CHAPTER NINE
CHANGING SLOWLY
1920s: Boom Times • Boosterism Impacts Little Italies • Growth in Copiague • The Confident Twenties • Sports and Recreational Activities • Socializing Institutions • Ethnic Theater • Social Service Agencies • Italian Entrepreneurs Help Glen Cove Grow • Italian Entrepreneurs in Patchogue

121
CHAPTER TEN
RELIGIOUS PERSUASION
St. Rocco, Long Island's National Italian Parish • Building the Church • Italian American Pastors • Other Italian Parishes • Our Lady of the Assumption • Our Lady of Good Counsel • St. Joseph Mission Chapel • The Church of SS Felicitas and Perpetua • Westbury and Port Washington Parishes • From Catholicism to Protestantism • Conclusion

141
CHAPTER ELEVEN
The Depression Years

Caught Up in the Anti-Alien Campaign • Survival Techniques
Coping with the Depression in Port Washington • Inter-Ethnic Discord in
Inwood • Promoting the Italian Language • In Behalf of Education •
Succeeding in a Difficult Atmosphere • Surge of Italianita
153

CHAPTER TWELVE
SEEDS OF DISTRUST
Clouds on the Horizon • Fascist Activity • The Call to Colors • Back Home •
Overcoming the Ambivalent Atmosphere • Loyalty Affirmed • Ethnic
Community Response
162

CHAPTER THIRTEEN
UNITY FOR ADVANCEMENT
Media Coverage • Dissension Within the Ethnic Community • District
Courts • Italo Balbo Visit • Influencing Italian Politics • Emergence in
School Matters • Upward Mobility
177

CHAPTER FOURTEEN
ESTABLISHING SHOOTS
Veterans Affairs • Community Involvement • New Levels of Italian
Community Presence • Manorhaven, Post World War II Italian Enclave •
Business
184

CHAPTER FIFTEEN
THE RISE AND CONSOLIDATION OF POWER
Republican Inroads in Patchogue's Little Italy • Inwood Republican Machine
• Mr. Republican on Inwood • Glen Cove Politics • Proletarians Become
Republicans • The Democratic Machine • Italians in Politics • Launching
Pad to Higher Office • Port Washington Republicans • Copiague Politics •
Westbury Politics • Overview
201

CHAPTER SIXTEEN
COMMUNITIES IN CHANGE
Trauma of Changing Neighborhoods: Inwood • Inter-Ethnic Contention •
Westbury's Changing School Population • Friction in East Patchogue and
North Bellport
End of the Settlement House • Changing Traditional Societies and Customs
• Decline of Ethnic Parishes • On-Going Immigration • Retaining Ethnicity
in Suburbia • Little Italy Endures in Glen Cove • End of Marconiville:
Beginning of Suburbia • Being Italian Amidst Suburban Pluralism • Italian
Identity in Patchogue: Today and Tomorrow

214
CHAPTER SEVENTEEN
CONCLUSION
225
PHOTO ESSAY
251
APPENDIX 1
257
APPENDIX 2
260
BIBLIOGRAPHY
269
INDEX

ACKNOWLEDGMENTS

It is sobering to realize that so many people were indispensable to the completion of this work. It is therefore a privilege and a pleasure to thank those who have helped bring this study into being.

With deep gratitude I extend my thanks to the dozens of interviewees, whose names are listed elsewhere, for helping unearth not only important information, but who have also enriched this study with a humane touch. Likewise, I am indebted to Richard Winsche of the Nassau Museum and Reference Library, Nicholas Falco of the Queensborough Public Library, Wallace Broege of the Suffolk County Historical Society and the staffs of Nassau Community College Library, the Center for Migration Studies Library, and the Westbury, Glen Cove, Port Washington, Lawrence, Copiague and Patchogue Public Libraries. I wish to express my appreciation also to John Tuthill, publisher of the *Patchogue Advance* for the opportunity to utilize his collection and to Wally Carmichael of the *Patchogue Advance* for his assistance. My debt of gratitude goes to a number of key people in several Long Island Italian communities for their personal support and for introducing me to others who were helpful, especially Joseph and Dominic Piscitelli, John and Michael Pascucci, Vincent Suozzi, Stephen Fuoco, Victor Yannacone, and Marie Contino. I want to thank, in particular, several colleagues and friends with whom I exchanged ideas and discussed the viability of the project and who read parts of the manuscript and made recommendations: Frank J. Cavaioli, Joseph Varacalli, Bruno Arcudi, Angela Danzi, Richard Renoff. A sabbatical granted by Nassau Community College enabled me to undertake extensive research throughout Long Island.

For their extraordinary support I wish to express my gratitude to the presidents and officers of the Long Island Chapter of the American Italian Historical Association, the Dell' Assunta Society of Westbury, the National Italian American Foundation and the Columbus, John A. Prudenti, Cellini, Italo Balbo, America, Donatello and Cabato lodges of the Order of the Sons of Italy. My heartfelt thanks also to Fred and Joseph Scalamandre of Freeport whose parents' life story is a singular account of immigrant achievement on Long Island and which is included in the appendix.

More than she realizes, my wife Julie, has been a source of strength and love over the years. Without her help this could not have come to fruition. In like manner, my thanks to my children, Frank, Mary, John and Christine for their encouragement.

To the staff of the Center for Migration Studies, especially the Director Lydio F. Tomasi, and editors Maggie Sullivan and Eileen Reiter, I owe a special debt of gratitude. Their interest, patience and encouragement in the laborious tasks of reading, analyzing and offering suggestions for re-shaping have been of immense help.

CHAPTER ONE
FROM STEERAGE TO SUBURB

"Italians Excluded", was the blunt, unmistakeable message included in a turn-of-the-century broadside which advertised property for sale in a Long Island community. No further explication was provided on the sheet, nor was any necessary—prospective property-owners need not fear the settling of the despised ethnic group in their midst. No other nationality or race was mentioned, not even those ethnic groups who regularly had been singled out for exclusion over the years. This blatant example of discrimination provided one dimension of the kind of reception awaiting Italians in suburban Long Island.

Ironically, Italian Americans came to be the largest single nationality group on Long Island only two to three generations later. The discrimination reflected in the above-mentioned notice was, fortunately, only one side of the coin. Simultaneously, other entrepreneurs and developers extended themselves in efforts to encourage the immigrant people to move to Long Island. An 1882 real estate advertisement in an Italian American newspaper, for example, promoted the virtues of residence in Deer Park to its readers. Within a number of years other real estate notices advertised "Italian" colonies on Long Island such as Colonial Springs near Wyandanch and Marconiville in Copiague.

The post-World War II exodus to Long Island established Italian Americans as the largest ethnic group numerically in the demographic region. However, even before this development, people of Italian extraction had carved out for themselves cohesive, humble but fruitful lives in a number of enclaves which originated almost a century ago. These were the forerunners of the large exodus to follow—the pioneers, as it were, who helped transform Long Island from a bucolic, unhurried rural place into the nation's foremost and vibrant suburb. It is the story of these Italian immigrants and their descendants that will be reconstructed in this volume.

For years the study of Italian enclaves has been a consuming interest of many works which have delved into and described life in the Little Italies of the nation's teeming cities. Accordingly, these works have iterated tales of settlement patterns in crowded ghettoes replete with accounts of confrontation with the viscissitudes of crime, poverty, poor health and exploitation in neighborhoods now shunned by ethnic groups who previously inhabited them. These studies also provided stories of the establishment of ethnic neighborhoods, of the struggle to eke out a living in a not always hospitable environment, of participation in the social and cultural institutions within the ethnic community as well as interaction with mainstream society. Emphasis on the type of life carved out by the immigrants in the large urban centers obviously was warranted for a number of reasons, not the least of which was the overriding fact that the vast majority of newcomers and their descendants lived in and made contributions to life in the big cities. Preoccupation with this experience, however, had the effect of developing a mind-set which equated Italian American history almost exclusively with urban history and thus precluded extensive investigations into the lifestyles and the assimilative patterns of Italians outside those demographic areas, particularly in the suburbs. It was assumed furthermore, that the forms of group life which characterized the large cities revealed a totality of mores, customs and experiences which could readily be applied to those who lived in the suburbs without further investigation. The impression is that old Italian immigrants were weak, poor, less-educated and unlucky—no recognition that these immigrants were likely to be the "strongest", those willing to take a chance. As the sociologist Joseph Lopreato has demonstrated in *Peasants No More* (1967), Italian immigration is symptomatic of a people on the move, a people striving for social mobility. This assumption, consequently, had the unfortunate result of neglecting alternate structures of settlement. At a time when the vast majority of Italian Americans resided in urban centers, city orientation was perhaps, justified. However, for at least a generation, Americans of Italian descent have come to inhabit homes in large numbers in the nation's suburban divisions and thus a gap exists with respect to what is known about their history outside cities. The present study recognizes that although a heavy movement from the cities into suburbia occurred during the post-World War II era, Italian Americans have had meaningful roles in the histories of Long Island suburbs long before the 1940s, indeed for the better part of a century. It is an history that encompasses up to five generations, yet comparatively little extensive research about them has been undertaken. It was to help fill the void that this study was commenced.

IMMIGRANTS IN SUBURBIA: LONG ISLAND'S ITALIANS

Immigrants in Suburbia: Long Island's Italians, will focus on the history and socialization of Italian Americans in six communities plus a few adjoining satellite localities on Long Island, New York, that have been home for Italian immigrants and their children for generations, indeed from the beginning of mass immigration in the 1880s. These include Inwood, Port Washington, Glen Cove, Westbury, Copiague and Patchogue. These communities, furthermore, have been reinforced by an ongoing flow of immigration to the present. Representing an estimated 25 percent of the population of Nassau and Suffolk counties, or approximately 700,000 people—a number exceeding the total population of many cities and some states—with one possible exception, they constitute the largest concentrations of Italian Americans in two contiguous counties in the United States.

In recent years the publication of a number of accounts of contemporary ethnicity have happily begun to close the gap in the literature dealing with the roles of various peoples in our pluralistic society. In their own right as well as for the insight they provide for incorporating the ethnic dimension into the forces which have shaped American life, these works validate the concept that the study of ethnic heritage is a worthwhile endeavor. As has been noted, extant literature on Italian Americans has been based on a preoccupation with city life. Even in the few instances when these works discuss Italian Americans in suburbia, they presume that such residency confers assimilation. Thus, Richard Alba in *Italian Americans. Into the Twilight of Ethnicity* concludes that, "...in general suburbanization was almost entirely associated with further acculturation and intermingling across nationality lines". No acknowledgement is given to the possibility of a meaningful ethnic consciousness or ethnic viability. However, in some instances settlement in suburbia came almost instantly upon immigration. To examine the persistency of ethnicity as a force in the history of Long Island Italian Americans is to make a valuable contribution to the realization that immigrant groups have survived as subcultures outside the cities. Thus, it is the intention of this study to expound upon the theme of ethnicity as a vital force in suburbia possessing its own sense of purpose, its own propensity for solidarity and its own history, even while accommodation and assimilation processes take place. In the course of this quest the staying power of ethnicity a century after the original communities were established will be assessed. Accordingly, several questions arise. How vigorously have Italian Americans maintained their sense of ethnicity? Have they been absorbed into the mainstream? How significantly have they progressed beyond the proletarian stage? Does the ethnic group still indulge in meaningful organizational life? Does their ethnic background set them apart from others in the community? Is their sense of ethnic identification more than mere nostalgia?

This work began in 1979 when I was awarded a State University of New York Research Foundation grant to conduct a seminar on ethnicity in suburbia. I then undertook the first indepth examination into the history of one of Long Island's oldest Italian enclaves. Encouraged by the results, I decided to proceed further to examine other old Italian communities in Nassau and Suffolk counties, quickly realizing that not all "new immigrant" people who came to this country in the late nineteenth and early twentieth centuries resided in the nation's urban centers. Thousands, indeed tens of thousands, settled in suburban areas of the nation that surrounded the great cities. For many it meant settling on Long Island, as that region was emerging as the quintessential suburb. In moving to this region Italian Americans helped shape the suburban environment and thereby conferred an Italianate ambience to the area.

To recognize ethnicity as a persistent force in suburbia might serve as an antidote to the more stereotypical views advanced by sociologists who stressed the conformist middle-class preoccupation of life bereft of a true sense of culture and mired in monotony and mediocrity. With respect to Long Island, it is to be noted that there are few published works which can be regarded as social histories; those that do exist abound with myths about uniform middle-class styles devoid of distinctive lineages and ancestries. Some of the better works which eschew such generalizations nevertheless are skimpy on social history. Edward Smit's fine study *Nassau, Suburbia, USA*, for example, while an important volume which recounts the transformation of the country from a rural to a modern, mature suburb, is concerned primarily with governmental, administrative, political and economic institutions. I propose instead, in the present work, to delve into the impact of suburban ecology, class structure, neighborhoods, lifestyles and other social/psychological influences which impinged upon these immigrant people. In the process of writing this book I have acquired an appreciation for the degree and extent to which suburban life has been influenced by Italian ethnic mores and customs.

Given the size of the population under study, a truly encyclopedic work was beyond my scope. Thus, an indepth research into the past and present of the oldest communities in which Italians settled, was undertaken. While not all-inclusive, this method at least has the merit of focusing on those villages, hamlets and a city which have seen several generations of Americans of Italian extraction in their midst and thus serve as valid field case examples. This volume will therefore concentrate on the history of those communities with identifiable ethnic roots. The research method employed was to uncover all available extant original sources pertaining to these communities such as deed records, taxpayer records, voter registration directories, business and civic group directories, records of ethnic organizations such as mutual aid societies, unpublished autobiographical accounts, company business files, church baptism, confirmation and marriage records, United States and New York State census records. Also examined were pertinent atlases, doctoral and masters theses, newspapers and a variety of published material ranging from books to articles. Furthermore, the above is supplemented with dozens of extensive interviews with individuals who were part of the history of these Italian enclaves and thus in a position to make perceptive observations. As such, testimony of a range of individuals has been recorded—from housewives to organization people, churchmen and churchwomen, businesspeople, students, retired people, politicians, judges and humble workers. These informants span the generations from the old-timers of the pre-twentieth century to those of more recent waves. This triangulation method—that is, employing a multiplicity of indicators—hopefully reduces bias possibilities and best approximates a complete picture. This methodology seems most useful and indeed indispensable if one is to glean information and insights into the ethnic group. Needless to say this has involved untold hours in libraries, individuals' homes, offices and streets both within and without the communities involved. It has been an enriching experience for me as the author, and I trust a useful experience for those who cooperated with me.

CHAPTER TWO
EARLY ITALIAN IMMIGRANTS

When Joseph Posillico and James Razzano left Durazzano and arrived in Westbury almost a century ago, they came upon a small, little-known rural hamlet. The native Americans called the area "Wallage", a name which was changed to Westbury by the English Quakers who moved into the area, thereby giving a lasting distinctive religious imprint. Throughout most of the nineteenth century Westbury remained a sparsely-populated insular farm locality with few businesses; a place of corn and wheat fields cultivated by Quaker farmers who, unlike their Long Island neighbors, farmed only to meet their own needs.[1]

This provincial world was, in fact, already changing when Posillico came to work on the developing estates then being constructed for some of the nation's wealthiest citizenry—the Morgans, the Winthrops, the Whitneys, the Phipps, *etc.*—who were intent on introducing polo, horseracing, autoracing and other glamorous pastimes of the favored class. These fulsome avocations required the building of ostentatious estates worthy of their lofty status, with the result that Westbury witnessed the erection of lavish mansions surrounded by acres of land in need of cultivation and beautification.

The sumptuousness of these estates, it seems, cannot be exaggerated. The Morgan mansion, for example, was situated on 200 acres that had formerly been a group of farms, including a water tower, lodge, squash court, swimming pool and racing stables (*Queens County Review*, February 7, 1899). The Harry Payne Whitney estate boasted of the largest private racing stables in the country. It was to work on the farms of these estates as well as to cultivate and to improve them that the Italians were first called into Westbury.

Durazzano, Italy, known for its gardening and landscaping, began to see a small exodus of its young men for Westbury by the 1880s, although it is not clear how they first learned about Westbury as a desireable work location. However, by the turn of the century, Italian immigrants emerged as the largest portion of workers on the estates and the nurseries in the vicinity.

The Italians who followed the footsteps of Posillico and Razzano were from three small towns in the vicinity of Naples—Durazzano, Nola and Saviano—and their surrounding villages. The majority of immigrants were from Durazzano, a little community of 3,000 people located on a mountainside 25 miles from Naples and a town which is busiest in June during cherry-picking time. Most of the inhabitants, at that time, earned their living by farming or engaging in a few service trades. The few Italians who migrated to Westbury in the 1880s formed a nucleus which increased over the next few decades. A residential settlement pattern emerged in which immigrants from Saviano and Nola established an Italian enclave in New Cassel, close to Westbury. Those from Durazzano congregated almost exclusively in the Westbury section known originally as "Nanny Goat Hill" and later as "Breezy Hill".

One of those early twentieth century immigrants was Anthony Razzano, the son of James Razzano. After his father's emigration Anthony was sent to work for a small firm which made wooden barrels. As a cooper he earned six cents a day placing wedges in the green wood being cut into shape for the barrels. Despite hs father's return to Durazzano, in 1913, Anthony decided to come to America himself that same year, following a pattern which had developed even before the turn of the century (Interview, Anthony Razzano).

In Westbury, the immigrants encountered a small, rustic community boasting only of a handful of houses and stores along with a blacksmith and a wheelwright shop on its main thoroughfare. Electricity was installed in 1902 and the Water District was organized in 1912. Storm sewers came later—after a disastrous flood in 1919 (*The Westbury Times*, July 10, 1952). Thus, work opportunities were available, but only in servile endeavors. There was no "gold found in the streets". There were, in fact, no paved streets.

Anniello Piscitelli came to Westbury in 1907. Now 89 years old, he recalls that when Post Avenue was only a dirt road, the only street lights were those illuminated by gas lit by a man who made the rounds every night. The streets were narrow and unpaved and required considerable maintenance (Interview, Aniello Piscitelli).

Some immigrants, like Anthony Razzano, were employed on Jericho Turnpike, then a sand road with numerous ruts and holes and barely wide enough for vehicles to pass each other. He and other Italian laborers filled the holes and poured heavy oil on the road to prevent dust from rising. They usually worked under Irish foremen who, for the most part, they remember with resentment for their arrogant attitudes (Interview, Anthony Razzano).

Italian immigrants in suburban sites such as Westbury seemed to have acquired the esteem of society somewhat faster than did their counterparts in New York City. In suburbia the immigrant group accounted for a relatively greater proportion of the total population at a much earlier period. For example, as early as 1915 Westbury Italian immigrants and their issue comprised approximately one of every six residents, while this same ratio was not achieved in the cities until a generation later. Another reason for the somewhat higher regard for suburban Italian immigrants revolved around the realization that there existed less of a mix of nationalities, that is, in suburban communities Italians frequently and significantly were one of only a few nationality groups in the settlement, whereas in large cities they constituted one of a plethora of ethnic groups of newly-arrived whose very size and diversity was cause for great concern to urban society. Thus, urban residents were more likely to regard with suspicion, if not treat with outright hostility, the multitude of nationalities, races, religions and cultures in their midst. By contrast suburban communities usually were comprised of only a few ethnic groups, heavily native born and minus the welter of strange and irritating newcomers that could be seen in the large cities. As a consequence, suburban communities could more readily become cognizant of the positive role of Italians in community development.

HOW THIS GARDEN GREW

Most Italians found employment in the large estates being developed or in the burgeoning nursery industries—chief of which was Isaac Hicks and Sons. Direct descendants of pioneer Elias Hicks, the Hicks family came to be one of Westbury's principal families providing civic, religious and economic leadership for many years. In 1853 Isaac Hicks established a 50 acre nursery business which, in time, became one of the most important firms of its kind in the entire northeast. As the business expanded, an increased work force was required—a force which at its peak numbered some 300 men, most of whom were Italians.

The nature of this work required that considerable time would be spent away from home in distant locations. As wealthy residents in the community increased their demands for the Hicks products, the nursery expanded to 400 acres hiring many Italians upon arrival from Italy and, apparently, even before they had obtained permanent housing. Seventy-two-year-old Edwin Hicks, recalls stories his grandfather related in which Italians built sod houses on the Hempstead Plains in the 1880s, much in the manner associated with the more familiar setting of the Great Plains in the American West (Interview, Mrs. John Emory; Edwin Hicks).

By the turn of the century, the flourishing horticulture business, together with the multifold activities on the developing estates, employed hundreds of gardeners, chauffers, and handymen. Migrants from Durazzano, Saviano and Nola had carved out a regular pattern of migration from the old country to the nurseries and estates of Westbury, thereby establishing the nucleus of an Italian colony on Long Island. Unlike the majority of Italian newcomers who entered American society through the filter of the urban experience exemplified by the classic Mulberry Street ghetto, the Durazzanesi, Savianese and Nolese moved directly into the rural environment. As such, they were spared some of the more pervasive indignities which befell immigrant Italians in the large cities.

SETTLEMENT INTERMEDIARIES

It is useful to compare settlement patterns of Westbury to those which applied to Italian immigrants in large cities like New York and in other Long Island suburban areas. The overwhelming majority of Italian immigrants of the late nineteenth century came to find better work opportunities. However, whereas there was no assurance as to specific employment in New York City, Westbury-bound immigrants had jobs awaiting them. Locating jobs in the Long Island suburb, furthermore, was accomplished without a role for the *padrone* or labor boss, while in the city immigrants frequently required intermediaries.

The role of the padrone in American urban society has been delineated by scholars who aver that for the most part padrones reflected the emergence of a class structure within the Italian enclaves of the big cities. As the *prominenti* of urban Little Italies, the padrones exercised enormous power in the immigrant communities because of their ability to link the new arrivals with work opportunities. Common consensus regarded these intermediaries as exploiters of the Italian Americans, who elevated themselves at the expense of their fellow countrymen. While there is some evidence that the padrone system was a part of the immigrant experience in suburbia as, for example, those who supervised large work gangs in extensive construction projects on Long Island, the evidence also suggests that padrone influence was extremely short-lived and rapidly overcome by the labor pattern that developed there, namely the role of supportive families which served as buffers to the wider society and which also served as the major means of locating jobs. Simply put, there was little or no need for padrone in the more accommodating Long Island suburban atmosphere.

Accordingly, the low profile suburban padrone precluded the establishment of extreme forms of the class distinctions and other social barriers to upward mobility. This is not to say that padrones were absent from the suburban experience, but rather that there was a more limited influence. Where they operated, they also frequently served as promoters of Italian settlement as, for example, in Port Washington.

PORT WASHINGTON SETTLEMENT PATTERNS

Settlement patterns which prevailed in Westbury were similar to those of Port Washington, Glen Cove, Inwood and Patchogue while a different model was followed in Copiague. In Port Washington, it was sand, the seemingly insignificant natural mineral, that was the improbable magnet which drew the first Italians to the town and accounted for more of them living in that community in 1900 than in any other location on Long Island except Inwood. The 120 Italians present there were primarily laborers in the burgeoning sand and gravel mines which operated in the community and its vicinity and which employed hundreds of workers, making it one of the few large-scale industries of Long Island.

Until the turn of the century Port Washington remained a rather sleepy village of a few hundred farmers and baymen surrounded by farms and landscape unmarred by the ravages of the sand industry. When the Long Island Railroad extended its tracks into Port Washington in 1898, the character of the town changed from a distinctively remote and rural setting to a suburban community.

There was no absence of local character in late nineteenth century Port Washington as some of the sturdiest and best-known Long Island families cast their collective lot with the little community. One was the Dodge family which traced its roots to colonial times. It was the Dodge estate that became one of the earliest sand pits, yielding a fine quality building sand which proved indispensable in the prevailing construction boom.[2]

Sand mining in Port Washington and the surrounding environs began around 1865 with over a dozen companies engaged in the activity at one time or another. Archeological research indicated that the rich Port Washington soil was ideally suited for use in mixing concrete, a commodity in increasing demand in the construction of New York City subways, skyscrapers, sidewalks and bridges. Because transportation costs were an important factor to the profitability of the sand business, Port Washington's proximity to the big city was highly desireable. Beneficiary of a spacious natural harbor, the location provided the basis for easy, direct access to the city as high capacity barges daily moved tons of Port Washington sand to construction sites. Local residents were aware of the great significance of the sand industry, boasting that many mangnificant city edifices constructed were traceable to the bare, bleak-looking banks of the Port Washington area, "for surely there is found no better building material than that which is taken from its coast hills" (*Port Washington News*, June 21, 1973). For such rewards from its sandy soil, which constituted its greatest single source of income, the local community was burdened with an unprecedented influx of foreign laborers. This was true especially in the early decades when raw muscle and brawn was utilized to lift shovels and move wheelbarrows from hilltops to schooners and scows tied along numerous harbors for the trip to New York City. Even the emergence of technological improvements in the early 1900s had little impact on the arduousness of the work. Sand mining remained so decidedly labor intensive and demanding that it was regularly avoided by local residents, necessitating the hiring of immigrant laborers including

Poles, Scandinavians, Germans, Irish and especially Italians (Williams, 1983).

That the work was difficult can readily be understood by realizing that during the 1890s there were virtually no machines to assist men in the labor; instead they were called upon to dig by hand and load sand onto little trains which ran on tracks crisscrossing the sand pits. To return home after a day's work of up to ten hours was to return in soot and steam blackened clothes and bodies, fatigued physically and mentally. After a number of years in this kind of activity men became physically spent, dispirited and less productive.

As the industry developed, specialization surfaced with groups of men assigned to perform distinctive tasks. Thus, almost all the machine shop workers were German, boatmen were Scandinavians, boat caulkers were primarily Italians from Trieste, *etc.*

The very preponderance of such a large body of foreign born in the area almost from the outset constituted a source of friction in both Port Washington and nearby Roslyn. Ironically, even though local merchants reaped financial benefit from trade with these workers, they still vented their spleen against them. A letter writer to a local newspaper voiced the opposition of many when he wrote:

> The representatives of Gallagher's bank on Tuesday said openly that nobody but a foreigner would do the work required, showing clearly that the more extensive is the Sand Business, the more the foreigners will be brought here...And the more undesireable persons we have here, the worse it is for the community at large. There is every indication that the laboring classes of Roslyn areas are as much opposed to the sand people as anybody...(*Roslyn News*, April 26, 1893).

This kind of lament, notwithstanding, the local populace was destined to see a continuing influx of immigrants. Pools of sand pit workers were brought from New York City and housed in company shacks (perhaps a total of 50 per shack) for which they paid rents ranging from $3.00 to $8.00 a month; some were sheltered in a large dormitory. To counter charges of exploitation companies offered idyllic descriptions of dormitory life: "The kitchen is a picture of cleanliness, the tables where the men ate nicely covered with oiled cloth, and the sleeping quarters quite satisfactory" (*Port Washington News*, June 8, 1928).

One of the first of his nationality to settle in the community was James Damita, born in the province of Avellino, who changed his name to James Marino and moved into the village in 1885. He quickly gauged the potential of the industry, becoming a pioneer in the sand and gravel business through management of the Crescent Sand and Gravel Bank (Interview, Albert Marino). Parlaying to his advantage his access to a large pool of Italian laborers by enticing his fellow Avellinese to move to Port Washington to work in the sand pits, he could be considered a benevolent pardrone operating a grocery store, a boarding house and a saloon which the men were expected to patronize. He married Potenza-born Stella Diranna, set up a home in Port Washington in 1895 and began to raise a family which by 1900 consisted of husband and wife, three children and 24 boarders. All the boarders were classified as alien "day laborers" who had been in the country for periods ranging from sixteen years to less than a year (*Port Washington News*, March 4, 1932). Other Italians who ran boarding houses in 1900 included Joseph Marino, Pasquale Fasano, Joseph DeMeo and Frank Aggeola. Indeed, 76 of the 120 residents of Italian descent in Port Washington at the time were boarders—thus validating the observation that many Italian workers were "birds of passage" here for a temporary sojourn before returning to their permanent homes in Italy. While a considerable number of local Italians did return many remained in the United States and became lifelong residents of the community.

It was likewise the attraction of work possibilities that dictated settlement configuration for early migrants to Glen Cove.

GLEN COVE SETTLEMENT PATTERNS

By the time the Italians began to settle there, Glen Cove was already two centuries old, tracing its English beginnings to 1668 when it was located on a grassy flat on the north shore of Long Island.

There is little indication that Italian immigrants were present in the area of Glen Cove prior to 1880 except for Mr. and Mrs. Gaetano Gitto who, upon coming to Oyster Bay village in 1876, became active in local civic activities and lived to be octogenarians (*Glen Cove Record*, March 25, 1926)). In addition, the 1880 federal census recorded one whose birthplace was Sicily and another, an Italian immigrant tailor by the name of Istitto, living in Oyster Bay village with his Irish-born wife and four children (*United States Census Tracts, Queens County*, 1880).

Italians in greater numbers began to settle in the general vicinity between 1880 and 1910. Oyster Bay, for example, had a sizeable Italian community either prior to, or simultaneous with, that which was emerging in Glen Cove. A systematic but informal pattern of settlement developed in which immigrants from certain villages in the Naples vicinity transplanted themselves in the Glen Cove area. Thus, in recognition that most were from the towns of Benevento and Paduli, Monsignor Canivan, pastor of St. Dominic Catholic Church in Oyster Bay, became well-versed in Italian language and customs and even made special trips to their ancestral hometowns (*Oyster Bay Guardian*, January 22, 1926). He was to play an important role in the later development of Glen Cove's Italian parish.

The proletarian roots of Italian immigrants to the Glen Cove vicinity were evident from the beginning and coincided with the acceleration of the industrial revolution of the late nineteenth century. During that period Italians began to arrive at various north shore locales where they served as a major segment of the work force for the area's industries and construction projects. The new roads to be built, the extension of the Long Island Railroad and the development and maintenance of large estates of the wealthy required significant immigrant labor of which Italians were to play a prominent role. On occasion a padrone located in Glen Cove's Little Italy would advertise in local papers that he could supply necessary laborers for construction projects, for excavating work and for other types of manual labor.[3]

As previously mentioned the padrone system was not a major feature of Italian immigrant life on Long Island. The close-knit Italian families, the relatively homogenous enclaves with common origins in a given town or province, and the generally more amiable, less pressured Long Island environment rendered unnecessary the use of padrones. The role of the family and the informal system of making contacts through relatives and *paesani* more than served the needs of the people. What pertained to the north shore communities of Port Washington and Glen Cove also was pertinent to Italian immigrants who were attracted to the south shore, as in the case of Inwood.

INWOOD SETTLEMENT PATTERNS

Inwood, is a hamlet located in the Rockaway peninsula in the southwest corner of Nassau County adjoining the borough of Queens in New York City. It is linked with the sister communities of Hewlett, Cedarhurst, Lawrence and Woodmere, collectively known as "The Branch" or "The Five Towns". Physically and legally part of the township of Hempstead, the area first saw colonial settlment in the 1700s. However, it remained sparsely inhabited until the 1870s when the peninsula was penetrated by the Long Island Railroad.

The transportation development quickly transformed the peninsula, which was now advertised as a desireable location within a one hour ride from the heart of New York City, "...and within that distance there are the most delightful and salubrious localities for both transient and permanent residents (*W.P.A. The Story of the Five Towns*; Pp.11, 34). Such inducements were bound to change the nature of the area radically. Whereas it previously had not been sucked into the dynamic flume of metropolitan New York life, Inwood now yielded considerably to the blandishments of the large city, maintaining, however, enough of a distinct genteel, suburban lifestyle to become attractive to many well-to-do residents from the big city who had come to know the area chiefly as vacationers, but were now prepared to make their year-round homes there. This indeed was evident in the growth of

Lawrence, Hewlett, Cedarhurst and Woodmere. For Inwood (previously called Westville), the boom was "...not so much because of the increased desireability of its real estate, but because its people reaped profitable return for their labor and produce in the neighboring communities" (*W.P.A. The Story of Five Towns*, p.34). In other words, Inwood was to become a service community.

Although Italian immigrants were to be well represented in the era of mass immigration, the first Italian immigrants preceded their coming by many years. The pioneer Italians undoubtedly were Joseph and Michael Vigotty (Vigotti), descendants from an old family in Piacenza, Italy, who fashioned extensive careers in the United States Navy. At the conclusion of the Civil War they retired and purchased handsome homes in Brooklyn and sizeable farms on Long Island—the latter probably a consequence of the marriage between Michael and a member of a prominent Long Island family. Michael owned a 40 acre farm in Woodmere and in 1866 for $3,000, Joseph purchased 22 acres of farmland in Inwood (*Nassau Land Records*, p.278). Their Italian ancestry seemed, however, to make little impact on their lifestyles and associational activities because they may well have been unaware of their ethnic heritage. They and their descendants into the sixth generation regarded themselves as either of French or Spanish origin until unearthed records revealed an Italian heritage.

The Vigottys constituted an interesting but atypical example of Italians in the area because the bulk of these people were proletarians from southern Italy. The 204 Italians listed in the 1900 Census indicated that virtually all were aliens, with only a distinct minority having taken steps toward citizenship. Most were renters and half were illiterate. The first large influx of Italians to Inwood in the 1890s became numerically the largest in Nassau County numbering 204 of the county's 746 Italians in 1900. They were proletarians who came to work in some local industries which had sprung up in the fishing boat industry, or as service workers for the neighboring wealthier towns.

All the Italian families were of the working class, with a total absence of representation in the professional and middle classes. Entrepreneurship was limited to a handful in minor peripheral fields with a single contractor enjoying the most influential position. More than half the Italian adult males were boarders. The traditional mode of Italian family life was evident in the predominance of housework for wives and even older single daughters— only one of the latter was gainfully employed outside the home. Data indicate that the vast majority emigrated in the 1890s and presumably settled in one of New York City's Little Italies prior to moving to Long Island. Among those entering the country before the 1890s and settling in Inwood were Batista Deliza (1879), Igilin W. Macolino (1880), Salvatore and Josephine Spina (1883), Batista Provenzano (1883), Dominick Rizzo (1885), Nicholas Fabrizio

TABLE 1

CHARACTERISTICS OF THE ITALIAN POPULATION
OF INWOOD, LONG ISLAND, BASED ON EXTRAPOLATIONS
OF THE UNITED STATES CENSUS, NASSAU COUNTY, 1900

Total Italian Population	204
Males (adults)	80
Females (adults)	38
Children	84
Boarders	41
Occupations:	
Gainfully employed	82
Day laborers	66
Section laborers railroad	1
Shoemaker	1
Barber	1
Grocery	2
Junk dealer	9
Contractor	1
Citizenship [a]	12
Home ownership [b]	7
Literacy [c]	48
Wives employed (day laborer)	1

Notes: a. Virtually all were aliens, with some who claimed citizenship possessing first papers, while others possessed second papers.

b. The bulk of the Italian population answered rentors to the question about home ownership.

c. Those who answered No to the query about literacy numbered 102.

Source: United States Census, Street Schedules, Nassau County, 1900)

(1885 and Beniamini Julian (1885). It is significant to note that five of the seven were Inwood homeowners by 1900 (*United States Census, Street Schedules, Nassau County*, 1900).

Early in the century Italians formed a substantial minority in Inwood, concentrated in the "Crow's Hill" section. Thus, in 1900, the 200 of 204 Inwood Italian Americans residing on three streets—Mott Avenue, St. George Street and Clinton Street—made a definite impact on older residents. Primarily rentors, within a few years the more industrious and more fortunate acquired, mostly from non-Italians, woodframe houses or the properties on which to build. Newspaper accounts provide a glimpse of the ethnic succession which was taking place through real estate transactions. In 1905 the *Rockaway News* reported that John Schettino and Francesco Martilotta acquired property in the area, the latter from a non-Italian. In that same year Carmine Capozzi bought a plot from Congressman William Willett while Augustino D'Agostino, Dominick Cavelli and Antonio Gallo purchased land from the Kelly family. Most of the transactions were handled by the Vincent Zavatt real estate agency. Of Italian descent, Zavatt became a banker and large real estate operator in the early 1900s, accumulating enough property to have a street named after him. In similar fashion, the Provenzano family came to own such considerable real estate that accounts referred to land on a "Provenzano Map" (*Rockaway News*, May 8, September 9, November 3, 1905; May 6, 15 and June 1, 1907). Numerous references to real estate transactions indicated that transfers occurred along intra-ethnic as well as inter-ethnic lines.

Early Italian Inwood settlers were from two regions of Italy—Calabria and Sicily. The largest contingent from Calabria included a major portion of Albanian Italians, whose ancestry distinguished them not only from Americans in general, but also from other Italians in that they were descendants from the Balkans in Eastern Europe who fled from Turkish invaders in the fifteenth century. Seeking refuge in Italy the Albanians established communities in Calabria, Puglia and Sicily where they were distinguished from the indigenous Italian population by language, dress and an Eastern-rite Christianity. In Inwood, Albanian Italians constituted a group within a group, an anamoly which confused local Long Islanders who referred to them by a variety of names: Albanians, Albanian Italians, Albanazians (the latter undoubtedly a corruption of the Italian term "Albanese"). Thus, they presented not only a duality but a problem of triple identification to outsiders. Within the Italian community there was less of a problem, however, since each was well-acquainted with the provincial backgrounds involved. Indeed, for some Italian Americans, there is still a question of acceptance of Albanians as "real Italians". Reflecting ancient animosities, some Inwood Italian Americans still categorically reject the notion that Albanese Italians are Italians. For their own part, in 1897, Inwoodites of Albanian descent formed their own Stella Albanese organization, a fraternal society which continues to function.

Less numerous and less conspicuous but nevertheless present among early Inwood Italians were Sicilians. Although by comparison to Albanian Italians there was less organizational activity, Sicilians nevertheless, possessed a strong attachment to the land of their forebears. Nothing exemplifies this more dramatically than their reactions to the devastating Messina earthquake of December 28, 1908 which claimed the lives of over 76,000 people.

> Along the Rockaway branch there are several colonies of Sicilians and Albanazians (Albanians) who are greatly excited over the terrible cata-

strophe which has befallen their home country. These are located in Lawrence and Inwood, and there is a small contingent of them in Far Rockaway near the Nassau County line. When the first news of the earthquake was received there, these people became greatly excited and as later and more terrible news arrived, the conditions bordered on insanity, some of the foreigners going so far as to pack up their belongings and make preparations to leave for the earthquake zone. Many of the Sicilians and Albanazians (Albanians), together with Calabrians, emigrated to America, leaving their families in Italy, and these are the more frantic. Many believe their whole families have been wiped out and have implored the Italian consul to aid them in securing news from their home country...In the belief that they might be able to locate some of their relatives, there are some who are on the verge of leaving this land to go to the stricken country. Their countrymen who have families here with them are doing all they can to console their bereaved friends, and subscriptions are being taken to forward to the sufferers from the disaster... (*Rockaway News*, January 6, 1909).

There is no evidence of the number of Sicilians who left Inwood during this emergency, although some undoubtedly did. The Calabrians remained and would be reinforced by continued emigration from Italy. In addition, many other poor southern Italians came to Inwood where they found employment in small industries and in numerous service occupations. It was a similar type of magnet, augmented by other promising possibilities, which drew people from southern Italy to other Long Island communities along the south shore. One must consider the ingenuity of real estate promoters both within and without the ethnic community. Accordingly Patchogue and its surroundings became the destination for a signficant number of Italian immigrants.

PATCHOGUE AND VICINITY SETTLEMENT PATTERNS

The choice of Patchogue and its environs as places of settlement represented an interesting phenomenon because these were located 70 miles from the heart of the immigrant metropolis in New York City. The selection of the Patchogue area was indeed fortuitous since, despite its considerable remotness, the location was the most important center of economic and commercial activity in Suffolk County. Situated in the middle of Long Island, along the south shore, Patchogue is one of the county's oldest villages—its incorporation in 1893 signalled a community on the rise, a village proud of its small-town life replete with busy markets, farming enterprises, recreational facilities and industrial establishments, and a wide-ranging assortment of activities which rendered it the most important center of its kind on the south shore between Babylon and Montauk, 70 miles to the east. Penetrated in 1868 by the Long Island Railroad, Patchogue marked the end of the line, the popular belief being that east of it lay only sandy, barren wastelands.

The history of Italian Americans in this area is more properly conveyed as their history in Patchogue, East Patchogue (also referred to as Hagerman) and Bellport, two villages and a hamlet within Brookhaven Township laying within a four mile radius from Patchogue. Brookhaven Township, with 229 Italians in 1900, housed the largest number of these immigrants in the county. The concentration of 128 Italian Americans in Bellport out of a total of 826 for the entire county made it the largest enclave on Long Island at the time (United States Census, Suffolk County, 1900). Bellport village, a well-to-do community, enjoyed a reputation as a small but beautifully situated area whose beaches and resort hotels afforded welcome diversion for countless summertime residents. Hagerman, by contrast, was a small hamlet located three miles east of Patchogue whose physical landscape was distinguished by unspectacular scrub oak fields—an area bearing sparse population by the end of the nineteenth century.

John Ciccia may have been the first permanent Italian American settler in Patchogue village, born in Messina, Sicily, in 1859. Apprenticed as a barber and pursuing a most unusual immigration route, at the age of eleven he made the acquaintance of a traveling Long Island seaman then temporarily anchored in the Messina harbor. The lure of the sea, coupled with notions of adventure and progress, were sufficient inducements for John to leave Sicily and come to Patchogue to live around 1870. Ciccia also followed a sea career. He married a non-Italian woman who bore him four children, all of whom he outlived (*Patchogue Advance*, January 6, 1919). Because of his atypical migration and because the move pre-dated meaningful Italian immigration to the area, it is not surprising to find little other reference to him within activities in the Italian enclave.

Hagerman was named after a local real estate speculator who sought prospective buyers for his woodlands among the teeming neighborhoods of New York City, including the old Little Italy of Mulberry Street, where Rosaria Stephani, a mid-wife for the Italian community, realized the real estate potential. Sometime in the 1860s she persuaded her husband Gaetano, an expressman, to purchase some of this property on Narragansett Street which he cleared and subsequently on which he built roads and a house. The Stephanis were the pioneer Italian family in the area; four sons erected their own homes on the same street when they married—for some years to come they were the only inhabitants on the block. In characteristic planting of family roots, it is interesting to note that their descendants continue to live there.

Corroboration that a land sale scheme was the catalyst for Italian penetration of the area also comes from the testimony of 82 year old Pat Felice, a member of one of Patchogue's oldest and best known Italian families, who recalled that his own family also desired to quit the congested city slums for Patchogue and an opportunity to live in the country on their own land. In their eagerness to acquire such land Italians frequently were exploited by promoters who took advantage of their ignorance of the territory as well as by outright falsification.

> Developers would sell their property to many. They called it Boomertown, had men cut it up (the land) into streets and placed false telephone poles and false hydrants to deceive the immigrants. Thus poor Italian immigrants bought the property. Most of the buyers were from Brooklyn and New Jersey. The land developers advertised in the Brooklyn *Citizen*. My father was in Brooklyn when we came here. I was born in Bellport and was three months old when we moved to Patchogue. I stayed in that house until we were married. A lot of Italian people remained in Bellport, however, where they built houses like the kind they had in Brooklyn. But many lost their savings. (Interview, Pat Felice; Joseph Stephani).

Although some lost their investment due to unscrupulous manipulation, a considerable number of Italians did purchase property in Patchogue and its vicinity. Moreover, they and their descendants, usually not without a struggle, were able to overcome difficulties and remain in the area. The same is true about Italians who began a distinctive colony in Copiague (Marconiville). The latter community differed, however, in that its founders were from northern Italy.

COPIAGUE—MARCONIVILLE

As in the large cities and the United States as a whole, Southern Italians constituted the bulk of immigrants destined to migrate to Long Island locales. This was certainly the case with Westbury, Port Washington, Glen Cove, Inwood, Patchogue and communities surrounding them. Interestingly, however, with Northern Italians predominating, the Copiague (Marconiville) story is significantly different.

Tucked away in the southwest corner of Suffolk County was a small community known until the 1870s as South Huntington, but then changed to Copiague—apparently a facsimile of an Indian name.[4] Whatever the origin, possession of its own appellation was necessary to distinguish it from its better known and much larger neighboring communities of Amityville to the west and Lindenhurst to the east. The latter had a substantial population, while Amityville enjoyed a reputation as a well-developed, stable and popular resort community whose stature was enhanced when it was incorporated into a village in 1895. Amityville's turn of the century lifestyle was spartan compared to today's standards—few homes had indoor plumbing or central heating while coal-burning heaters and kerosene lamps were the order of the day (*Amityville Record*, March 13, 1936).

Although a United States Post Office was opened in 1903, Copiague was not large enough for incorporation and survived as a six mile square hamlet stretching from the Great South Bay on the south to Old Sunrise Highway to the north. Dissected by the Long Island Railroad into northern and southern portions, the latter contained a larger population, of old stock Americans, while the northern portion, which consisted of farms, remained sparsely populated.

As late as 1893 the future Copiague boasted of few residents—the reminiscences of one old-timer recalled only thirteen houses on Montauk Highway (Merrick Road), the main thoroughfare. Old Copiague was then a tiny community of homes with stretches of open country, green woodland and acres of salt meadows surrounded by a serenity and quietness that abounded in such measure that the insignificant hamlet betrayed little indication of the imminent growth to come.

Yet even as a sedate country atmosphere prevailed there were signs that changes were in the offing. Surely the economic activities in the nearby communities of Lindenhurst, Amityville, Massapequa and Farmingdale indicated important developments for Copiague as well. Old farm holdings were being sold and divided into smaller plots for small industries and manufacturing establishments, which attracted new immigrants, including Italians, to work as farmers or on various projects.

By the turn of the century a small but distinctive Italian presence had emerged in the region with some pioneers establishing themselves permanently. Perhaps the earliest nineteenth century Italian to settle along the south shore of Suffolk County was Giovanni Starace who emigrated to the United States in 1866 on a 90 day voyage in his own 60 foot sailing ship. Starace married a daughter of the Bailey family of Patchogue. His son Achille became a major importer of Italian food products and succeeding heirs have been influential in the history of Amityville.

A few Italians had entered farming activity in the 1880s, including Dominick Botta of Genoa who immigrated in 1879, began operating a farm in Bethpage in 1883 and subsequently became one of the most successful farmers on Long Island (United States Census, Street Schedules, Suffolk County, 1900). His son Joseph purchased a steam gang plough which was acclaimed as the first of its type to be used in the area, and which enabled Botta to plough fifteen acres a day and daily deliver two vanloads of green corn to New York city markets. Botta became a millionaire as his holdings—300 acres—increased in value over the years and were later sold to New York State which developed the land into the famous Bethpage Golf Course and Polo Grounds (*Amityville Record*, August 16, 1912; Interview, Carmine Izzo).

Other success stories include that of Dominick Posillico, who for years was a factor in Farmingdale's Italian community, just to the north of Copiague, by his operation of a boarding house and saloon (he also served as a deputy sheriff). Posillico then entered the construction business, laying the foundation for his sons to carry on and develop the largest construction firm in the country (Interview, Joseph Possillico). The high value Americans placed on visible success by dint of hard work rendered individuals such as those referred to more acceptable to the host society thereby leading to accelerated social integration.

Far different, however, was the lot of those Italian immigrants who were not so fortunate—an impression easily gleaned from newspaper accounts which sometimes reported their misfortunes. For example, in 1913 two Italian women were arrested by a local proprietor for stealing potatoes. Deputy Sheriff Posillico placed bail for the individuals (*Amityville Record*, September 26, 1913).

From the beginning, Farmingdale's Italian colony attracted unfavorable press coverage. A news item in 1901, for instance, upbraided the ethnic group for the inhumane practice of Sunday birdshoots for profit. Although the newspaper reporter admitted that he had not actually witnessed the actions, it was enough that he saw Italians wearing feathers of jays and larks in their hat bands. "It is about time this was stopped. It is evident that these men have no regard for the Sabbath" (*Southside Signal*, April, 1901).

For a short period of time Italians by the hundreds were present in an area northwest of Copiague in what was then called Central Park and later Bethpage. They were there as a consequence of interest in a new racing sport—automobile races—which was under the local patronage of multimillionaire William K. Vanderbilt II who spent fulsomely to build the Long Island Motor Parkway, destined to be hailed as the nation's most modern road. Designed as a non-stop concrete road, it was intended exclusively for automobiles and featured special racing facilities which for years attracted large crowds (Smits, 1914). While Vanderbilt provided the leadership and financing, the labor and muscle were primarily Italian as a newspaper report of the inauguration ceremony indicated. "A spectacular effect in connection with the work was the turning loose of a large group of about 100 Italians, who prosecuted vigorously the work of construction...". While they worked on the right of way, Vanderbilt pressed an electric button which blew up many trees and the Italians quickly removed them using giant stump pullers to clear the land (*Long Island Enterprise*, June 13, 1908).

It is interesting to note that the prevailing stereotype of Italians as complacent, docile laborers did not receive verification with respect to the Central

Park workers. After a week's work on the parkway several hundred of them went on strike over perceived exploitation. The strike was short-lived and may well have been a protest against *padronismo* as against management. A local newspaper report intimated that selfish maneuvering of Italian workers by labor bosses was a probable cause. That is, since hiring bosses received $2.00 for every hand hired, they encouraged a rapid turnover, sometimes dismissing employees after only a few days. Reports also indicated that padroni charged extortionist prices for supplies (*Long Island Enterprise*, June 20, 1906).

Many Italians were employed in the late nineteenth and early twentieth century construction projects then underway in the region, such as the construction and paving of Merrick Road. Italian and Polish immigrant labor formed a substantial portion of the workforce in the construction of the Brooklyn Water Works in Massapequa which was designed to serve as a reserve water supply for New York City. These were days of "pick and shovel" workers and even as Italians became prototypes for this kind of labor, they accomplished impressive construction feats interspersed by human tragedy. On one occasion an Italian laborer on the water works project fell into a chain bucket and was crushed to death. In a gesture of ethnic/worker solidarity, his fellow Italians started with shovels and knives in hand for the engineer's shanty in the belief that he was responsible for the mishandling of the machine. When the engineer ran away, the workers then surrounded the mangled body of their co-worker, preventing the local undertaker from touching it until the dead man's relatives arrived from Brooklyn to claim him.

Although the identity of the first Italian to settle in Copiague is elusive, it appears that the farm land that was the site of the future Marconiville passed into the hands of speculative real estate companies, one of which, the Sovereign Realty Company, was presided over by Nicholas Cimino in 1906. A map of that year showed that of the few streets in the area, a couple bore recognizable Italian names, suggesting that a predisposition toward *Italianitá* was already evident although not yet widespread. By 1908 the company had accumulated considerable property and had begun to build homes with sales going mostly to Italian Americans. Another Italian American, builder John Gennovario, also constructed a few expensive cottages which were to be surrounded by sodded grass and a floral base. The names of his customers also indicated sales to Italian Americans.[5]

Whoever the first Italian in Copiague may have been, John Campagnoli was undoubtedly the catalyst for Italian settlement in the community. A wealthy northern Italian, educated as a graduate mining engineer at the University of Bologna, and owner of a well-known bicycle company in Italy, he also served in the diplomatic service of his country, representing Italy in America. In that capacity he is said to have arranged for the purchase of coal from Pennsylvania for Italian industries. As a result of this activity he became interested in Long Island property and proceeded to buy some scrub oak land north of the Copiague railroad station. Assuming the vice-presidency of the Manhattan-based Sovereign Realty Company in 1908 and realizing the potential for development, in 1909 he became president of the company and moved his family into Copiague, determined to guide its growth (*Long Island Enterprise*, July 3, 1909). Land sales to the Bernagazzi and Giorgini families were followed by their movement into the community. Thus, within a few years a small number of Italians became inhabitants of the Long Island hamlet. Iola Giorgini, one of the community's oldest residents, recalled that when she came to live there in about 1910, there were a few Italians who worked as laborers in the area either on local farms or as gardeners for the Brinckerhoff Manor, one of the largest land holdings in the area. The likelihood is that these anonymous Italians were from the Mezzogiorno (the Italian South) (Interview, Iola Galuzzi).

If the southern Italians were unknown, those from northern Italy were not. Originating in the Romagna province, the Romangnoli began to move into Copiague around the time of Campagnoli's appearance with many of them relatives or friends from the old country. The Tassinari, Giorgini, and Bernagazzi families, for example, having first settled in New York's Little Italies, later relocated to Copiague. The suburbs held promise of owning their own homes and lands, thus approximating the kind of lifestyle associated with the more comfortable class.

The entry of early Italian immigrants into the several Long Island communities was the origin of the Little Italies which came to fruition locally. Although these enclaves functioned virtually as self-sufficient ethnic entities, they also were in communication with each other, intermixing on appropriate occasions. Feast-day celebrations found interaction among contiguous Italian communities such as the Italian colony in Oyster Bay frequenting Glen Cove's Little Italy during St. Rocco's Day festivities while Farmingdale's Italians visited Copiague or Westbury's Italian sections during the Feast of the Assumption. Likewise, suburban Italian residential patterns indicated instances of families establishing themselves first in one Italian enclave with subsequent moves to another nearby Italian community. This was the path followed by a number of families whose first Long Island homes were in North Bellport (Hagerman) but who eventually moved into homes in Patchogue's Little Italy.

Lure of the land, desire for home ownership and ample work opportunities accounted for the attraction of the first Italians to Nassau and Suffolk Counties. These humble beginnings of the late nineteenth century, in which newcomer Italians numbered very few, were nevertheless destined to grow and become permanent places of settlement into succeeding generations, as will be seen in the next chapter.

FOOTNOTES

[1] For the history of early Westbury and its Quaker roots, *See*, J. O'Shea, "Our Westbury Heritage", *Your Westbury, 1932-65*, 1965; *The Westbury Times*, July 10, 1952. *See also, Nassau Review-Star*, June 11, 1952.

[2] The early history of Port Washington is treated in S. Kaplan, *The Dream Deferred: People, Politics and Planning in Suburbia*, New York, 1977. *See also, New York Herald Tribune*, April 21, 1963; C. Wysons, "A History of Port Washington", *Port Washington Post*, American Legion, 1939.

[3] *See, Oyster Bay Guardian*, July 20, 1913 for advertisement by Locust Valley Italian-American contractor featuring "Laborers furnished" appeal.

[4] For background information on Copiague, *See*, E. Eide, *Copiague, Your Town and Mine*, Copiague Board of Education, 1971. In later years efforts by Copiague "boosters" to incorporate as a village came to naught. *See, Amityville Record*, March 25, 1927.

[5] *See, Suffolk County Records, Date of Incorporation*, Liber 22, p.22 and *Long Island Enterprise*, June 13 and August 8, 22, 1908, for early history of the Sovereign Realty Company. Perhaps the first Italian American to own property in Copiague was Charles Segale whose name is recorded as purchasing land from the Sovereign Realty Company in 1906. *See, Suffolk County Deeds*, Liber 600, p.448, and Liber 690, p.281, 1906.

CHAPTER THREE
SETTLEMENT

Settlement patterns followed by Italians who moved into Long Island were similar to those of immigrants in Italian enclaves throughout the United States. Here, as elsewhere, immigration was a personal choice in which individuals relied on their own resources.

Beneficiaries of assistance from neither government nor private agencies, Italians developed a support system which emphasized intra-family and *paesani* relationships. Individual sojourners usually set out for a Long Island destination because of recommendations from relatives or townspeople who had preceded them. Rarely did they decide to settle in a particular community in the absence of such considerations. Finding someone they knew from the old home town already settled in a town, male newcomers frequently made their abode with them as boarders until they accumulated enough funds to secure other housing arrangements.

THE BOARDING HOUSE

The typical boarding house was owned by a member of an ethnic group utilizing some rooms of his home to board others of his nationality. The informal network of relationships developed through membership in larger family structures or as a result of contacts based upon a common hometown residence proved an important factor. Individual Italians would scrape together sufficient money to purchase their own homes and to make ends meet as well as to be of assistance to their relatives and paesani, would rent a room or two to the newly-arrived. This was the case with Nicola Piscitelli who purchased a home on Hicks Street in Westbury. His son, Dominick, remembers the frequency with which the bedroom he shared with his brother was put to use for new arrivals from Durazzano. Through letters exchanged beforehand or through the word of returned emigrants, Durazzanesi journeyed directly to the Piscitelli house upon arrival in the Long Island suburb and remained for periods ranging from a few days to a few months. Necessarily spartan, boarding houses nevertheless served as half-way houses between renting and home ownership; they served also as buffers in the otherwise harsh social climate of the strange new world. Nicola's home was always open to fellow Durazzanesi towards whom he felt a special obligation. During periods of financial straits, boarders of long duration would pay $3.00 a month for the amenities of a real home (Interview, Dominick Piscitelli; *See also*, G. Morino, 1978).

Those newly-arrived from Saviano and Nola followed a similar pattern in New Cassel, which was contiguous to Westbury. Pre-World War I boarders paid from $2.00 to $3.00 per month—amounts which were lower than those paid by lodgers of other nationalities. Among those who settled in New Cassel early in the century were Pasquale Simonetti, Carmine, Anniello and Giuseppe Catapano, Fred Tufaro, and Nicola Sommese. Frank Weli boarded thirteen men at $2.00 a month for which the men received a bed and meals, although the food was purchased by the boarders. It was estimated that, in 1905, a good table in the Westbury area could be had for a cost of $1.75 per week per person for raw food supplies (*Hicks Labor Record*). The boarding system was of mutual benefit to people with minimal economic means. It constituted a small but welcome additional income for the few homeowners and it afforded a place of warmth and understanding for the newcomer among people of his own kind who spoke the same dialect, ate familiar foods and worked in similar occupations. The system persisted well into the 1920s, as exemplified by the Pascarella house on Fifth Avenue which was home for twenty-four Italians who paid $3.00 a month for beds and cooked meals, when boarders supplied the food. John Monteforte recalled that he and his father slept in a room with six others and that the house had three such bedrooms with eight men to a room (Interview, John Monteforte).

The boarding house system had other interesting side benefits. For American-born Dominick Piscitelli it afforded an opportunity to acquire first-hand acquaintance with names his parents had long bandied about, kept him informed about events in Durazzano, and in general enabled him to understand the newcomers. The experience also gave him more familiarity with the language and mores of the old country.

Further insight into the boarding house operation is reflected in the career of Ralph Lamberti, who at 85 years old recalled his early days in Port Washington. Born in Torella di Lombardi, Avellino province, in 1897, and aware of the job possibilities in Port Washington because his own father had once worked in the sand mines before ultimately returning to Italy, Ralph decided to emigrate. As soon as he turned sixteen and was thus legally independent, he journeyed to Naples and boarded a boat for the two week trip, happy in the knowledge that he would find in America the work opportunities lacking in his home town. Entering the Long Island community in 1913, he went to work in the sand pits earning $1.75 per day, a daily wage which compared favorably with other options and which provided steady employment in addition. As a boarder with James Marino, like other sand company workers, he was expected to take his meals in the Marino boarding house. Ralph remained there for two months but found the cost too expensive since boarders were also expected to spend money in the proprietor's bar (Interview, Ralph Lamberti).

Boarders learned to provide for themselves. The absence of restaurants and their natural inclination toward frugality led them either to cook simple meals for themselves or arrange for the wife of the boarding house owner to cook for them. Lonely sojourners resorted to occupying boarding houses not only because of economics, but also because it provided a reasonable approximation of the old country. To be together with people of their home villages who spoke the same dialect, shared in common traditions and partook of the familiar foods of their region enabled them to cope with an otherwise hard dispiriting existence. Catherine Cocchiola's description is revealing. "My mother sometimes would cook for our family and they (the boarders) ate with us. Other times my mother would start the gravy and when they came home they would finish their own meals, cooking their own macaroni". For recreation the immigrant workers whiled away their time playing bocci ball or cards at the tavern nearby. "Furthermore, since everybody made their own wine, they would frequently stop in for a drink".

THE MARINOS: PORT WASHINGTON LEADERS

Operation of a boarding house served as a vehicle for upward mobility for some. James Marino of Port Washington, for instance, enjoyed prominence in the community at large becoming a deputy sheriff of Nassau County—a position frequently and conspicuously given to leaders within Long Island Italian colonies undoubtedly in order to assure law and order among the ethnic element.

James Marino was also an entrepreneur with a keen business acumen acquiring, apparently at a low price, such large village real estate holdings, that in time the street on which they were located was named after him. In 1904 he built a stone mansion utilizing his sand bank employees during the normally slow winter months when demands for sand industry products tapered off. Virtually all the material to build the mansion came from his sand bank and the stone was cut on the site by his men. Upon completion the building measured 60 feet by 50 feet, and contained a basement, two floors and an attic. The roof was of red tile. The handsome Italianate showplace with large trees lining the roadway and surrounding house was a mark of success few Italians in America had achieved so rapidly (Interview, Albert Marino, *Port Washington News*, July 9, 1970).

The extensive Marino holdings provided places of residence for various immigrant people. In April 1907, the *Port Washington News* reported that a fire destroyed a combination barn and dwelling on James Marino's property on Middle Neck Road, forcing out the Italians who were sleeping there and the two Polish families who occupied the other building to flee. (*Port Washington News*, April 3, 1907).

Marino's successful sand mine operation proved an inspiration to his cousin Joseph, who emigrated from Nusco in Avellino to Port Washington in the early 1890s. Like James, Generoso DiMita changed his name to Marino and also operated a sand bank, a general store and a boarding house to accomodate paesani.

Despite emulation of one relative by the other, James and Joseph Marino each went on his own and one can only speculate how extensive their holdings might have been had they cooperated in joint ventures rather than engage in competition. As it developed, both men lost heavily during the Great Depression and were left with only fragments of their earlier fortunes.

SETTLERS FROM STURNO

Migration to the several Long Island Italian enclaves followed a pattern which, after the initial location, soon became a well-worn path to a burgeoning immigrant settlement. Once a firm connection was effected by earlier pioneer immigrants, successor paesani immigrants traversed an identical road as in the instance of Italians who settled in Glen Cove.

Glen Cove's Italians came principally from Sturno, a small mountainous town in the Avellino area 30 miles from Naples. Common belief holds that Vito Capobianco, a stoneworker, was the first to migrate to that Long Island town. A worker on an expansive estate then being erected, his letters told of existing job opportunities and thereby underscored the value of the written word as a spur to emigration—a phenomenon readily acknowledged by immigration historians.[1] One analyst of nineteenth century immigration cites a variety of sources about the New World such as guidebooks, gazeteers, geographies and histories which became accessible to Europeans. However, as great as was the authority of the printed word, it paled before that of the personal letter, which was at once more personal and reliable, and generally spoke in glowing terms about the abundant possibilities in America, while providing much useful information for prospective immigrants.

Another account has Filippo Capobianco as the first Italian to settle in Glen Cove. His grandson, Carmine Capobianco, now in his seventies, related that his grandfather emigrated from Sturno to East New York in Brooklyn where he settled in 1896 along with others from his hometown. He subsequently moved to Glen Cove lured to the suburbs by employment on the Long Island Railroad. The Sturno—East New York—Glen Cove pattern was followed by others like Alexander Stanco who arrived in Long Island about the same time as Filippo Capobianco. On the other hand Catherine Cocchiola stated that in 1899 her father left his hometown of Frugento, a town near Sturno, and came directly to Glen Cove to join his paesani already settled there, including the Capobianco, Fusco and Stanco families. Other early comers followed still other odessies such as Jimmy Limongelli who came from Paduli and worked with fellow townsmen in Pennsylvania coal mines. Finding mine conditions less than promising, Limongelli returned to Italy for a few years before he once again decided to try his luck in America—this time in Glen Cove.

IMMIGRANT LABOR ON THE ESTATES

Known for its verdant fields set amidst natural beauty, by the turn of the century Glen Cove attracted wealthy New Yorkers who had adorned the city with palatial homes and were arbiters of its culture. They were now in search of other locations for additional residences, at first for summer recreation purposes and increasingly as permanent homes. Among those who established exquisite Glen Cove estates were the Woolworths, the Pratts, the Graces and the Morgans. The development of a large estate required much manpower. Consolidating large tracts of land (1,100 acres), Charles Pratt developed his estate with the help of hundreds of Italian immigrant laborers and gardeners. Nor was Pratt the only wealthy landowner to use immigrant labor. The practice was emulated by others in nearby Brookville and Locust Valley. Developers of extensive properties encompassing hundreds of acres each, this elite class required the services of a numerous retinue for household needs and for maintenance of the grounds. Italian immigrants were well-qualifed to perform these tasks. From experience and disposition they possessed valuable knowledge about working the land, having demonstrated their skills at stabilizing marshland soil, an expertise which was utilized in Italian farm communities in America. In Glen Cove, estate owners welcomed Italian steadfastness and devotion to the land and engaged them in occupations which often developed into lifetime tenures so that even when estates terminated their existence as family residences, old Italian workers remained. Sturno-born Sylvester Cangaro gained employment in 1903 as gardener on the Brookville property of financier William A. Prime. Cangaro's love for the land was such that when the property came under the ownership of Mrs. Meriweather Post he remained. Known as "Hillwood", this estate enjoyed years of horticultural fame becoming "...one of Long Island's show-places largely through the ceaseless attention of Mr. Cangaro", who was credited with planting most of the original shrubs, trees and ivy which graced the main buildings (*Long Island University Magazine*, 1970, p.36). In 1951, Long Island University acquired the property setting the stage for the creation of C.W. Post College. Cangaro continued as head gardener into 1970 when he died at the age of 91.

As already discussed, many Italian immigrants to Long Island worked on local estates for years, even a lifetime. Such service afforded an opportunity for steady employment at reasonable rates for many and on occasion it was the beginning of the story of personal success in America.

CONSTANTINO POSILLICO: ESTATE OWNER

One of the best examples of a local immigrant success story is that of Constantino (August) Posillico, son of the first Durazzanesi to come into the Westbury community. Born in Italy in 1883, Constantino arrived in America in 1898, and began to work indefatigably to raise a family which eventually reached eight children. Although the beneficiary of little formal education, he possessed a strong natural intelligence and determination to succeed. Accordingly, in the early years he would come home to the boarding house after twelve hours of grounds work and, resisting the temptation to relax, he would pore over his English-Italian dictionary for hours. One night fellow boarders drinking coffee in the downstairs kitchen heard a thud upstairs in his room and, fearing the worst, rushed up to find that he had passed out from the combination of work and study. He strove to affirm the adage, "You put your hands in dirt and you will be successful". Upon arrival in the village he worked as a handyman, gardener and chauffeur for various estates. In time, he became superintendent of the Martin G. West Estate and for a few years the entire Posillico family lived in a building on the estate grounds. Mildly successful in such a position, Constantino remained unsatisfied. In 1927, he rented a house and property on Post Avenue where he began to develop a combination construction and landscaping business, enjoying a modicum of success through his contacts in the Westbury Horticulture Society (Interview, Joseph and Fred Posillico). While Constantino was developing the construction and landscape enterprise, his wife and children established a small live poultry business where local residents could purchase chickens and turkeys slaughtered by Mrs. Posillico. Older residents of the village still remember the chickens that roamed the length of the Posillico property on Post Avenue. Constantino then concentrated on developing the construction firm which engaged in a variety of tasks from building homes to supplying top soil. The equipment was kept in the family garage until family fortunes improved in the 1930s.

Constantino possessed uncanny business acumen, investing in property along Old Country Road at a time when it was strictly a rural roadway and esconced in a setting in which only a hopeless optimist or a truly farsighted individual could predict growth and development. At first the development of Posillico's Old Country Road property was very modest—a hot dog stand, a gasoline station, and a construction business. He built a house for his family on the land, and in time, as age and education permitted, his sons became active in company affairs. The prescient Posillico saw even greater possibilities for the land, envisioning the locus for a large shopping center. His prognostication has proven to be eminently valid. As new stores for the center were being constructed, the brick family house had to be moved back on the property. With continued prosperity, Posillico now was able to purchase the very estate in which he had been employed many years before. Posillico proceeded to divide the estate property, setting aside land for all his children to build their own homes. Currently, several of them live in handsome homes on the property of the old estate which is penetrated by a street named after the elder Posillico—August Lane.[2]

The Constantino Posillico story was not typical. More likely settlement patterns were accounts which were reflective of very modest attainments, patterns which saw Italians originate their economic ascension to, at best, a lower middle class status. Such was the experience of Italian settlers of Patchogue who acquired less than desireable land as their introduction to suburbia.

SCRUB OAK SETTLEMENT IN PATCHOGUE

Italian immigration patterns to Patchogue followed a three-step sequence: 1) temporary residence in one of New York's Little Italies; 2) moving to North Bellport or East Patchogue; 3) settlement in Patchogue. This was the sequence followed by the Stephani and Felice families. Frank Felice, the head of one branch of the numerous local Felice clans, had emigrated from Italy to Brooklyn as a teenager, where he married in 1892 and with his immigrant wife, moved into Bellport where he worked as a mason. After 37 years of Bellport residency, the Felices moved to Patchogue in 1929 (*Patchogue Advance*, August 27, 1942).

As the pioneer Italian family in the Patchogue area, the Stephanis were in a position to encourage other conationals to follow in their footsteps. In emulation came the Mailer (Mele) family, who emigrated from Lorenza in northern Italy to New York's Mulberry Street in the latter part of the 19th century, purchased land in East Patchogue in the 1880s for $5.00 per lot, and subsequently built the family home. Small, spry and still energetic despite her 95 years, Catherine Mailer Stephani told of her background: born in Little Italy in 1889, her family moved to Long Island in 1896 after her father had completed the house. In time she married one of the Stephanis; she and her 75 year old son Joseph continue to live in the house built by her husband (Interview, Catherine Mailer Stephani, December 12, 1984).

For many an Italian pioneer into the Patchogue area, the Roe name constituted the important connecting link at the turn of the century when Patchogue was on the brink of major expansion. The proprietor of large land holdings of scrub woodlands in and around Patchogue, Austin Roe also operated a well-known hotel (*Patchogue Advance*, March 29, 1962). His son Justus became a formidable factor when he coupled his inventive abilities with his public position as road commissioner and invented the steel tape measure. In time, the Roes built a thriving business manufacturing surveying instruments. It was not surprising therefore, to find Italian newcomers to the region working for the Roe family, if not in the manufacturing end, certainly in the agricultural/ land-use end. This was the route followed by a number of Calabrian immigrants such as the Lotito and Mazzotti families (*See,* Femminella, 1968).

Born in Terranova di Sibari, Calabria, fifteen year old Louis Lotito migrated to the United States, worked as a waterboy on the railroads in the Buffalo, New York, area and, after several years, in the mid-1880s came to Patchogue as a farmhand on Roe's Farm. An ambitious young man, in time he came to purchase the land where he was first employed. Over the decades his descendants went on to become principal factors in the vicinity.

In 1896, two year old Rose Mazzotti, also born in Terranova di Sibari, was brought to the United States in the first of three transatlantic journeys over ten years before the family settled here permanently. Rose confirmed the power of informal chain migration in which pioneer settlers spread the word to friends and relatives who followed their lead. The Mazzotti family came to Patchogue "because there was an uncle, my mother's Uncle Lotito, and we went to work on the Roe farm where we spent three years. There were only a few Italians here then from my hometown" (Interview, Rose Mazzotti Romeo).

The Mazzotti family came at the request of "Uncle Lotito", caretaker of the Roe farm, who needed more manpower and who shared his house with the relatives, thereby providing Rose with an opportunity to glean her first impressions about life on a Long Island farm at the turn of the century. She remembers a house with no electricity, served instead by kerosene lamps—it was her duty to keep the lamps cleaned and filled. Heat was provided by a coal stove with the coal stored in a covered bin outside the kitchen. Transportation was by bicycle, horse and carriage or sleigh in the winter. Other chores entrusted to young Rose were helping her father deliver milk, sewing and mending for her family and scrubbing the wooden floor. Not much time was left for play and even if there was time, girls of her era were discouraged from "unladylike" athletics and gymnastics.

The other Italians then present in the Patchogue area were the Stephanis, Garafolas, Lotitos, Gruccis, Felices, Prudents, Fuocos and Gazolas. When Rose's father learned that Mrs. Gazola had had convent training in Italy, he sent Rose to the Gazolas where she lived for a time learning the womanly arts of etiquette, cooking and sewing from the older woman. It is clear from

Rose's testimony that her Uncle Louis Lotito was the earliest Italian to reside in the Patchogue village and that because of his instigation many others from the Calabrian hometown came there (Interview, Rose Mazzotti Romeo).

The Romeo family, for example, related to the Lotitos and from the same village, emigrated to East Patchogue and eventually settled in Patchogue village. In time dozens of Romeo family members became inhabitants of the village, including Frank Romeo whom Rose had known in Italy when he was eighteen years old and she nine. Because of Rose's tender age, her parents regarded Frank's enamoration of Rose a premature infatuation. Frank arrived in New York City in 1902 "with no money, no family, no job", but with the help of hometown paesani he obtained employment as a contractor's helper finishing sidewalks. After learning that his beloved Rose lived in Patchogue with her family, Frank resumed his courtship even if it meant undertaking strenuous 65 mile bicycle rides on weekends from New York City. However, he soon moved to Patchogue and gained employment as a stone mason and a bricklayer—crafts which he had learned in Italy from his father. On January 16, 1910, when he was 25 and she was sixteen, Frank and Rose were married and proceeded to raise a family of eight children.

Cosenza-born Antonio Fuoco was the head of a pioneer Bellport Italian family. Entering the country in the 1880s, he learned of the availability of cheap land in the Patchogue vicinity, and bicycled over 50 miles each way on weekends to inspect and purchase land in what is now North Bellport. Antonio Fuoco was the first of his nationality to establish himself in the northern part of Bellport where in due course he constructed a four room family house for his wife, daughter Elizabeth and three sons. Although illiterate, Antonio's natural business ability enabled him to expand his house and purchase additional property until, in time, he became the largest local Italian real estate holder. His twelve room rustic brick house stands as an eclectic home which accommodated not only family needs as in the case of bedrooms, kitchen, *etc.*, but also housed a general store serving the immediate neighborhood. The second floor hall, a large room perhaps 60 x 25 feet, was the location for many a community function such as club meetings, political conferences, weddings and even funerals for local Italian families too poor to rent commercial funeral parlors. He stored hay and other farm supplies in a large barn adjoining a spacious field which was the site for ball games and local celebrations such as on Christmas Eve when local Italians commemorated the event with a huge bonfire. It is no surprise that Fuoco Avenue became the center of the growing North Bellport Italian enclave which increased from 128 in 1900 to 415 in 1915 (*See, New York State Census, Brookhaven Town*, 1915).

It is interesting to note that a significant number of pioneer families capitalized on their early arrival by developing businesses in the community. Immigrant John Ginocchio, who was probably the first of his nationality to own a business in Patchogue, opened his ice cream and confectionary store in 1890. For years the intersection in which the store was located was known as "Ginocchio's Corner". James Stephani and Frank Romeo both became active in road construction, gaining credit for building some of the more important roadways in Suffolk County. Pasquale Felice and his sons were also contractors in Patchogue's Little Italy, however, the Felice name is best known locally for starting a restaurant which still endures and which is considered a habitue of town politicians.

A penchant for business enterprise was a concomitant of Italian presence on Long Island. The business drive was important for self-improvement and economic advancement; it was also helpful for the development of an entire community. Nothing illustrates this better than the example of Marconiville (Copiague).

PROMOTING MARCONIVILLE

Promoters of real estate have always functioned along the cutting edge of American settlement. Whether it was in the American West or in the outlying suburbs of large cities, land promoters were present to entice buyers to purchase real estate. This activity led to the influx of various groups, including Italians, to Long Island. With an ingenuity that approximated that of the shrewdest hucksters of the day, Giovanni Campagnoli, one time classmate of Guglielmo Marconi and owner of land he dubbed "Marconiville", utilized every opportunity at his disposal to foster his land venture. Thus, whenever the famed inventor came to the United States, Campagnoli seized it as an opportunity to advertise his Copiague property. For the tiny Marconiville ethnic enclave the personal visit or even the possibility of a Marconi visit was regarded as an auspicious occasion.

The first Marconi visit, planned for early 1913, found Campagnoli assiduously advertising the projected appearance in the real estate sections of the Italian language press (In *Il Progresso Italo-Americano*, January 11, 1913). There is doubt that this projected visit actually occurred, however, since there was no further mention of it either in the local media or in the standard Italian language newspapers. Marconi did come to the Long Island town in 1917, during which time he was serving on an Italian government mission which endeavored to rally sympathy and support within the United States for his home country, then embroiled in World War I.

Tito Tranquili, born in Florence and a young, newly-arrived immigrant to Copiague at the time, remembers the occasion well since he was one of the few men in town with a driver's license and was therefore approached about his availability to drive Marconi to the Long Island hamlet (Interview, Tito Tranquili, July 1, 1980). Greeted by an excited audience, Marconi responded with vibrant emotion that he had never received such a reception. He kissed the young Bernagazzi girl who presented him with a bouquet of flowers and then posed for photographs. Later, with cries of "Viva Marconi, viva il genio Italiano", ringing in his ears, he returned to New York City (*Il Progresso Italo-Americano*, July 17, 1917).

In 1927, Marconi made another visit to the hamlet which bore his name. Accompanied by his wife and important business leaders, he addressed a large turnout at the Marconi Community League Clubhouse which was bedecked with Italian and English banners prompting Marconi to announce his pride in being in such a progressive community (*Amityville Record*, October 21, 1927).

Although these visits attracted many non-Italians from within and outside of Copiague, they were especially significant for the Americans of Italian descent since they represented marks of noteworthy distinction. For an ethnic group not enjoying prominence within the Long Island setting, it proved heartwarming, if even for a few hours, to be associated with a globally esteemed figure.

Operating his real estate office in New York City and advertising his development in the Italian language press such as *Il Progresso Italo-Americano*, *Giornale d'Italia* and *Bolletino della Sera*, Campagnoli spread the word about Marconiville far and wide. Aware of the discontent of many of New York City's Italian-American population in being forced to reside in congested urban quarters, and congnizant of their long-harbored dream of obtaining their own land, Campagnoli emphasized the unique opportunity Marconiville represented. His advertisements appealed to their desires for home ownership by coupling it with the equally desirable goal of living among fellow ethnics in a "...singular Italian village". One of his agents scoured Italian colonies as distant as Virginia in efforts to interest fellow countrymen to buy lots in the area.

Campagnoli had some initial success with northern Italians such as the Giorgini family which had previously lived in East Harlem and Belmont, the Little Italy of the Bronx. Octagenarian Iola Giorgini was a seven year old girl when her family purchased property from Campagnoli and built a home in Marconiville. While her father and uncle, who were among the earliest Italian residents of Marconiville, worked in New York City, Iola and her contemporaries became the first generation of Italian youngsters to grow up in that suburb.

Iola remembered the village as numbering perhaps a few hundred, most of whom were from the older portion, south of the tracks. This group held a low opinion of Italians. In retaliation, the Italian element derisively referred to old-stock southerners as "clam diggers". Iola went to Copiague's elementary school and followed that with high school in Amityville, since Copiague did not then have its own upper level school. In the prevailing social pecking order, Amityville residents were "snobs" in their relations with the Copiaguers while the older Copiague residents similarly looked down their noses at the Italians. In an unusual display of educational prescience together with a strong sense of ethnic roots, Iola's father supplemented her formal education with private tutoring in Italian. With the exception of the latter point, Iola's story of movement from the city to the suburbs is not atypical of other northern Italian Marconiville settlers. Italian residents of other ethnic enclaves underwent similar socialization.

Most of Campagnoli's promotional effort was directed at southern Italian enclaves in New York City and the surrounding metropolitan region. An interesting example of this was to enlist a saloon proprietor's aid on Linden Street, in the Bushwick section of Brooklyn. Because of his frequent contacts with local residents this business became the vehicle through which various Copiague property purchases were effected. Some bought lots they lost only a few years later during the Great Depression. Others, such as Antonio Gorgone, made an initial down payment, followed it up with subsequent payments and finally moved into the community. Antonio Gorgone, 72 year old son of the senior Gorgone, related the account of how his father first heard of Marconiville from the Linden Street saloonkeeper. He remembered also that Campagnoli, who held the house mortagage, became over-zealous in reminding mortgagees to make their payments—sometimes leading to unpleasantness. Thus, when Campagnoli came repeatedly to the Gorgone home for payments, the by now angry Gorgone refused, producing receipts of payments which entitled him to his property deed. Gorgone's combativeness probably was due also to a feeling that the developer had misled him. Gorgone was originally shown a model home in a very desireable location in the heat of the summer when conditions were dry. However, he had been sold property in a swamp-like area. Undaunted, in 1917 Gorgone completed building his house and moved in his family (Interview, Antonio Gorgone).

JOHN CAMPAGNOLI

John Campagnoli proved to be an assiduous promoter personally supervising the development right down to the laying out and naming or changing of street names in order to effect an Italian ring to them. The result is that Copiague bears more street titles named after historic Italian figures than any other settlement in New York and quite probably the nation. To travel through old Marconiville is to pass street signs featuring names such as Verrazzano, Mazzini, Verdi, Dante, Marconi, Vespucci, Caboto, Colombo, Pio Nono X and Garibaldi, not to mention those named after some of the early Italian families in the community such as Campagnoli and Barcellona.[3] That Campagnoli was determined to create a distinctive Italian community in the suburban setting was clear. As he noted:

In 1913, I founded on Long Island in the locality called Copiague, a village which, in honor of the inventor of the Wireless Telegraph, I christened Marconiville and which, with very few exceptions, is inhabited exclusively by persons of Italian birth including well-to-do businessmen, merchants, contractors, skilled and unskilled working men, all of them prosperous and law-abiding (the majority citizens) and people who are proud of the progressive career of the village (Vacca, et al., 1948).

Totally committed to the project, Campagnoli became a naturalized American citizen and converted his pleasure automobile into a truck in order to transfer building materials (*Amityville Record*, June 21; September 27, 1912). A peripatetic man, Campagnoli could be seen inspecting houses under construction, making certain that sidewalks were layed properly and that a clean and tidy appearance prevailed.

By the 1920s Campagnoli had built a magnificent two-story home. Replete with traditional Italian architectural designs and trimmings, constructed from material largely imported from the old country, it consituted the transplanting of an edifice of the Italian elite in the United States. Long-time next door neighbor Renato Giorgini recalled its magnificence. "I remember he had all those statues that were brought from Italy encased in the walls. There was a house for the servants and a garage". The house featured a downstairs kitchen, a dumbwaiter to hoist meals to the upstairs dining room, a large fireplace in the living room, dazzling terazzo floors, Italian-style bathrooms constructed with imported tiles and a large enclosed porch with glass walls (Interview, Renato Giorgini). It was easily one of the finer examples of Italian architecture in the area and the most impressive house in the community. Campagnoli's son Hugo maintained the house for a time after his father's death. Subsequently, it was purchased by Our Lady of the Assumption Parish which used it for religious education classes. Eventually it was vacated, condemned and demolished.

Local Italians possessed ambivalent feelings about Campagnoli. To some he appeared to be too strongly motivated by material considerations, precluding a sense of friendship and sympathy poorer Italians like to see in their leaders. Since his sales were largely on the basis of down payments, he also retained mortgages on the properties entitling him to reclaim them should mortgagees forfeit. Accordingly, he badgered those in arrears and on occasion, reclaimed homes. Other early Italian settlers held, however, more positive impressions about the man. MaryAnn Megna Rudolph (Ridulfo), for example, related how her father held Campagnoli in the highest esteem. She had fond memories of how effusive Campagnoli was in his gratitude to her whenever she would bring him a basket of fruit and vegetables from her father's expansive garden.

Among the edifices Campagnoli constructed was a hotel on property he owned on Dixon Avenue and Great Neck Boulevard, which he named in honor of Guglielmo Marconi. The hotel went through several ownerships before being completely destroyed by fire in 1925 (*Amityville Record*, June 12, 1925).

Extending beyond real estate, Campagnoli's self-appointed leadership affected the social and cultural life of the community. *The Amityville Record*, the major local newspaper although preoccupied with its own village, did, nevertheless, report Copiague events, especially the activities of the long-established population. When activities of local Italian Americans of the pre-World War I era were reported they were usually the social activities of the Campagnoli family, revealing a picture of a family with extended friendships and contacts within and without the community. Birthday parties for the Campagnoli children were attended by Italian friends such as the Giorginis, the Bernagazzis and by non-Italians. Among the out of town visitors who frequented the Campagnoli home were an array of personalities which bespoke of familiarity with the "right people": Boston society members, leading Italian professors, important Italian newspapermen and members of the Italian nobility. Parties hosted by the family revolved around genteel and sophisticated activities such as listening to piano recitals and operatic arias. Furthermore, the family partook of cultural events in New York City such as attending the Metropolitan Opera House. Education and proper upbringing of the children received high priority. The two sons were formally educated in local public schools and both attended New York University—one becoming an engineer, the other a medical doctor. Clearly this was not the typical, poor, uncultured Italian immigrant style so characteristic of the masses of the time.

The Campagnoli family was an exception to the more traditional story of Italian immigrants on Long Island. The simple fact was that the masses could not aspire to partake of the same amenities as those enjoyed by the Campagnolis in the early part of the century. The vast majority were not destined to go to college or to imbibe in the more elevated expressions of bourgeoisie suburban life. The majority considered their settlement in suburbia perhaps an improvement over residence in the thickly-settled Little Italies of the city, however, they did not regard movement to the suburbs as a panacea. Transplantation from urban to suburban settings might provide expanded opportunities for economic and social growth. However, the overwhelming perception of Long Island Italians throughout the first half of the century was that of a working class people. Within these parameters settlement in the suburbs was seen as a step in the right direction.

We have seen settlement in suburbia pursue a predictable course of following leads first developed by family members or paesani, and then making necessary accomodations consistent with meager resources. Settlement patterns produced a phenomenon of attempts to transplant village customs from the old world to suburban places usually after temporary residence in a classic city Little Italy. Securing compatible residences for living was naturally intertwined with employment possibilities. So long as jobs were present it was feasible to develop ethnic neighborhoods. It is this topic which will now be treated.

FOOTNOTES

[1] *Newsday Magazine*, July 4, 1976. Although this account mentions a carpenter named Chiucholo, Catherine Cocchiola maintains that name was erroneous, and that it undoubtedly was her father Anselo Cocchiola who should have been cited. Interview, Catherine Cocchiola, February 28, 1983. With regard to the indispensable role played by immigrant letters which furnished information to prospective immigrants, *see*, Marcus Lee Hansen, *The Atlantic Migration*, New York 1961, Pp. 152-153, and Maldwyn Allen Jones, *American Immigration*, Chicago 1961, p. 100.

[2] Constantino came to be known as "Gus" or August, which he eventually adopted as his own name. Interview, Joseph and Fred Posillico, March 9, 1979.

[3] Regarding Italian street names, *see, Map of Section The Brinckerhoff Manor, Copiague, Long Island, Suffolk County*, surveyed by Birdsall Johnson, 1906, which shows very few streets in the area and only two recognizable Italian names such as Verdi and Margherita Avenues. This suggests a predisposition toward Italianitá evident before Campagnoli became president of the Sovereign Realty Company.

CHAPTER FOUR
UNITY FOR EMPLOYMENT

Hungry for work opportunities on Long Island, Italian immigrants found such abundant employment that by 1900 they constituted the largest portion of foreign born laborers. Filling jobs at the lower end of the economic ladder, they proved to be indispensable factors for the development of various industries. Most of the work involved the use of learned skills such as working the soil and other forms of outdoor labor. Accordingly, as stated in Chapter 2, Italian immigrants in Westbury became the principal work force on the burgeoning estates and the flourishing nurseries, chief of which was the Hicks Nursery Company.

Hicks Nursery

Employment with the Hicks company enabled Italian immigrants to learn the techniques of transplanting huge trees—work necessitating careful coordination and raw brawn of men and horses.

Hours were long and the pay small in the pre-World War I era, averaging ten hours a day, six days a week at the rate of $1.50 to $1.75 a day. The weekly pay fluctuated between $9.00 and $11.00, with additional allowances for extraordinary conditions as, for instance, when the nursery sent workers to plant trees on important estates in locations as far away as Rhode Island and Virginia. Out-of-state work meant staying on the job and away from home and family for days, weeks, even months. Thus, from November 1905 to April 1906 Anniello Daddio, Jemi Buffalino, Mike Mayo and Tony Naples were sent to work in the Jamestown Exposition, a national showcase then being developed in Norfolk, Virginia (Many names of the immigrant workers were either English phonetic approximations or their Italian counterparts or deliberately changed; the labor records reveal, however, their nationalities). Accompanied by a black foreman the Italians were supplied with blankets, mattresses and pillows and $2.00 per day salary, and other extras. The men purchased their own food at an Italian store in Hampton, Virginia (*Hempstead Sentinel*, April 9, 1908).

In 1906 the nursery sent six Italians to work for five weeks at the McAlpin Estate in Morristown, New Jersey, during which time they boarded with families in the Morristown Italian colony. This prolonged separation from their families in Westbury proved too intolerable and, contrary to company policy and at company expense, they returned to their homes on Easter Sunday. Although critical of the action, the company refrained from punitive measures, merely noting the infraction on the company labor records (*Hicks Labor Record*).

Employment on the estates and the Hicks Nursery was primarily an individual act between employer and employee. There is no indication that the padrone system, utilized by many Italians elsewhere as a means of obtaining employment and frequently an exploitative experience, was in usage in Westbury. Rather, there evolved an informal association between family members and *paesani*. Thus, jobs and residences were realized through word of mouth, advice and knowledge of friends and relatives. As such, it is not surprising to find more than one family member working for the same employer.

Little organized labor activity was evident among Westbury Italians in the estates and nurseries. As Aniello Piscitelli put it, "No strike, no union in those days". There is no trace of organized union activity in the Westbury vicinity in the early years of the century. Edwin Hicks, who became engaged in his father's business in the 1920s, had no recollection of union activity throughout his years with the firm. Discussions with participant estate and nursery workers affirm the prevailing accepted thesis that the Italian immigrant role in the organized labor struggles which convulsed American life during this period was slight. Their low profile in formal labor unions, led to a somewhat erroneous conclusion that most of the immigrant's were intent on their own personal survival and that of their families. "To eat and sleep today and tomorrow was the limit of their ambition as it had been in the arid land of their birth" (Amfitheatrof, p.73). It was almost as if they failed to comprehend the potential power of their solidarity. Yet, this evaluation seems too harsh for Italians of Westbury because, in fact, on one occasion in 1906 they banded together for their mutual benefit albeit in the absence of a formal union.

At the time, the Hicks Nursery employed 55 men—35 of whom were Italians—who were paid an average of fifteen cents an hour, working ten hours a day, six days a week, thereby earning between $9.00 and $10.00 per week or $408.00 a year. This was supplemented by nine storm days and eleven days annually for paid absences, for a total of $438.00 a year. Regarding these wages too meager and the hours too long, fifteen workers struck the company on August 20, 1906, and the records indicated that several others were leaning toward the strike. All the strikers as well as those who considered joining in the move were Italians including the leaders: Jemi Lazzarino, Tommy Somma, Mike Mayo, Joe Ross and Frank Coppola (*Hicks Labor Record*).

Marcus and Joe Daddio became deeply involved, to the extent of offering the use of their homes as assembly places where strikers could discuss strategy. The ethnic familial linkup was evident in the realization that three Daddio brothers were prominent among the strikers. Their domestic physical proximity seemed to served them well in their determination to strike for just demands. On the other hand, the strike found some families split over the issue as in the instance of the Yanuchis (Iannuccis) who numbered Rocco Iannucci as among the "loyal" workers, while Jemi Yanuchi was an aggressive strike leader. Interestingly, Poles, Germans and blacks were listed as "loyal". Of the forty men who were not listed as among the strikers, fifteen were "loyal" Italians, while the attitudes of five other Italians were "unknown". The strike lasted from August 20 to August 25, 1906 and at least one leader (Jemi Yanuchi) was discharged for insubordination. The workers won a wage increase seeing their salaries rise from fifteen cents to seventeen and a half cents an hour. This was not necessarily extended to newly-hired men, especially teenagers who more likely received $1.00 per day (*Hicks Labor Record*).

The low wages for the period under review must be measured against its own time in American history and against average wages for comparable work in Italy. Comparison with wages earned by Italians elsewhere is revealing. During this same period Italian workers in St.Louis earned between $1.95 and $2.23 per day while in Buffalo's canneries they were earning from $1.25 to $1.75 per day and workers in the Louisiana sugar fields averaged $1.40 daily (*See,* McLaughlin, 1974; Scarpaci, 1975). Accordingly, Westbury's pay scale was in line with national averages and much higher than the prevailing wages in Italy which found *contadini* (farm laborers) and *braccianti* (hired day laborers) working for 40 cents a day.

Wages did not rise rapidly in the nursery industry so that in 1913 when the Hicks Nursery firm was once again beset by worker demands for a shorter work day, management responded with a proposal which included an increase in wages for 26 employees from $9.00 to $10.00 per week, and for fourteen men to be advanced from $10.00 to $10.50 per week, while still a third group saw an increase from $10.00 to $11.00 weekly. The firm was unwilling, however, to reduce the number of hours per day maintaining that its customers would not accept less than what they had originally contracted. The only concession was to decrease the Saturday workday by one-half hour. The normal workday began at 7:00 a.m. and concluded at 5:00 p.m. Time involved in going to and from the place of employment, frequently extended the work day to more than eleven hours, six days a week. The company asserted that workers should express gratitude for being employed at the nursery since it provided them, their families and the entire community with great benefit. Furthermore, it did not grant increases to all the employees. Anthony Piscitelli, for example, was refused a request for a raise with a letter reminding him that he should consider himself fortunate to be gainfully employed in year-round work, rather than seasonal employment, which characterized employment elsewhere.

The *ad hoc* activity of nursery workers in Westbury was matched by action in other large-scale Long Island businesses such as the Long Island Railroad. In this instance, however, there was the benefit of a formal labor organization.

LONG ISLAND RAILROAD

The Long Island Railroad played a major role in employment opportunities for Italian Americans on Long Island from the 1880s on, hiring them to extend the lines into the more remote parts on the island as well as for general maintenance work. Although by the turn of the century Italians could be said to have become the major ethnic group within the work force, they were not always welcomed. In 1890, acting upon the complaints of some influential passengers, the line prohibited Italians from riding in coach cars, confining them to the smokers instead (*Amityville Record*, March 3, 1944).

Many a Marconiville Italian American worked as a laborer on the Long Island Railroad. Antonio Gorgone's father, for example, was a laborer who worked for a time on local farms, then in factories, and finally for the Long Island Railroad where he became foreman of a gang of laborers—mostly Italians whom he recruited to work in a variety of maintenance and clean-up operations. This was the beginning of railroad employment for three generations of Marconiville Gorgones. Antonio himself began with the transportation system as a young man and remained on the job for the rest of his working life, retiring finally after 49 years. Now, in retirement, he keeps abreast of railroad developments through his son who continues the tradition (Interview, Antonio Gorgone).

Despite the employment of large numbers of laborers by big industries on Long Island, more Italians worked in factories and shops which frequently employed only a handful of people. Employment in these modest-sized facilities enabled many an Italian family in Marconiville to eke out a living.

SMALL FACTORIES

By 1917, work opportunities in Marconiville expanded as a result of the opening of small factories. For example, in 1914 Tavermina and DiGiuseppe of Brooklyn began manufacturing women's skirts in a new plant which employed 35 people. This was welcome news to the growing local job-seeking Italian population. In the next three years two more firms started Copiague clothing manufacturing factories which employed dozens of people (*Amityville Record*, July 17, 1914, May 10, 1940, July 2, 1959).

In 1915, one of these, the Colin pants factory, became the focus of a major dispute with far-flung ramifications. At a time when New York City garment workers were engaged in a militant effort to unionize his plant, Colin started his Copiague operation in an apparent effort to reduce production costs. A city garment workers' union sent organizer Lorenzo DeMaria to unionize the Long Island pants workers—an effort which met with success and resulted in a Copiague strike action. What ensued was a three-week work stoppage finally ending when employers acceded to the union demand for a $2.00 per week raise and a decrease in the workday to nine hours (*Il Lavoro*, July 14, 1917).

The strike revealed not only the natural antipathy existent between labor and management, but also the intriguing machinations on the part of a small clique of Italians in Copiague who, although not connected with the factory, was ready to sacrifice worker objectives by advising them not to strike. Indeed, union sources charged actual collusion between factory owners and this reactionary element within the Copiague Italian community. The union asserted its determination to unionize the plant. Although the dispute was eventually resolved favorably, there was no public revelation about the membership of the anti-union group.

CONSTRUCTION WORKERS ACTIVITY

It was axiomatic that expanding American communities were in the utmost need of manpower. For many on Long Island this meant tapping the large immigrant labor pool in New York City: Polish, Italian, Russian, *etc.* The Italians came to play an indispensable role in building and transforming Glen Cove into a modern suburban center. In 1900 they were employed as laborers in the construction of Glen Cove's new St.Patrick's Church and, although poor and in dire need of work, they were not so docile that they would not fight for what was rightfully theirs. On August 15, 1900, they struck the construction building firm because, over a protracted period, the contractor had failed to pay them. Tired of empty promises "...until driven by desperation and in the absence of the contractors they threatened to blow up the building". It was no idle threat:

> It required the greatest tact on the part of Senator Norton and the presence of Sheriff Wood to allay the passions of a gang of Italians at work at the new St.Patrick's Church and avert serious damage to property and perhaps loss of life, on Tuesday...they called the priest in charge...away from the confessional, and after considerable parlaying they succeeded in pacifying the men and they went peaceably away. There has been considerable complaint along this line for some

months but this the first outbreak (*Oyster Bay Guardian*, August 17, 1900).

The local press made no further mention of the matter, leading one to suppose that it was resolved favorably for the workers.

To meet the needs of an expanding village, local Glen Cove authorities approved the construction of a water works which saw a general construction firm hire dozens of New York City Italian laborers. It was the prevailing view that these people could be had for low wages and that their docility assured no interruption in the work schedule. Troublesome workers, even if they consisted of an entire work gang of a given nationality, could easily be replaced by a gang of another national background, thus precluding worker solidarity. Much to the surprise of observers who were inclined to characterize Italian immigrants as inimical to the labor movement, on April 29, 1903, the workers went on strike for an increase to $1.50 per day. Because they were engaged in laying large four inch pipes for the water works on Glen Street, a main village thoroughfare, this brought great consternation to local leaders. Wishing to prevent a complete work stoppage, the contractor acceded to their demands and they returned to work. However, they promptly struck again—in behalf of a nine hour day. This time management refused to make concessions and proposed to replace the strikers with new city workers—a task which resulted in a standstill for many days. The company actually did engage a new work gang of 75. However, upon arriving at a terminal point in Queens, the latter was met by a delegation of strikers who persuaded them to go back to New York City. The company's effort to hire Polish strikebreakers likewise was frustrated. Finally, on May 9, when a new gang was brought in, they were driven out of the trenches by the striking Italians.

> They were persuaded to work at 1 p.m., but the strikers again drove them off. On Friday evening the leader of the strike was arrested and on Tuesday was sentenced to thirty days. The strikers expressed a willingness to return to work on Saturday at the old terms of $1.50 for a day and they were taken back and a large gang is now at work (*Oyster Bay Guardian*, May 1,8, 1903, May 15, 1943).

Only a partial victory, the incident nevertheless illustrates that Glen Cove Italians were prepared to fight for just wages and hours. The editor of the *Oyster Bay Guardian* saw the event as a potentially serious harbinger of things to come because it threatened to interrupt a number of work projects and also held out the spectre of violence causing a "...stench in the nostrils of all conservative men" (*Oyster Bay Guardian*, May 1,8, 1903). The paucity of other similar instances of labor militancy is perhaps due to the limited number of local mass industries and the greater likelihood that the local Italian laborers worked estates or construction projects outside the locale.

SAND MINE WORKERS

In an era when little attention was given to the welfare of workers, Italian Americans suffered their share of misfortune due to accidents or deaths. Thus the community of sand bank workers and their families stood in constant dread of accidents which befell men all too frequently in the late 19th and early 20th centuries. One estimate was that every year saw two to three deaths due to sand mine accidents and several accidents causing injury on the job (Shenton, 1982). Not all victims were of Italian ancestry, of course, as Poles, Scandinavians and others suffered the same fate. The following account provides the sense of alarm experienced upon learning of an accident.

> Chief Snow and men hustled to the bank where they found the most deplorable scene they had ever witnessed in this vicinity. A large sand washing machine 100 feet high, with a storage capacity of 25,000 tons, a mass of wreckage while eleven men who had been working upon or near the machine were lying here and there where they had been pulled out of the ruins by their fellow workers. It was a horrible sight to look upon, and it made many present, who, like Chief Snow had seen many sad sights in their time, feel faint at heart. Without the slightest warning the massive structure separated itself from another and crashed to the ground, carrying death and injury with it...one Jerry Lorenz, an Italian, being killed outright...(*Port Washington News*, June 25, 1910).

Reference to Italian victims over the years underscores the relevance of recurring tragedies to the ethnic group. In May 1929 Dominick Larriga, an employee of the Goodwin-Gallagher Sand and Gravel Company, was killed in an accident when a sand pit locomotive ran over him. In August 1932, 46 year old Tony Natale, described as one of the ten best workers in the sand mines, was suffocated when a huge amount of sand fell over him. In May 1935, Mauro DeMeo, 56, was killed when he fell into a hopper (*Port Washington News*, May 10, 1929, August 5, 1932, May 3, 1935). Sand-mining accidents were respectors of neither age nor experience, as the case of 67 year old Charles Salerno illustrates. Arriving in Port Washington in 1905, he had been a sand worker nearly all his life when, in December 1949, he was injured in a cave-in at the sand banks. He received a shoulder injury, nursed it at home for a day and returned to work. Less than two months later he was killed instantly when he either lost his footing or got his coat caught in a sand feeding machine (*Port Washington News*, January 27, 1950; Interview, Helen Dejanno).

Industrial deaths decreased in the post-World War II period although the work activity still causes its share of injuries. Santo Bassi, 57, who came from Trieste to the Port Washington sand mines in 1957, considered himself lucky that in his 25 year tenure he was able to work in an activity he loved since childhood—the maintenance of ships, a trade he had learned in his native land. Upon employment in the sand mines in Port Washington he became a caulker, eventually becoming foreman over 22 men who performed similar duties. In time, fiberglass boats began to replace the older wooden crafts, requiring re-assignment to other boat-related tasks. Unfortunately, in 1982 Bassi fell from a post and broke a leg. A year later, walking with the aid of a cane, he realized he could never return to his former job since the type of work he performed required sure footing and stability.

Poor and desperate for work, Port Washington's Italians were not, however, docile or passive employees who were putty in the hands of exploitative employers. Rather early in the 20th century these workers demonstrated a refreshing degree of solidarity in tackling the power of the sand magnates. The issues were bread and butter ones in 1908 as 150 Italians struck the sand pits demanding a 25 cents a day wage increase over the $1.50 standard pay of the time. It is a salient point to note that although many nationalities were represented among the employees, only the Italians walked out—a development which reflected the ethnic division among the ranks and which was a favorite technique used by employers bent on preventing labor unification. The singular action on the part of the Italian immigrant workers stands as indisputable testimony to a labor committment, and to a willingness to join in a common enterprise to improve their lot.

The cohesiveness of ethnic ties served to cross company boundaries as the strike proceeded to affect all workers in the screening operations of all the sand companies in town. With the usual media penchant for associating strikes with violence, the local press spread the word that the strikers threatened physical harm should strikebreakers be brought in. For their part the sand companies maintained that the long-planned strike agitation implied that outside influences were fomenting disorder. The use of 150 local firemen deputized by authorities along with 50 men brought in from the Federal Detective Agency broke the strike. Clearly the strike-breaking forces made the difference, intimidating strikers who were actually outnumbered by these hostile forces including some whose association with law enforcement was dubious. Despite a newspaper pre-occupation with probable violence, only two or three Italian strikers were actually apprehended with weapons, although 125 strikers were arrested. Commenting on the supposed threats of violence, the *Port Washington News* said, "It didn't look as if the Italians meant to do any real fighting".

It was reported that those arrested lost their jobs and were fined up to $40.00 for disorderly conduct, significant sums considering the rate of contemporary wage scales. Many were forced to borrow from their countrymen while some went to jail until the fines were paid. The strike lasted five days and the dismissed workers were replaced by other foreigners, mostly Poles brought in from Garden City and New Hyde Park. Little sympathy was extended to the strikers although some newspaper accounts did mitigate their criticisms, "...and right here in Justice, the *News* must say that the strikers behaved themselves like men from the beginning of the strike to the finish" (*Port Washington News*, May 23, 1908).

In returning to the sand pits they accepted prevailing labor conditions of $1.75 for a ten hour day, six days a week, minus job security. As one veteran miner put it, "You had to work because when you went to the sand pits in the morning, there was a bunch of people there waiting. If you did not do your job or work hard enough, the bosses would put their hands in their pockets, pay you off and get somebody to replace you" (Interview, Ralph Lamberti). Although the 1908 sand workers strike failed in the immediate sense, especially since the workers remained unorganized until the 1930s, in another sense the 1908 incident was not a total defeat, but rather a necessary step to sensitize the public to the needs of local workers.

The lot of Italian immigrant families in the sand banks was indeed one of hard work and sacrifice, as the stories of Josephine DiLeo Caminera and Helen Salerno Dejanna illustrate. Josephine's father was born in Torella di Lombardi, the home of most early Italians of Port Washington. He came to the Long Island town originally in 1896, returning to Italy several times before he married and settled in Port Washington in 1902, becoming a sand bank worker. In time he brought his family from Italy. Josephine remembers life as a young girl on Shore Road, the site of the Hesah home—a company-owned estate of some 50 rooms—where several Italian families who worked for the O'Brien Sand and Gravel Company lived and rented two rooms for $4.00 per month. Inured to self-sufficiency, the Italians operated their own farms on which they raised chickens and grew vegetables and fruit, thereby minimizing outside purchases. One of the residents owned a cow which supplied milk for all the families. Frappoalo's Bakery delivered Italian bread to the families except in deep winter when the snows made the roads impassable. During those occasions Josephine's or Helen's father would make the long trip to the bakery and return with a sack of 40 or 50 loaves to supply the neighboring families. Josephine's father remained a sand bank worker until both his legs were broken so badly that one was amputated in 1942. Charles Salerno's career followed a slightly different course. He left the sand banks for work on ground maintenance in one of the estates—a job which failed to satisfy him. He then returned to the sand banks which had become his life's work—this loyalty and attachment also ended tragically when, at the age of

67, he was killed in a work related accident (Interview, Helen DeJanna).

Conditions for sand workers did improve over the years as companies undertook steps to meet the educational needs of their employees' children with the creation of schools and playgrounds. Gradually most of the families were able to leave company homes and move into the town proper becoming renters and home owners.

In 1938, Italian American sand workers struck again, this time achieving success albeit due to altered circumstances. First, they had learned the bitter lesson of the importance of universal organization rather than relying on only those of Italian background to support them as in 1908, and consequently they joined and rallied behind an Irish American leadership. Secondly, they exploited the contemporary pro-labor atmosphere which prevailed during the New Deal years. For example, the North Shore Italian American Society scheduled a public meeting wherein a state representative explained, in Italian, the procedures for applying for unemployment benefits (*Port Washington News*, September 23, 1931).

Organizational efforts suffered from abundance, however, and a jurisdictional dispute arose. Thus, while most sand workers joined the S.E.M.E. (the union of Steam Electrical Mechanical Engineers, Local 1), a rival independent union, the Operating Engineers of the American Federation of Labor, succeeded in obtaining contracts with some quarries thereby posing a serious challenge to the S.E.M.E. Interestingly, management seemed receptive to unionizing, at least that was the case with the Colonial Sand and Gravel Company, then leased by Generoso Pope, owner and publisher of *Il Progresso Italo-Americano*, the largest Italian American daily in the country. A staunch union man, Al Marino nevertheless fondly recalled being welcomed as the union representative by Pope who, contrary to the advice of his own company lawyers, accepted the union.

> When we went to his office in the city, I remember he had a big desk and sat in a big chair and said to us "Well, what kept you so long, I was expecting you. I came to the country broke. I may have to go back broke but I'm not going to let men starve. They are going to get a good wage". He was no problem for us at all. Our troubles were amongst ourselves, between the unions (Interview, Al Marino).

In the course of the dispute between the rival unions, 1,400 workers were idle for nine weeks as violence occasionally punctuated the 1938 strike resulting in the development of internecine arguments which endured for years. Mimmia Frommja, for example, convinced that support for the union was the only way to alleviate intolerable working conditions, went out on strike, was arrested, and spent a night in jail. The law enforcement official was Assistant District Attorney Albert DeMeo of Port Washington. Frommja was further upset when he learned that his daughter was to marry DeMeo's nephew.

Although interethnic in character, the Italian Americans clearly took the lead in protesting undesireable working conditions. Thus, local Italian American organizations protested loudly to the county District Attorney over his office's widespread use of deputies to foster strike-breaking activities. Finally, the strike was settled in August, 1938, as the workers joined the A.F.L. local, obtaining considerable local autonomy. The successful outcome of the labor dispute led to vastly improved wages and working conditions and ushered in a period of stability to Port Washington's sand banks, a period which was to last 45 years.

WORKERS OF THE SOIL

How to feed oneself and one's family? The question was uppermost in the minds of Italians in Patchogue, Hagerman and North Bellport, for although no longer confronted with the brutality of crowded slums, they could never avoid the task of earning a livelihood. Workers of the soil in the old homeland, they were among the fortunate few destined to break the surface of the waiting earth in the new land. They were, as Oscar Handlin puts it,

> Among the multitudes that survived the crossing, there were now and then some who survived it intact enough in body and resources to get beyond the port of landing and through the interior cities of transit. Those who were finally able to establish themselves as the independent proprietors of farms of their own made up an even smaller number (Handlin, 1951).

Thus, in the Patchogue vicinity a few Italians became the owners of their own farms, while others worked as tenant farmers or farm hands. Obviously propagandistic in nature, the claims of a self-help group in Bellport contain some truth as it advertised the potential for profitable truck farming awaiting landowners in the vicinity. "There is a great future for the neglected land on Long Island, and if this company carries out its plans the people who develop the Bellport property will be the first to profit by their enterprise" (*Patchogue Advance*, August 5, 1915). Likewise, many in North Bellport gained employment as handymen and gardeners for older, more affluent and even wealthy Bellporters in the southern portion of the village (Interview, Elizabeth Fuoco).

SMALL INDUSTRIES

Italians in Patchogue were fortunate in that the presence of industrial enterprises rendered it one of the largest manufacturing centers on Long Island. From the 1870s, the shipbuilding industry, which saw several firms constructing dozens of vessels, emerged as a major activity. A case in point was E. Bailey and Sons, which began producing lumber in 1869. They then expanded into ship-building, relocated on the Patchogue River and secured government aid to dredge and deepen the river and to install a breakwater at its mouth. At its height the firm employed 250 people, including many Italians as carpenters. Work on the Long Island Railroad also brought Italians into the Patchogue vicinity since the village was the eastern terminus of the line. When, in 1881, the railroad line was extended still further eastward, more laborers were needed, the majority of whom were Italians (*Patchogue Advance*, April 12, 1945).

Lace-making was another kingpin industry in Patchogue. Scottish entrepreneurs found local water so ideal for bleaching purposes that they formed the American Lace Manufacturing Company to produce crinoline (*Patchogue Advance*, February 2, 1962). They hired immigrant workers, including Italians, in large numbers from Patchogue to Bellport. By 1915 the lace mill constituted the largest single place of employment for the ethnic group, accounting for at least 48 Patchogue village Italian American residents.

ORGANIZING LACE MILL WORKERS

Front page advertisements enticed young ladies fourteen years or older to apply to the American Lace Manufacturing Company for "good wages and guaranteed work" (*Patchogue Advance*, December 5, 1909). The minimum age notwithstanding, many a girl began toiling at the mill at a much more tender age. Catherine Stephani actually began when she was twelve years old. At the time she worked in the mill (1901-1902) she walked a distance of three miles from home to mill and labored eight hours a day for $2.50 per week (Interview, Catherine Mailer Stephani). Rose Mazzotti Romeo worked in the folding room briefly as a fifteen year old girl where she earned three cents an hour in a fast-paced activity keeping the machines threaded (Interview, Rose Mazzotti Romeo).

Rose Pascuzzo went to work in the lace mill in 1922, sometimes bringing home work so she and her mother could earn a few cents more by stripping and separating sections and returning the finished parts to the factory (Interview, Rose Pascuzzo).

Ralph Tomassone retains a memory of his mother and grandfather working at the lace mill. Born in 1922 and raised on Waverly Avenue near the manufacturing plant, Ralph recalls the street scenes near the end of the work day. "When they came out of there you could not do down the street because of the crowd. They needed a cop to direct the traffic early in the afternoon

TABLE 1

OCCUPATIONS OF ITALIAN AMERICANS
IN PATCHOGHUE, NEW YORK, 1915.
NEW YORK STATE CENSUS, BROOKHAVEN TOWN, 1915.

OCCUPATION	NUMBER
Auto driver	1
Baker	2
Barber	7
Bartender	3
Bayman	1
Bookkeeper (lace mill)	1
Bootblack	4
Bicycle dealer	1
Bricklayer	1
Cake maker	1
Candy store	1
Carpenter	6
Carpenter's helper	1
Cigar store	1
Confectionary store	1
Contractor	2
Fruit dealer	2
Gardener	1
Grocery store proprietor	2
Hotel keeper	1
Housekeeper	103
Florist	1
Janitor	1
Junk dealer	4
Knife grinder	2
Laborer	32
Lace mill[a]	45
Lace mill laborer	2
Long Island Railroad	3
Long Island Railroad foreman	1
Milk peddler	1
Mason stone	3
No occupation	3
Plaster	2
Plumber	1
Retired farmer	1
Shoemaker	4
Stonemason	2
Storekeeper	1
Tailor	6
Truckman	1

Note:
   a. An interesting aspect of employment patterns found Patchogue Italian American young women aged 14-21 more likely to be employed outside the home than in any other Long Island community, undoubtedly because of the presence of the lace mills.

TABLE 2
ITALIAN AMERICAN POPULATION GREATER PATCHOGUE AREA 1915

PATCHOGUE	653 = 9.4 PERCENT OF TOTAL POPULATION
EAST PATCHOGUE (HAGERMAN)	94 = 37.6 PERCENT OF POPULATION
BELLPORT AND NORTH BELLPORT	415 PERCENT OF POPULATION
TOTAL FOR ALL THREE COMMUNITIES	= 1,162

Source: New York State Census, Brookhaven Town, 1915.

TABLE 3
ITALIAN AMERICAN POPULATION GREATER PATCHOGUE AREA 1925

PATCHOGUE	865 = 11.5 PERCENT OF TOTAL POPULATION
EAST PATCHOGUE	571 PERCENT OF POPULATION

Source: New York State Census, Brookhaven Town, 1915.

en the early shift let out". To those of an earlier generation, tenure in the mill was a prerequisite to entering the wider working world, with local people referring to it as the "college" upon whose termination of employment one was said to have "graduated". Frank Lotito who worked in the lace mill from 1933 to 1941, recalled the walkout in which his sister was deeply involved along with other untrained fellow ethnics.

> We started the union ourselves but we did not know what we were doing. Then professional unionizers came. But everyone did go out. I was there when the firemen shut the steam down...They shut the steam down and everything stopped. It was like a funeral. Even the engines were dead (Interview, Frank Lotito).

In March 1941 the American Lace Operators began a concerted effort to organize the employees at the Plymouth-Patchogue Lace Mills, successor to the American Lace Manufacturing Company. An April vote demonstrated that the movement had majority worker support, thereby precipitating strike action when management remained adamant in its refusal to acquiesce to union demands. A strike ensued in June which led to a complete shutdown of operations. Albert Benicase, the son of a veteran Patchogue Italian family and the main figure behind the union effort, and a strike committee, brought about a complete shutdown of operations for eight weeks when on October 10, 1941 it was concluded with a one-year contract which called for pay raises for 550 employees (*Patchogue Advance*, April 11, June 6, 27, October 10, 1941). Satisfaction with the results was not universally shared as indicated by the caustic comments of an editorial which stated, "On such issues the rich labor lords and their well-paid field hands and the criminal racketeers in the system fatten" (*Patchogue Advance*, April 21, 1941). This criticism notwithstanding, the union remained a fixture until the mill ceased operations in the 1950s.

The early Italians found work wherever it was available within and without the community: gardening, farming, shipbuilding, lace-mill hands, *etc.* Whether it was employment as seasonal laborers on Long Island farms and nurseries or whether employed as factory workers or skilled craftsmen, it is clear that the Long Island experience confirms the interpretation that economic causes prompted Italians to come to America. They came to Long Island essentially not because of a vague migratory sense, but because the emerging suburbs had urgent need of labor. They not only served as necessary laborers, but also showed that they, too, were willing to fight for workers rights, that in fact that they were prepared to do what was necessary to advance the cause of labor in their locales. Most of their self-improvement efforts were of the *ad hoc* variety, therefore leaving seemingly little lasting benefit in the form of on-going labor unions—the railroad and sand workers being the exception. Their activity in behalf of their rights earned them ill will on the part of nativists who were already disposed to a negative image of Italian newcomers. Like other "new immigrants" of this era Italians were, in the public mind, connected with asocial activities, a subject to be dealt with in the next chapter.

CHAPTER FIVE
CRIME AND VIOLENCE

Association of criminal activities with Italian immigrants and their descendants has been an on-going problem for the ethnic group for over a century. Even before the emergence of mass immigration in the mid-1880s, American newspaper readers could find frequent accounts of criminality in Italy. Apparently finding a receptive reading audience, reporters outdid each other in highlighting the ubiquitous criminal orientation (*See*, LaGumina, 1973). A *New York Times* story in 1875 is typical as it described the increase in the number of Italians brought before the police courts of New York City as in proportion to the immigration of Italians from the south of Italy.

> It is to this latest addition to our Italian population that the Italians belong who are now so frequently guilty of crimes of violence. They are extremely ignorant, and have been reared in the belief that brigandage is a manly occupation, and that assassination is the natural sequence of the most trivial quarrel.

In analyzing the relationship between crime and American life, students of the subject aver that each ethnic group has had involvement with criminal activities as part of the process of striving for recognition and success. Accordingly, it would seem that Italian Americans were at a stage analogous to that followed by other ethnic groups.

While there was little manifestation of concern about Italian Americans and crime in most of the Long Island communities under study, on occasion it did surface.

THE BLACK HAND

Because it fostered open speculation that the Black Hand, a turn-of-the-century sinister Italian criminal organization, was active in Glen Cove, it is interesting to note a 1907 event which recounted an occurence at midnight, January 29, when a heavy explosion caused windows to crash and china to fall. Upon investigation, the cause of the disturbance was to be found in an Orchard Street house occupied by a grocery store and also containing apartments which functioned as sleeping quarters for a large number of Italians. The building had been the target of violence previously, thus encouraging the opinion that organized crime was operative within the ethnic group. "The popular opinion seems to be that the building in the populous section of the village should not be leased to this class of tenants as they apparently have no regard for the sensibilities of their neighbors, and in some cases make life a burden to them" (*Oyster Bay Guardian*, January 1, 1907).

Although the first two decades of the twentieth century were years of heightened criminal activities in major Italian colonies throughout the eastern part of the country as local hoodlums preyed upon their unfortunate countrymen, it did not seem that the underworld had such an influence within Glen Cove. The prevailing view of those who had spent their entire lives in the community was to deny the existence of criminal organizations like the Mafia. "I never met people like that in my life. Growing up in the Orchard there were no extortionists terrifying storekeepers and businessmen. It may have happened in the big cities but it never happened here" was the way a former mayor of the city put it (*Newsday Magazine*, July 4, 1976). This does not mean there was a complete absence of violence, but that the crimes were committed by individuals rather than as part of organized criminal activities.

Reportage of certain incidences gives credence to the view that anti-Italian prejudice was not absent in Glen Cove. Not as pervasive or as blunt as in the big cities, it was, nevertheless, present in the form of demeaning attitudes and terminology as a July 1916 instance demonstrates. Local constable McCahill, arrested two Italians among a crowd of laborers who had attacked a "burghers" car as it passed along a newly-improved road which the laborers had just completed, and who were convinced that premature usage would cause damage. The use of the word "Wop" by reporters covering the story offended local Italians who rebuked the newspaper, whose feeble excuse that the newspaper was merely repeating word usage—underscored insensitivity to the Italians.

More so than any other community on Long Island, more so even perhaps than in New York City itself, one could find in the Inwood newspapers a steady stream of law violation references. In an age when journalists were uninhibited either by laws or ethnic sensitivities, they produced headlines which blared the cold, grisly facts of violence which detailed in almost clinical fashion the degrees of hatred manifested by Italians engaged in crimes leveled against both Italians and non-Italians. As early as 1896 Italian immigrants had come to the attention of law enforcement authorities in Inwood for disturbing the peace of the community. Altogether, twenty were arrested, fined and jailed in May of that year for making Sunday a day "...hideous to the people living in the neighborhood by singing, swearing and shouting...The doings of the Italians on Sunday have made a nuisance and a disgrace to the place" (*South Side Observer*, May 22, 1896). The attitude reflected in that unkind newspaper description rendered it no surprise to learn that the media source followed up the event with dire warnings against increased Italian immigration. "The almost unrestricted immigration laws of our country operate to provide a refuge for the ignorant and the criminal classes of Europe that bodes no good for the future of this country (*South Side Observer*, July 12, 1896). With unrelieved regularity, blatant headlines and incendiary descriptions which would be regarded as highly prejudicial and incredibly offensive in the present contemporary atmosphere, were then common fare. As the economist/ scholar Robert Foerster put it there was a disproportionate American attitude toward the Italian record in crime not so much because of the number of offenses as because of an uncanny and fearsome disposition.

> Elemental natures seem at work. Abduction, kidnapping, rape, stand forth and the newspapers glory in the details. The knife is used by men in their senses, by sober men: and a startling record of homicides or of attempted homicides appears. It is the Old World way. That the victims are themselves Italian, and that the roots of the dispute lie in the past or in a misadventure of love, is insufficiently realized. The strangest manifestation has been in the "Black Hand" outrages...A man of means receives a scrawled missive bearing the sign of the black hand and the inexorable demand that a stated sum of money be privately conveyed to the nameless writer. The robber is as good as his word. Death by the knife or the bomb, the blasted home or store, is the proof which comes too late (Pitkin, 1977).

Prior to the First World War, Black Hand activity flourished in Inwood with newspapers regularly reporting its depradations as illustrated in a 1907 attempt to bomb the home of banker Vincent Zavatt.

> The neighborhood of the Italian quarter of Inwood was rudely awakened last Saturday night about 2 a.m. by an explosion that nearly cost the life of Vincent Zavatt, his wife and child...Investigation showed that a stick of dynamite had been placed at the front door and a fuse attached. The explosion tore out the door and the frame smashing windows and starting a fire which was soon extinguished. Mr. Zavatt, when he saw the flash of light, went to the bedroom window and called for help thinking the house was on fire but his only answer was shot from a revolver which imbedded itself in the building about ten inches from his head...Mr. Zavatt, who is a well educated Italian and a large property owner, is interpreter in the county courts of Nassau. He has been instrumental in having culprits brought to justice and it is

probably his work in this line that has caused the cowardly attack. Rumor has it that Black Hand letters have been received by other parties of Inwood, although the rumor has not been confirmed (*Far Rockaway Journal*, August 16, 1907).

The *Rockaway News* covered the same event with the front page headline "Black Hand at Work", and further speculated that the attack on Zavatt may have been in retaliation for his role in causing problems for two Italian American neighborhood saloonkeepers. It also told of Zavatt responding to the shot fired at him by seizing his own "doubled-barreled shot gun and fired in the direction that the shot came from..." The *News*, account is revealing also as it described the recollections of Inwood resident Frederick Sprague, a relation of the important Republican leader, who upon hearing the explosion, looked out his window and saw two men walking hurriedly away from the scene. "Not knowing the nature of the trouble and supposing that an ordinary Italian fight had been in progress and that these two men were sent by authorities, Sprague did not bother with them" (*Rockaway News*, August 14, 1907).

If indeed intimidation was the perpretrator's objective, the courageous Zavatt indicated he would not be cowed into submission:

> I haven't an enemy in the world that I know of and I don't know of any reason why anyone should want to do away with me, with the exception that I have always done my part in running down criminals among my countrymen. I never was afraid of anyone and this affair does not scare me. Some time in May, I had several complaints from the more ignorant class of Italians that a number of young Italians were demanding money from the laborers under threats of death if they refused. I was also informed that this gang used Costanza's place on Henry Street as their headquarters. One day I met Costanza and had a conversation with him, telling him that if I could get the slightest evidence I would have him arrested...(*Rockaway News*, August 14, 1907).

Zavatt's remarks were not the result of exaggerated pride for he soon became Deputy Sheriff in the community, providing local enforcement officials with the welcome opportunity of obtaining the assistance of an important member within the ethnic group. Over the course of the next few years Zavatt became instrumental in the apprehension of several notorious local outlaws, being credited in at least one instance for the breakup of a large gang of Italian outlaws. His activities brought him into contact, furthermore, with Italian enclaves in nearby communities where he earned a reputation for bringing to justice murderers, extortionists and other criminals.

CRIME AND MELODRAMATIC JOURNALISM

Organized criminal activity, in fact or alleged, was not the only kind of transgression reported. There were, in addition, numerous activities of violence of passion which purportedly reflected an elementary nature. Typical headlines suggested the contents of these stories: "Slashed With a Razor", "All for a Woman's Honor, Joseph Fucci Shoots James Renzulo and Salvatore Russo of Inwood for Defending Woman's Name", "Stabbed during Quarrel", "Italian Shooting Fray", "Another Italian Holdup", "Shot Down by Italian on Mott Avenue", "Murderer Makes His Escape". Some of the crimes were of the simple robbery nature such as the report of an Italian American chicken thief or a gang of Italian Inwood boys who stole plumbing material and disposed of it to an Italian junkman from Inwood (*Rockaway News*, May 18, 1907; June 13, 1908; July 14, 1909; May 18, 1910; January 10, 1912). The articles provided detailed accounts of the incidents with all the particulars of depravity and insensibility perpetrated by the malefactors. In one instance a trolley car operator was attacked by an Italian from Inwood over objections about paying his fare. As the conductor resumed collecting fares,

> he was suddenly attacked by the Italian who pulled a razor from his pocket and began slashing the conductor. One of the slashes made by the drink-crazed Italian cut through the clothing of Hicks, including a ghastly looking wound reaching from his left shoulder down his back and side, nearly to his hip (*Rockaway News*, January 20, 1906).

The delineation of criminal events may perhaps offer much information on the asocial aspects of Inwood Italian life in the early part of the century, but they are also helpful in providing insight into the prevailing sentiments among Inwoodites concerning foreigners in their midst. The violent incidents constituted a ready backdrop for the melodramatic comments of imaginative journalists. While non-Italian violence was also the subject of journalism, there was a decided emphasis on depradations connected with the Italian ethnic group. The shooting of an Italian in Inwood's Little Italy in 1910 is a case in point.

> Michael Patuso, the victim of the first affair, was sitting on the porch of his home on Smith Street, about ten o'clock. He was quietly smoking his pipe and thinking no doubt about his native Italy which he had left only two years before when he came to this country...Suddenly he heard the sound of approaching voices. He recognized the men as compatriots as they were talking in Italian. They were plainly in an angry mood, as their voices were high-pitched and quarrelsome. It was also apparent that they had been drinking and that their passions had

been inflamed by the liberal use of intoxicants. As they came before the house Patuso was sitting on the porch and was greeted with a volley of Italian abuse. Then some one in the crowd pulled a revolver and started shooting at him. This example was followed by several others in the party who obviously thought Patuso made a first-class target for revolver practice (*Rockaway News*, July 29, 1910).

The article then proceeded to tell of another shooting in the same neighborhood that very same night. Acts of violence naturally were newsworthy events and therefore within the province of the journalists of the day. However, the frequency of such reportage and the repetition of similar events could lead one to conclude that there existed a preoccupation with Italian Americans and violence, a preoccupation which dwarfed attention paid to criminal associations involving other ethnic groups.

By 1911, criminal activity was so brisk that Inwood opened its own lockup instead of sending its prisoners to jails in nearby towns as had been the custom previously. In December, 1911, Italian immigrant Salvatore Lombardo, from Far Rockaway, killed a man in self-defense during a quarrel in which the victim had made malicious remarks about Italians, causing Lombardo to take strong offense and thus precipitating the argument which led to the slaying (*Rockaway News*, December 23, 1911). In another instance the wrongdoing reported was in the form of sexual molestation as a newspaper reported a tale of two Inwood girls "frightened to death" by two Italian men intent on assaulting them—an incident which so provoked the girls' father that he threatened to indulge in "...gun play if his daughters are again molested by the swarthy Sicilians" (*Rockaway News*, September 8, 1911). Sometimes violence was visited in the form of retribution upon those who forgot their families in Italy, as in the case of Fortunato Fiore who was attacked by knife wielders in August 1913, apparently because he "...has not forwarded money to his wife and children in Italy for a long time" (*Rockaway News*, August 9, 1913).

There is evidence that the *Omerta* code was adhered to in Inwood. Briefly put, the code required that an individual seek his own redress of grievance even if the private retribution extended to being victimized rather than appeal to law enforcement authorities for aid. "In obedience to these rules even the most respectable among the common people would never testify if he had been a spectator to a crime..." (Pitkin, 1977). In February, 1906, an Inwood Italian was shot in the foot at a wedding celebration, and unfortunately, despite what seemed to be a minor wound, contracted lockjaw and subsequently expired. During his entire stay in the hospital, he refused to disclose the identity of his attacker. In July, 1909, an Italian was injured by a co-national during a shooting fray, but refused to name the assailant—a pattern of behavior which elicited a reporter's comment: "With the usual reticence of the race the injured man declined to say anything about the affair other than it was an accident and that he was shot by friend" (*Rockaway News*, February 7, 1906; July 3, 1909).

LAW ENFORCEMENT

The extent of the criminal activities in Inwood attracted the attention of law enforcement authorities and public officials across the county and state. Consequently, prompted by New York Governor Sulzer, these officials frequently took action against local malefactors (*Rockaway News*, February 5, 1913). Such was the case in March 1914 when county officials authorized raids of Italian-owned saloons in Inwood after receiving complaints that the proprietors sold liquor to minor children causing them to come to school intoxicated. Although virtually all of the saloons in the Italian section were raided, only one was found guilty. Saloon proprietors and customers generally reacted to the intrusion good-naturedly, prompting positive assessments about the area. So far as any outward evidence would show, the Italian section is in a most peaceful and law-abiding frame of mind (*Rockaway News*, July 14, 1914). Even while this assessment was being made, however, the prevailing speculation was that the absence of widespread law violations was probably the result of saloonkeepers being forewarned of the pending raids.

One reason for the high volume of law violations undoubtedly was the practice of carrying revolvers and other concealed weapons. Whether this was prompted by activities in the Italian enclave is uncertain. However, in 1911, Nassau County passed an ordinance prohibiting the sale and carrying of revolvers and other concealed weapons. This was the objective of a local judge who launched a series of raids on Inwood, inflicting heavy fines and imprisonment to anyone found with a weapon. This energetic activity elicited hope that the gun-carrying practice was being terminated—a prophecy unfortunately too premature. For several years following, newspaper reports continued to provide accounts of gun toters having scrapes with the law.

A 1918 historical assessment of Inwood's violent reputation, by observing that a majority of the town's 4,000 inhabitants were Italians, is enlightening:

> Until recently and for a period of years the rough horseplay of the old baymen was overlooked on account of the gunplay of the foreigners and the name of Inwood for quite a while conjured up thoughts of dark deeds of violence...The lawlessness of the bad parts of Inwood has been greatly overcome of recent years mainly owing to the zealous efforts of the priests there who set themselves the difficult task they have so well performed...(*Bellot*, 1918:81).

This bit of optimism notwithstanding, revolver-associated wrongdoing in Inwood continued to attract attention not only throughout the county, but also on a state level. Much to the chagrin of Nassau County law enforcement officials and apparently in response to citizen complaints originating in Inwood and Lawrence, state troopers came in to "clean up" the village. Led by a state trooper corps commander known for his effectiveness in dispatching criminals, state troopers arrived in Inwood on January 13, 1925, making known their intention of remaining until they completed their task. In addition to the residents' complaints of lack of sufficient protection in the area, there was speculation that the move may also have been precipitated by an incident which took place the previous New Year's Eve in which discharges from revolvers and rifles marked the occasion in the Italian section. Finally, "...the fact that (there have been) two fatal shooting matches, a holdup and a score of robberies in the village within the past two months is believed to have an important bearing on the presence of troopers" (*Rockaway News*, January 17, 1925).

State police were involved in at least one major roundup of what was described as a "large and organized band of robbers". Working on information about a planned burglary, the troopers staked out a home whose cellar was stocked with wine. When the perpetrators attempted to rob the premises, they were seized by the troopers. The subsequent trial found that six of the men were guilty of a "charge with having drawn lots for the commission of a crime after the manner of the Mafia in Italy" (*Rockaway News*, December 2, 1925). Despite denials to the contrary the accused were branded members of the notorious organization and sentenced to long prison terms.

Whether or not it could be attributed to the presence of the state police in 1925, there was a discernible decrease in criminal activity except for violations against the prohibition laws. With the enactment of the Volstead Act, the country officially went "dry" in 1920. Inwood, like many another community, hosted its share of law violators who were engaged in the business of illegally making liquor. In May, 1925, an explosion in a still operated by an Italian on Henry Street shattered many neighborhood windows, throwing the Italian colony into a panic and also costing the man his life. Upon arriving on the scene, law enforcement authorities found yet another still nearby and promptly proceeded to confiscate the paraphenalia associated with it (*Rockaway News*, May 30, 1925).

Reiterations of a profusion of criminal depradations in Inwood's Italian community as reported by the local press, render inescapable the conclusion that violent and/or criminal behavior was too frequently part of social life in the early phase of Italians' Long Island history. In these instances news reporters could not always resist the temptation to characterize the events along lines of ethnic stereotypes. The brutal murder committed by a "jealous boomertown (Bellport) Italian, invoking the unwritten law, butchered his wife with an axe. Very coarse work. A stiletto would have been just as effective and more picturesque", was the description of an insensitive reporter which discounted any pretense at objectivity concerning a 1911 deed.

> He will no doubt be indicted and convicted of murder in the first degree ...The fiend committed his crime and seemed satisfied because he had gotten rid of his wife. When brought before Justice Green for a hearing on Tuesday afternoon he was seemingly quite at ease, regardless of the practical certainty that he must go to the electric chair for his crime. The court room was jammed with people, a majority of them being Italian, who were especially interested in the case on account of the nationality of the principals (*Patchogue Advance*, July 14, 1911).

Demonstrating a deep interest in the case, Italians who were present in large numbers at the trial were rumored to be armed and therefore were forced to undergo the indignity of a search which in fact failed to bring to light a single weapon (*Patchogue Advance*, February 2, 1913).

On July 12, 1913, Carl Gentile, an enraged immigrant, was apprehended for shooting his son-in-law Sam Palmer, a "well known member of the Italian colony", for terrorizing his whole family and brutally assaulting his wife, who was Gentile's daughter. Palmer even threatened Gentile himself. Neighbors acknowledged that the unpopular Palmer, a lace mill employee, was a known wife-beater (*Patchogue News*, July 17, 1913). Interestingly, at court hearings it proved to be very difficult to obtain witnesses to divulge that they knew about the shooting. "The witnesses seem to be afraid of earning the enmity of the principals or their friends" (*Patchogue News*, July 25, 1913). Because of insufficient evidence, and in view of the widespread belief that Gentile had acted in self-defense after being shot at by his son-in-law, Gentile was set free. In the meantime the constable issued a stiff warning to Palmer, whom he drove out of town (*Patchogue Advance*, December 6, 1912).

There were other instances of crime and violence associated with Italian immigrant life on Long Island. However, with the exception of Inwood, the extant press is bereft of organized crime in the vast majority of Italian neighborhoods. It would be speculative to assert with definitiveness as to the causes of the prevalence of crime in Inwood. One would have to consider the combination of poverty and proximity to New York City as possible factors. Physically closer to the big city than any other Long Island Italian enclave, Inwood's Italian population probably shared in the dubious spotlight of public attention then accorded to criminal activities in the city's Little Italies. In the latter instances the public was treated to repeated stories of violent acts committed by Italian immigrants. It would be unusual to expect that the readership would expect these asocial acts to cease upon reaching the limits of municipal geographical lines.

Aside from Inwood, instances of crime and violence in other Long Island Italian neighborhoods, although relatively minor, probably could be attributed to a similar type of dispiriting poverty along with frustration at the inability to cope with the complexities of an alien culture. Unfortunately the heritage of preoccupation with the seamier aspects of socialization helped create a climate conducive to prejudice and discrimination.

CHAPTER SIX
PREJUDICE

It was the lot of new immigrants to be confronted with varying degrees of prejudice. Grounds for negative prejudgements varied from low regard for the newcomers' culture including their social, religious and linguistic features, to fears that immigrant innundation would tax American service systems, debase the body politic and retard the American labor movement. In addition to these pejorative evaluations, Italian immigrants also had to endure other damaging stereotypes—that of perverse criminal inclinations. In the main, Italian-Americans were the targets of prejudice in its severest forms in the big cities where discrimination was blatant and often vicious. Italian American residents of suburban Long Island, while spared from the worst excesses of discrimination, nevertheless did experience some.

NEGATIVE CLIMATE

Even when Long Islanders acknowledged their need for Italian immigrant workers, they nevertheless confessed misgivings. The absence of much evidence that the misgivings were based on allegations that the Italians were displacing other workers locally leads to the conclusion that newcomer Italians were regarded as a mixed blessing.

For all their hard work, local observers viewed these newcomers ambivalently. Thus, although these observers valued Italian work contributions, they were less sanguine regarding the kinds of Americans these newcomers would make. "Italy is still sending over swarms of her people who risk the hazards of new fortunes in the United States...the steamships of the Mediterranean bring us hosts of steerage passengers to Ellis Island", was the criticism in a local paper which cited the respected *New York Herald Tribune* as its source. The *Sea Cliff News* went on to report that some of the Italians were typical "birds of passage", that is, that they earned their livelihoods in America but returned to Italy to live off their savings. At the same time the observer did refer to many Italians who remained in this country. However,

> the many persist in remaining Italian in heart and soul, in habits and sympathy and ways of living and refuse to cast their lots in this hemi-

sphere to the end of their days and become American...But the passion for the old scenes and the old conditions appears to be almost indistinguishable among the descendants of the ancient Romans (*Sea Cliff News*, May 30, 1903).

Negative assessments of Italian Americans on occasion led to offensive remarks about some of the groups' most cherished practices, as, for example, the commotion attending feast celebrations. One irate 1910 letter writer from Port Washington received prominent newspaper coverage when he castigated town officials for permitting these celebrations to take place on Sundays, averring that the activities constituted an infringement upon the rights of others and an improper observation of the sabbath day.

> If our Italian neighbors desire to worship with so much fervor-enthusiasm and noise, if requested they will doubtless be willing to do so at a time and place where it will not be an annoyance to a large number of citizens who wish to spend their Sundays in quietness and peace. If our town officials have not a proper regard for the fitness of things on Sunday, it is high time that they made room for others who have higher ideals as to what is meant by American liberty and real service to the people (*Port Washington News*, October 3, 1910).

Too obvious an Italian name could become the basis for discrimination in local institutions like the church and the school. Accordingly, it was the source of friction in Glen Cove's St.Patrick's Church while the institution was under the direction of an unsympathetic pastor. One of the oldest parishes on Long Island, St.Patrick's was organized by the Irish Americans of the late 19th century and remained staffed by Irish priests and nuns who operated the parochial school. Although adherents of the same religion, Irish Americans and Italian Americans experienced a measure of inter-ethnic conflict, precipitated by an Irish pastor who made little secret of his animosity to the newcomers. Not even the sacrifices made by poor parents to send their children to the parochial school spared them from prejudice, according to recollections of an old-time resident. "I remember going to St.Patrick's School. There was Fr. Cross, who once he knew we were from the other side of the tracks almost wanted to push me down the steps. Even years later, when I became involved in the Knights of Columbus, I would never go there because of his dislike of us. We were always hated" (Interview, Lewis Capobianco).

Of course, discrimination was not confined to the parochial school. One could meet it in the public schools as well. Sometimes prejudice reflected itself in overt and arbitrary decisions on the part of school teachers to change Italian names. Octogenarian Nora Limongelli Mamorale tells of beginning public school with her mother's warnings ringing in her ears. "Don't let them change your name" she admonished, "because that's what they do here". Forewarnings notwithstanding, when Nora started school the teacher found Assunta Maria Margerita Limongelli too long and too un-American—Nora was more suitable...it became her name from that point on, although in her senior years she continues to use her original appellation on official documents (Interview, Nora Limongelli Mamorale).

Forewarnings of name-changing were not idle concerns on the part of Italian parents who had seen altogether ample examples of involuntary alterations of Italian names not only on the part of schools but also in the workplace. The simple fact was that either because of pronunciation difficulties, illiteracy or a display of superiority, native Americans did not always call Italians by their Christian names. Misspellings were frequent and serve as a sober comment on the effectiveness of phonetics. Thus, Ianucci would likely come out as "Yanuchi". Also surprising was the widespread use of Anglo-Saxon and Celtic names like Sullivan for Salvatore, Williams for Villano, Kelly for Colicchio, and names like White, Ross, *etc*. One may speculate that this proclivity for Anglo-Saxon appellations reflected a conscious effort to avoid identification with a "foreign-sounding" name due to anticipated discrimination, or it may indicate resignation to the adoption of an easier appellation in order not to be subjected to the ridicule and humiliation of misspelled names which frequently became the lot of newcomers in America's midst.

Long Island Italian Americans also experienced prejudice of a social/political nature. Thus, in Copiague the very name of Marconiville, became the center of controversy which manifested unmistakeable prejudicial overtones.

PREJUDICE IN COPIAGUE

Throughout the years John Campagnoli, the builder who first developed and named the area, championed the legality of the Marconiville name since the Babylon Town Board, in whose jurisdiction Copiague lay, had approved it. Campagnoli furthermore opined that Marconiville should be considered as separate from Copiague proper, an opinion in which he was joined by the *Amityville Record* which agreed to call the area Marconiville in future references (*Amityville Record*, August 18, 25, 1922). It proved a phyrric victory, however, since the Italian community was split on the issue, with some Marconi Community League leaders taking sharp issue with Campagnoli, openly challenging his version of the relationship between Marconiville and Copiague and rejecting any notion of separateness. These critics maintained that "...Marconiville did not exist as anything but a name for a real estate development for John Campagnoli..." (*Amityville Record*, September 28, 1928).

The idea that by promoting the name of Marconiville he became a divisive force for the community was a great disappointment for Campagnoli. The embattled entrepreneur repeatedly argued his case producing a petition signed by 105 Italian residents of Copiague, addressed to the Postmaster General to the effect that he should authorize a change in the name of the local post office:

> The Postal Authorities have unofficially recognized the existence of Marconiville, delivering mail regularly when so addressed; the Political Authorities both Federal and State, the Draft Board, the Board of Supervisors, the Board of Health have adopted and use the name of Marconiville in circulars, in official papers, in road and crossing signs; and the Long Island newspapers as occasions arise, refer to it always as Marconiville (Vacca, 1948).

This situation reflected the unsympathetic atmosphere toward the designation of a community name which had a decidedly foreign ring to it. In an intensely pressurized climate of the nativist 1920s, it was imperative to divest "un-American" ties as quickly as possible and to assimilate.

Leaving no stone unturned Campagnoli appealed for help in his name-changing crusade to Salvatore A. Cotillo, one of the most prominent Italian Americans in the New York State Legislature. Likewise, he appealed to the Long Island Lighting Company, the local utility, to change its addresses for bill payments to read Marconiville instead of Copiague. Finally he tried to influence the local public by stating his position in a letter to *The Amityville Record*.

> Marconiville can boast of a striving club, named the Marconi Community League, housed in an up-to-date clubhouse with all improvements. In the last two years at least forty new homes have been erected, showing the extraordinary advancement since it was founded by Campagnoli in 1908. It was a long struggle to bring this about: to have electricity and gas and telephones installed when other sections of Copiague were without...It seems more fitting that this little advanced community should be named Marconiville as a memorial to one of the most famous scientists of the era (Vacca, 1948).

Campagnoli's efforts, notwithstanding, Marconiville was not destined to be a separate entity from Copiague and, after a number of years, virtually ceased to be the title reference to the community except in the nostalgic recollections of old residents.

As for the Marconi Community League, it thrived during the boom years of the 1920s but declined during the Great Depression. After several lean years of imprudent management the organization was forced to divest itself of the clubhouse which was sold to the Bernagazzi brothers who, in turn, sold it to a commercial firm. The building still stands, housing a factory, but betraying little indication of its Italian past.

Friction between the northern and the southern sections of the village persisted, improving finally in 1924 as the disparate sections found themselves rallying around efforts to enlist community support for the building of a new high school. That all elements in the community endorsed the project was symbolized by support given to the community-wide Christmas program that year. "...it will show a new harmony of interest between the sections of the north and south of the track which for several years have worked at cross purposes in common rivalry" (*Amityville Record*, November 21, 1924).

AMERICANIZATION PRESSURES

Prejudice visited upon the Italians was undoubtedly a reflection of the intense nationalism of the 1920s as the nation rejected a major internationalist role and worried about safeguarding itself against hordes of foreigners swarming onto American shores. These years saw the enactment of the most stringent immigration restriction laws with the passage of the National Origins Quota Act in 1924 which severely restricted Italian immigration. Keeping out "undesireables" was only part of the problem. Other Americans were determined that newcomers from southern and eastern Europe must be made to shed their backgrounds and assimilate into American society for the integrity of the country. Accordingly, an Americanization program was lauched with the expressed objective of teaching foreigners the English language and American customs. Historians of immigration have shown that the effort was advanced by exhortation, cajoling and high pressure tactics amidst dire predictions for the nation's future unless all were Americanized.

The Americanization movement was in full evidence in the Copiague vicinity with Amityville in particular featuring locally-sponsored programs. Surely participation in the programs was to be regarded as good citizenship—a view not to be lost in Copiague especially among the older, native population, as it judged its Latin neighbors to the north. An indication of the pervasiveness of the Americanization issue can be seen in the front page coverage the local paper gave to an exhortation by a clubwoman on the kind of loyalty and patriotism to be expected of all Americans, even the most recent newcomers.

> After the foreigner has established himself in our country the first thing of course is to make him acquainted with our language, for it is only by a clear understanding of it that our ways, ideals, and customs can be made an integral part of himself. He must be made to feel that he has not come here to dig our ditches or to perform other menial tasks, but that he is entitled to all we are entitled to because we are citizens of

this great country...In our striving to make Americans we must ever bear in mind that Americanization should be made so attractive to the foreign born as to create in him or her a desire to have it and accept it gladly. The women of America should be made to feel that they have a great part in the process of Americanization. They can enter the homes of the immigrants, teach them how to make their homes ideal American homes, how to care for the children, how to conform to American customs. This is a task that requires much loving sympathy and patience and each American woman should be proud that to her America has delegated the great task of binding close together her many people into one. Now that the right to vote has been granted to women, each of us should strive to make our foreign sister see that voting has to do with the business of living...Americanization cannot be dropped at this critical time. Both the men and women of America should see that the children in our public schools are firmly grounded to the principle of patriotism for they are the foundation of our future America. If we are to have America for our homes we must be American one and all...(*Amityville Record*, April 16, 1920).

PREJUDICE IN THE FIRE DEPARTMENT

Copiague figured prominently in another example of prejudice in the highly nationalized atmosphere of the 1920s. In this instance prejudice led to discrimination over the location and construction of the town fire department, surely one of the more important institutions in the hamlet, and the major local vehicle through which community involvement and political participation took place. As one veteran Copiague politician put it,"...at one time or another everybody belonged to the fire department...it was the only organization in town of any substance" (Interview, Daniel Curcio).

Firehouse politics was evident from the beginning as the construction of two Copiague firehouses at a cost of $80,000.00, one in the north, the other in the south, indicates. According to a prevailing view only one firehouse was really necessary, but the sole facility would "...let in the north side in the councils of native politicians". Emphatically, the leadership in the south was determined to avoid this role for the north—which is to say for the Italian Americans. It was charged, furthermore, that the firehouse built in the Marconiville section was inferior to that of the facility in the south both in size and character. Officials of the Copiague Fire Department, who were from the older area of town, inferred that they were being more than fair to the Italian section since that area only represented at best one-seventh of the total taxable value of the village. A significant response to these views was made, interestingly enough, by the non-Italian chairman of the Copiague

Voters League who castigated the southern Copiaguers for their prejudicial treatment of Marconiville, making the relevant point that in the democratic electoral process representative government is based on people not on property values. The southern townspeople were chastised, furthermore, for a charade of fairness which in reality did not obscure their employment of dubious methods to insure dominance over the Italian area (*Amityville Record*, September 28, 1928).

The most evident manifestation of ethnic discrimination at work was to be seen in the election of five fire commissioners exclusively from the south side, despite efforts expended by Marconiville leaders to create the fire district in the first place. The state of affairs so agitated the Italian community that in 1928 it rallied to the support of one of their own in the election for fire commissioner as William Bernagazzi handily defeated an incumbent fire commissioner from the south side who was running for re-election. Furthermore, two other Marconiville leaders, Michale Galuzzi and Anthony Curcio, were given important posts in the department as clerk and inspector, respectively (*Amityville Record*, September 28, 1928).

THE KU KLUX KLAN AND ANTI-ITALIANISM

Anxiety and intolerance also affected post-World War I Patchogue in a variety of ways. One was in the form of cries of alarm from national figures who warned against an immigrant tide which would undermine the American social fabric. Thus, Patchoguers could read in their local paper that prominent individuals urged great caution against the intermingling of native Americans and the newly-arrived. It was the activity of the Ku Klux Klan in the general vicinity during the 1920s which constituted a pronounced example of nativism, however, as the hate-filled organization initiated hundreds of new recruits, spewing forth inflammatory accusation against the subversive Catholic parochial school system and in general denouncing Catholics, Jews and others. A crowd of 5,000 attended a KKK and a Kamelia meeting in a field north of Yaphank in July 1924 to hear a speaker condemn the Masons for cooperating with the Knights of Columbus Catholic fraternal organization. At another meeting attended by a large audience an eloquent Klan speaker deprecated Catholics, waxing venemously when speaking about the "dago Pope" (*Patchogue Advance*, April 16, 1920; March 16, 1923; *Patchogue Argus*, July 21, 1921 and May 7, 1925).

Identification with the KKK was openly public, moreover, as in the case of a West Sayville Reformed Church pastor who was "a member of the Klan in spirit", and who allowed the KKK to use his pulpit, justifying it on the grounds that the congregation had voted for it" (*Patchogue Advance*, December 1, 1922). On more than one occasion the KKK marched down Patchogue's Main Street and otherwise demonstrated considerable influence

—developments which rendered it less than shocking to learn that the Klan had become an important factor in local elections, especially school board elections. In 1924 the organization boasted of a key role in defeating a Catholic candidate for election to the Bellport School Board—a sober reminder of its power to affect the political atmosphere (*Patchogue Advance*, March 21, 1924).

But Italian Americans were not easily threatened even if they were impressed by the large turnouts. A scheduled Klan lecture in March, 1923, was the setting for allegations against Angelo Milano on the grounds of disorderly conduct at the door of the meeting. Brought before a local justice for trial, the court was unable to proceed due to its failure to secure a jury from among the prospective jurors called and the spectators assembled; with one exception all interrogated for the duty were well aware of and critical of the Klan's activities. Despite this, the repressive KKK atmosphere was so pervasive that many years later, in the early 1940s, new Italian residents to Patchogue sensed that an anti-Italian climate still pervaded the village (Interview, Fortunata Yannacone).

Renato Giorgini remembered the nature of prejudice when he ran for the Copiague school board. The event revealed much about the influence of narrow forces locally—namely the activities of the Ku Klux Klan which was then in a vicious anti-Catholic stance and heavily involved in many school board elections on Long Island. "When I was elected to the school board", he reminisced, "they were burning a cross outside my house".

THE IRONY OF DISCRIMINATION

Discrimination, the negative end result of prejudice, sometimes had beneficial effects for the affected group. Accordingly, discrimination against Westbury Italians served as a catalyst to the determination to build a clubhouse. At the time, the Knights of Columbus, a Catholic fraternal organization then largely made up of non-Italian Westbury residents, had recently built a clubhouse on Maple Avenue. In the hope that a common religious heritage as well as personal membership in both the Knights of Columbus and the Dell' Assunta Society would render the former amenable to the latter's request to utilize its facilities, Dominick Piscitelli approached the fraternal order with the request. Much to his dismay, Dominick's request was rejected, an action which convinced Dominick that ethnic prejudice was at the core of the problem. "What the Knights of Columbus did was wrong. They discriminated against us, yet we were both Catholic. But because we were *guineas*, we were discriminated against". However, adversity had its own internalizing effect which can sometimes serve to intensify resolve. As Dominick mused, "In retrospect, it was the best thing that happened because it forced us to build our own hall" (Interview, Dominick Piscitelli).

WORLD WAR II LEADS TO DISCRIMINATION

The atmosphere of World War II complicated issues of acceptance of an ethnic group whose origins were traced to an enemy nation. Accordingly, the war years and the immediate post-war years found Long Island Italian Americans once again forced to deal with the consequences of prejudice.

The outbreak of World War II in September, 1939, had a deleterious effect on community relations in Westbury, as village officials attempted to restrict or at least discourage local Italians from celebrating their traditional feast days. Thus, in 1940 the village board of trustees passed a resolution which strongly discouraged "celebrations and ostentations of any nationalist type or nature other than distinctly American". Although it did not single out the Italian element, the not too subtle message was clear—their celebrations were regarded as being less than American and at least one organization—the Durazzano Society—succumbed to the pressure by reducing its annual celebration to nothing more than a church service at St.Brigid's on July 4. As John Monteforte explained, his society did not think that the wartime atmosphere was an appropriate time for traditional celebrations (Interview, John Monteforte).

The Dell' Assunta Society, however, was of a different mind, rejecting the village board's depiction of its celebration as a nationalistic affair maintaining instead that members of the society "...are a purely religious group. The celebrations we hold are in honor of the Blessed Virgin and have nothing but religious significance". President Dominick Piscitelli pressed the board for its regular permit to hold the procession adding: "We certainly would not carry Italian flags if the village board objected and we would change the color of the bunting around the booths" (*Westbury Times*, June 28, 1940; Interview, John Monteforte, February 9, 1979). Failing to obtain the board's approval, the Society applied to the towns of Hempstead and North Hempstead, both of which approved permits for the parade and the holding of fireworks outside the physical limits of Westbury village but close to it. The 1940 feast of the Assumption was held, in a subdued manner, minus Italian flags and colors and without blazing street lights.

In 1941 much of the same battle ensued. Emboldened by a Westbury American Legion resolution which denounced nationalist events, Westbury village authorities rejected the Dell' Assunta application for a festival (*Westbury Times*, June 25, 1940). Issues of American allegiance and loyalty to Italy were matters of importance elsewhere in the vicinity as, for example, in nearby Mineola, where a chapter of the Italian American Federation of Republican Clubs lashed out against foreign influences and urged the teaching of Americanism in an apparent reaction to another Italian American civic club which had refused to march in a Memorial Day parade because Italian flags were barred (*Westbury Times*, July 12, 1940).

The rejection by civil authorities notwithstanding, Dell' Assunta Society President Piscitelli and Vice-president Alfonso Ianucci immediately appealed and, through the backing of Judge Dwyer who argued in their behalf before the New York State Supreme Court, gained a reversal of the village order. Village officials then tried to get the Society to divert its regular march to a street other than Post Avenue on the grounds that it might be "offensive to some portions of the village's population" (*Westbury Times*, June 25, 1940). The Society refused to be deterred and eventually obtained permission to use its traditional route.

The war, nevertheless, did have its effect as the feast celebration became a faint approximation of the *festas* of former years. Vivid colors were paled, bright lights that decorated the booths were eliminated and the gaity of the crowds diminished. The parade continued to be held but other festive notes such as gaudy streamers of lights across streets, huge votive shrine candles, outdoor stands where broiling and sizzling continental delicacies used to be sold were gone. The old flavor of the festivals would have to await the conclusion of the war.

The Village board's decision to prevent the parade was considered rank discrimination by Piscitelli who refused to accept the interpretation that what was essentially a religious affair be deemed nationalistic—an interpretation in which he was upheld by civil authorities outside the village. The fact that Italy was an enemy of the United States during the war was no grounds for painting all Italian-descended Americans with the brush of disloyalty. So far as he was concerned they were Americans and were entitled to full citizenship rights without being relegated to second-class citizenship because of their Italian backgrounds (*Westbury Times*, September 10, 1942). The irony of the situation was that as soon as the war began Italian Americans came to represent a significant portion of Westbury's young men inducted into the armed services. Moreover, a number of them paid the supreme sacrifice. In April 1942, Frank T. Tufaro, a sailor, was reported missing in action—the first Westbury serviceman to lose his life in defense of the country (*Westbury Times*, February 27, November 1, 1940). It was always a sore spot for local Italian Americans to be denied permission to carry on meaningful traditional customs, yet realize that Italian names were so numerous among the village's roster of Westburyites serving in the armed forces.

LOYALTY IN THE FACE OF DISCRIMINATION

The irony was further compounded when Italian aliens, whose sons were in the service, were required to register as enemy aliens. The drive to register aliens in Westbury was perhaps one of the most intense of its kind in the country as between 250-300 were registered, most of them long-time residents who had neglected to obtain citizenship. "Most were elderly, who came to this country minus the educational privileges so general here and about the only charge that can be made against them is one of negligence" was the interpretation of the local newspaper (*Westbury Times*, Undated articles in Dominick J. Piscitelli scrapbook). Any understanding of the true sentiment of the immigrant generation would have readily disposed of intimations of disloyalty. Some insight into this mentality may be discerned in the crude but sincere sentiments of an Italian-born Westbury barber who kept a diary and whose simple account of his entry for December 7, 1941, Pearl Harbor Day, stands as eloquent testimony to immigrant patriotism:

December 7, 1941

172 Post Avenue
Westbury Barber,

 I am Italian Born--
 Thank you, Uncle Sam, for giving me a home
and
 letting me become an American.
 I am proud to be one of you and I shall
help in every possible way to keep America
on top of the world.

American Citizen A. Cesare (Diary of Antonio Cesare)

 Italian Americans in Westbury could find other instances of discrimination. In the estimation of many, an effective defacto discrimination was the reason why few Italians worked in the local bank or served as policemen before World War II. Likewise, those who served in the volunteer fire department were numerically limited, although a second headquarters was opened in the New Cassel area in which Italians predominated. For Italian Americans to aspire to positions on the Westbury school board was to be preposterous, just as it was fruitless to look for them within the political realm. The "establishment" of pre-war Westbury had, in fact, little room for people of Italian background in prominent positions.

 For people like Dominick Piscitelli, while war-time discrimination rankled, it also served to confirm a determination to overcome unfair obstacles and re-double efforts to succeed. Even while in the service, for instance, he retained his dream of running for higher office, anti-Italian discrimination notwithstanding.

But I remembered the prejudice so much that while in the Sea Bees service during World War II, lying awake in my cot at night, I would promise myself that when I got back to civilian life I would run for office. I did not care whether I would win or lose—I was going to run (Interview, Dominick Piscitelli.)

THE POST-WAR DISCRIMINATION

In 1949 a major controversy over a proposal to change the street names in Copiague and thereby terminate their Italian origins engulfed Marconiville. Whether this development was the result of anti-Italian animosity engendered by World War II when Italy was an enemy nation is a matter of speculation. However, at least one complaint expressing embarassment over the spelling of Italian street names reached the Town of Babylon Board in 1945. Most interviewees denied any unusual ill feelings against Italians during the War and point with pride to the large number of servicemen the community produced. In addition to service in the active armed forces, Copiague Italian Americans played other meaningful roles on the home front during wartime by participating in a wide variety of civic works.

The move to change the street names was traced to the Copiague Lions Club which circulated a petition to that effect on the grounds that most area residents favored the idea. It is interesting to note that the Lions Club member and well-known leader Anthony Curcio spearheaded the petition. The Lions Club successfully persuaded the Planning Board of the Town of Babylon of the desireability of name-changing based on convenience and the avoidance of duplication with similar names in other communities. Consequently, a name-changing resolution was endorsed by the town board—locus of local government for the unincorporated hamlet (*Amityville Record*, November 18, 1949; Interview, Daniel Curcio). While a case could perhaps be made about the difficulty of spelling some Italian names, the argument about duplication was patently specious. Names such as Marconi, Caboto, Garibaldi, Mazzini, Pio X, among others, are so rare in all of Long Island, indeed throughout the nation, would be insured exclusiveness, regardless.

It was more likely that name-changing advocates were embarrassed at identification by address with Italian-sounding nomenclatures. It was also probably due in part to a residue of animosity between old Copiaguers in the south and Italians to the north (*Amityville Record*, March 31, 1950). In the revived nationalistic period of post-World War II America, it seemed eminently more desireable to be associated with Anglo-Saxon English-sounding titles. Some examples included the proposal to change Amerigo Vespucci Avenue to Brinker Avenue and Dante Avenue to Derry Street. Surely such changes were bound to outrage Italian Americans and others who professed to retain what was referred to as "those sweet sounding old

Italian names". Name-changing protagonist hopes of accomplishing their goals quickly, before opposition surfaced, were to be frustrated because aroused Copiaguers, in their vehement opposition to the entire project, effectively organized into *ad hoc* groups linked with local civic organizations and resoundingly denounced the move. Led by Rocco L. Moies, protesters appeared before the town board in large numbers, claiming anti-Italian discrimination as the real motivation behind the plan. Charging that the board had acted too hastily after being misled by the Lions Club whom he likened to the bigoted Ku Klux Klan, the fiery Moies declared: "We don't intend to be bossed around by the Lions Club...A group of men tried this 25 years ago, only then they wore white hoods". Other spokesmen opposed to name-changes cited high costs to businessmen and unneeded confusion. So determined were the outraged Copiaguers that the chastened Town Board rescinded its stand and ordered the retention of the old names. It was an unusual display of ethnic solidarity which the local press explained in another way: "Residents Make Town Say Uncle" (*Amityville Record*, March 31, 1950).

Despite Anthony Curcio's involvement in the matter, the dispute over the name changes, was more truly a classic confrontation between Anglo-Saxon and Latin. The action of a Babylon Town judge, who opposed Moies because of his attack on the Lions Club of which the judge was a member, is revealing. The indignant but insensitive judge berated the Italian American leader for impunging the name of the benevolent organization, while simultaneously acknowledging no regret that Italian Americans had been insulted (*Amityville Record*, April 7, 1950).

The Campagnoli era, however, was fading and the newer second and third generation Italian Americans probably favored the name changes, according to the local newspaper:

> Now, Italian is a Latin language but English is the current tongue of Copiague and shortly was to become such through all Marconiville when a new generation had had schooling. English has a good deal of Latin about it but perhaps not enough to affiliate with the sounds of the Italian as these sounds are embraced in the names of the streets. Marconiville became Copiague. Now after forty-five years its sons and daughters are represented in the social, the professional and the business life of all Copiague, although the families of most of the Italian immigrants still are prone to build homes in the Marconiville section, which lies to the north of the railroad tracks. We know many of the second and third generations and admire them for their loyalty to American ideals and customs. They are bright. They are energetic. They are adaptable and that is the characteristic which leads us to suspect that some of them are not entirely hostile to a purpose which

the Copiague Lions Club had in mind when it decided to find out whether the people of Copiague as a whole would not like to see the renaming of some of Marconiville's streets to bring in just a bit of Anglo Saxon color...The contest is interesting. The strife by the Old World to inculcate its speech and habit into sections of the American scene has always given us interest. Throughout the whole country the friendly feud had been going on and is still going (*Amityville Record*, April 14, 1950).

Understandably the Babylon Town Board was sorry it ever got involved and was content to return to the *status quo* which meant the retention of the original Italian names. The matter produced ill-feelings which lasted for a considerable period of time; a generation later the names persist and few recall the earlier squabble.

The existence of prejudice is an enduring dilemma for America. It appears, perhaps as a perversity of human nature, that individuals already established in a locale perceive the newly-arrived as inherently lacking in the qualities which they, the natives, possess. Generally out of fear combined with ignorance, those already entrenched in society see foreigners as strange, alien and different—surely unmistakeable marks of inferior cultures. Italian immigrants to suburbia would confront such attitudes and were required to deal with these feelings of ambivalence toward them. Even though milder in form than the discrimination experienced by their counterparts in the big cities, it was understandably something they did not enjoy. While prejudice never fully disappeared from the suburban scene, with patience and hard work Italian immigrants and their descendants would slowly but surely overcome the obstacles which were the results of prejudice. Certainly they would not allow such negative attitudes to deter them as they sought to establish themselves as full and productive inhabitants of suburbia. In short, they were determined to plant their own roots.

CHAPTER SEVEN
ESTABLISHING ROOTS

By 1900 the several Italian American communities that had been planted had matured to the point where they constituted solid foundations for the development of viable ethnic enclaves. Accordingly, Inwood, Port Washington, Glen Cove, Westbury, Patchogue, North Bellport and Hagerman were recognizable and emerging Little Italies. Only slightly later they were to be joined by Copiague (Marconiville). It was in these enclaves that Italian immigrants and their issue fashioned distinctive life styles and established their roots in American society. Called by a variety of descriptive names these neighborhoods constituted genuine reflections of Italian immigrant life on Long Island.

THE ORCHARD

Glen Cove's Little Italy, called the "Orchard", was a triangular piece of land in the southern part of the city. A small area seven blocks square, its narrow streets are slender and small and filled with modest homes. Carmine Capobianco, who was raised in the Orchard and still resides there more than 70 years later, recalls the area as containing wooded lands, cornfields and apple orchards (Interview, Carmine Capobianco). The name derivation was traced to the 1860s when its farm lands and apple orchards were run by individuals with distinctly Hibernicized and German names.

The Orchard's transition was the end result of the expansion of the Long Island Railroad inching its way along the North shore and which employed immigrant labor. Some of these laborers were housed in barracks on the Murphy property in the Orchard—the place through which the first Italians became acquainted with Glen Cove (*Glen Cove Record*, April 28, 1960).

Some years later more laborers came to dig trenches and lay heavy concrete pipes by hand for the village waterworks, while others were employed in the construction of St.Patrick's Church. Simultaneously, representatives of the nation's wealthiest families began to acquire property on the beautiful North Shore, intent on further enhancing their holdings by erecting baronial mansions which were destined to become glittering centerpieces of Long Island's fabled "Gold Coast". Lured by the prospect of employment on these estates more Italians quit the teeming and stiffling tenements of New York City's ghettoes in favor of a rural setting which was more in keeping with the old country they had left behind.

Bringing with them old world skills as gardeners, laborers and stone masons, they were prepared to work hard and live frugally and thereby save sufficient funds to bring over their wives and families. Some went back to Italy or to the older Little Italies in New York City, married, returned with their brides, and purchased small parcels of land from the old farm families in the Orchard thereby beginning a new community. Descendants of estate workers generally recall that their parents and grandparents painted a positive picture of working for estate owners who took an interest in their employees and their families, providing them with clothing and medical care.

Construction of houses in the Orchard was frequently a family affair in which use was made of available resources such as stones dug from the nearby fields or foundations and lumber salvaged from existing buildings and barns no longer in use. Most of the early efforts at homebuilding produced small wooden-framed houses which, far from luxurious, were nevertheless functional and accommodating. Perhaps the first to build a three story brick home in the Orchard was Neil Abbondondolo, who included provisions for a bar on the ground floor (Interview, Lawrence Abbondondolo).

OLD WORLD TRADITIONS IN GLEN COVE

Immigration patterns in Glen Cove comported with traditional interpretations regarding male predominance in the initial phase of immigration. However, as soon as the early arrivals had established themselves, they called for their families to join them. Mary Limongelli Renaldo's description of what it entailed for her mother and her siblings, provides significant insight into the potentially traumatic experience. She tells of her father preceding the rest of the family to Long Island, but missing them so much he sent for them.

> They came over but did not know where Glen Cove was, and my sister tells the story of how the family had tickets pinned on with their names and where they were going and who they were supposed to go to. A man put them on a train and when they got off at Glen Cove, my mother, who had a lot of nerve, asked a man for help. It happened to be an Italian from the Orchard named Carmen DiLeo, who knew my father and directed the family to the house. In the meantime my father was in New York City looking for them.

Italian immigrants learned to adapt to living in American homes which, in that era, meant, for example, depending on cistern wells to catch and store rainwater underground. Gas was manufactured in a nearby gas plant and heat was provided by potbellied stoves, around which children would gather to warm themselves before dashing to frigid upstairs rooms. Each home had its private outhouse in the backyards requiring utilization of potties in the middle of the night.

Italians brought with them many of the old world traditions such as a rich legacy of wine making—a legacy that continued with fervor and pride. Every October witnessed a familiar ritual: varieties of grapes from muscatel to zinfandel were crated and shipped in from California and sold in local fruit stores which specialized in the crop. Then would come grape crushing in decrepit wooden presses, the soft pop of carbon monoxide bubbles as the fruit fermented and the enlistment of upright oak casks to store the newly-made beverage. Virtually every Italian home in the Orchard had a cool cellar for storage purposes and the practice continues among a considerable number of Americans of Italian descent in Glen Cove to this day.

Long Island was not so sunny as the Italian peninsula, an environmental verity that required adjustment for the early immigrants, most of whom worked outdoors. Winter was the most severe season of the year since it necessitated work termination for laborers and construction men perhaps as early as Thanksgiving or most certainly by Christmas, with work resuming the following spring. Each family grew its own vegetables and then carefully buried some in the backyard to assure enough food for the long winter. Cabbages in particular were preserved this way with roots left outside of the ground while the rest of the vegetable remained buried. Demonstrating resourcefulness and efficiency, Orchard residents also raised hogs and poultry, mainly chickens, on the tiniest of backyard plots. The more prosperous had cows. With the commencement of winter the efforts of the entire community were mobilized and any man with expertise, such as the local butcher, was enlisted in the slaughtering process. The residents then made their hams and sausages which were preserved outdoors during the cold winter months.

GROWTH OF GLEN COVE'S LITTLE ITALY

Glen Cove's Italian population experienced phenomenal growth prior to the outbreak of World War I. Whereas they numbered perhaps two dozen in 1900, that figure jumps to 1,163 in 1915 (U.S. Census, 1900). Thus they were over ten percent of the 10,502 total residents of Glen Cove. Of the 1,663, 566 were females and 440 were boarders. In addition, 1,053 were aliens while 610 possessed American citizenship.

For Glen Cove at large the emergence of an extensive Italian settlement in the Orchard necessitated a process of acquaintance and adjustment to alien mores. The process did of course ensue, although wrapped up in associating

Italian customs with the quaint, the romantic and the exotic, as illustrated in a 1917 newspaper account:

> ...Pepper hangs in long red bunches in the kitchen. Watch their faces, their snappy dark eyes, their hands and their shoulders...Hear them talk and above all hear them sing. Have you ever been to "De Orch" on a summer night when a great white moon floods the skies and earth with magic lights? It is too late now but make up your minds to go next summer. If you want to see the real thing in Italia...They know how to play anywhere—and to dance—anywhere—and to make music—anywhere, but they choose the street under the moonlight.

They were occasionally misdirected, opined the news reporter, but all that was needed was to show them the right direction and they would be fine. Thus, even while the focus was on strange alien ways it nevertheless reflected a more open attitude of acceptance than in the large cities.

> There are 56 peppery Italians in the Orchard Clean-up club and you ought to see them using their mother's brooms on the streets...Once a month there is a party and prizes. Sometimes they even clean themselves before the party...just have a little patience and they'll wash off the neckline one of these days (*Glen Cove Echo*, December 15, 1917).

Funeral practices were among the more interesting customs carried on by Glen Cove's Italian populace. As southern Italians they were descendants of regions in which local mores, with their provincial-based variations, persisted long after unification of the country. To the peasant world of the late 19th century death was a deeply personal experience which could not be entrusted to detached outsiders. It was a phenomenon in which the family and close neighbors played an intimate role. Before the extensive use of funeral parlors, wakes were held at the homes of the deceased, although a pervasive sense of guilt on the part of the survivors, which so characterized an earlier period, had undergone much transformation. There were very few funeral parlors in 1925 in the neighborhood when Mary Renaldo's father died, he was embalmed and waked at home in typical Orchard fashion. The family stove was put out as was the custom, with neighbors assuming the responsibility of cooking for the family, staying with them and sharing the bereavement around the clock. Visitors who came to pay their final respects left some money for the family.

Virtually all borders were aliens who were likely to return to Italy after a stay; however, a considerable number re-emigrated to resume their jobs. Just as in Westbury, the boarding house served a useful function for immigrants providing a place of acceptance at moderate cost amidst familiar people, even relatives, along with partaking of habitual foods and carrying on of old-world customs. It also enabled boarding house keepers to earn a modest income while paying off mortgages. Many an Italian home in the Orchard served as a place of residence not only for immediate family members but also for up to 25 boarders. Amato Famigletti, for instance, had ten lodgers in 1915, a figure that was surpassed by Angelo Cocchiola who housed as many as 25 at one time.

FAMILY PROFILE

Surprisingly, despite the well-founded reputation for large families normally attributed to Italians at the turn of the century, Glen Cove families numbered an average of 2.3 children per household. The lower fecundity rate was not necessarily attributable to a suburban characteristic. One factor which may serve as an adequate explanation for this phenomenon is the presence of relatively young married couples who were just beginning their families rather than the predominance of older established families. In addition, it was evident that many had not yet brought their entire families here, so the real total of children per family was not altogether revealed. Thus, one can examine with benefit other characteristics of the population which are closer to the image. Accordingly, of 228 wives, all listed housework as an occupation—a clear manifestation of a domestic-oriented society which did not tolerate married women working outside the home. This domesticated condition, moreover, largely pertained to the young unmarried but working-age Italian American females. Of twelve in the upper teenage category who were unmarried, ten listed housework as their occupations, while one listed factory work and another a maid as their occupations—the latter apparently was here without family and lived in the residence of her employer—an experience very unusual for Italian American females of that time (*New York State Manuscript Census*, Nassau County, 1915).

Because of inferior locations and improper care, early twentieth century immigrant neighborhoods frequently became the centers of serious health problems which attracted widespread attention.

ALARM OVER HEALTH DANGERS

In 1910 the Italian government, concerned about health and sanitation within Italian communities in the United States and acting upon the findings of Dr. Antonio Stella, established a health clinic in New York City. Although somewhat milder than in the big cities, by 1915 worry over dangerous living conditions was prevalent among health authorities on Long Island. Aware of the association between cleanliness and disease, local civic groups launched a clean-up campaign that urged Glen Cove residents to expurgate and paint their buildings to produce a spotless village. Clean-up posters were circulated and reproduced in Italian. Large newspaper advertisements, in Italian appeared in the local press announcing the launching of the campaign for May 5-7, 1915, along with instructions regarding how buildings should be cleansed in the quickest manner possible. These missives exhorted immigrants to join in the efforts to produce a sanitary and beautiful town (*Glen Cove Echo*, May 1, 1915).

Conditions in the Orchard were indeed terrible. A depressing neighborhood dump, plainly visible to the unfortunate inhabitants, underscored the almost total lack of public services for the area. For years the dump had seen the accumulation of all sorts of undesireable items such as tin cans, ashes, dead cats and dogs, offals of butchered cattle—refuse which produced the most offensive odors. With reason, Italian residents complained bitterly of the stench which intensified during warm weather or when caught up in unfavorable winds. This assessment of the awful conditions were virtually conceded by the town health officer whose confirmation of the gravity of the situation was prompted not so much over concern for the Italians as it was for protecting the rest of the community. Thus, he was grossly offensive with his statement that he "considered the dump the best thing that the Orchard had...", since its location at that site precluded its unsanitary spread throughout the rest of the general area (*Glen Cove Echo*, May 27, 1916). He then proceeded to complain about insufficient town laws to deal with the problem.

Concern over health matters had a causative effect on organizing the Italians. With the encouragement of settlement house workers from Glen Cove's Neighborhood House, in May 1916 an Italian neighborhood club with a membership of 50 was organized to serve as an outlet for social, cultural and civic functions. It was evident that much of its early activity was concerned with health and sanitary problems. The second meeting, for example, featured the New York Department of Health Sanitary Supervisor for Nassau and Suffolk, whose talk was entitled "Dirt and Sickness", a program highlighted by illustrations through stereoptican views (*Glen Cove Echo*, July 7, 1916).

Strenuous efforts to prevent calamity notwithstanding, the unhealthy environment proved overwhelming and newspaper reports told of widespread diphtheria in an Orchard tenement inhabited by fifteen to twenty families (*Oyster Bay Guardian*, August 13, 1915). In December, 1915, a state health official called the conditions in Glen Cove, especially in the Orchard, "public scandal". Curiously, but revealingly, a local official used the occasion to make humorous remarks. Despite attempts at levity during the meeting it was undisputed that there was a genuine danger inherent in the spread of the disease from Glen Cove. It was reported that the citizenry of the community was doing all in its power to stamp out the disease and that physicians were donating their services, however, it was also admitted that there existed a potential public outcry about expenditures of public funds for a clinic in the afflicted areas (*Oyster Bay Guardian*, December 31, 1915).

Despite warnings from health officials, some town authorities and local newsmen remained incredulous regarding the seriousness of the epidemic. The *Oyster Bay Guardian* used words like "overzealous" to describe the evaluation made by state health officials. "It is not that the people of the town are unwilling to provide all that the State authorities exact, but they are asking themselves why so much greater necessity for all this now than a few years ago?" (*Oyster Bay Guardian*, January 14, 1916). One can only speculate that this reluctance to spend public money to control the health menace was a measure of an unwillingness to divert substantial tax funds whose initial and main beneficiaries were immigrants. As it was, the pathogenesis would not allow authorities to put off the matter. With the elapsing of only two weeks more, the town health officer reported twelve new cases of diphtheria and three deaths from the disease in the Orchard. Alarm over health conditions spread to nearby communities in the summer of 1916. Oyster Bay's wealthy class now sought to contain the spread of *infantile paralysis*. No less an illustrious figure than Oyster Bay's most prominent citizen, former President Theodore Roosevelt, became personally active. At the behest of the Town Board, Roosevelt offered suggestions as to ways and means of cleaning up the area, recommending that a large committee be formed and that some Italians be placed on it "...in order that they be taught that cleanliness and order was for their good and was their cause as well as the cause of Americans" (*Oyster Bay Guardian*, July 28, 1916). The recommendation was adopted unanimously and subsequently the committee suggested an inquiry into the feasibility of erecting an isolation hospital near Glen Cove. Conditions in the community were considered so grave that celebration of the annual St.Rocco's feast had to be postponed.

Over the next few months health conditions in the general vicinity so deteriorated that the Town Board declared a state of quarantine in the Town of Oyster Bay which prohibited anyone under sixteen years old from entering the town without a certificate of health confirming the absence of a communicable disease. Simultaneously, a report highlighted over-crowded conditions in a number of homes in the town in which as many as five families lived in one-family houses—in one case as many as 89 people lived in a single family home.

Italian Orchard residents were far from complacent—not simply waiting for outsiders to help them in their misery but prepared to take matters into their own hands. All but a small minority pledged monthly sums of money for garbage removal thereby winning the plaudits of the *Glen Cove Echo* which was so pleasantly surprised that it offered to publish the names of the Italian contributors (*Glen Cove Echo*, September 2, 1916).

By 1918 local newspapers devoted less attention to the menace posed by health and sanitation habits in the immigrant areas. Apparently either the worst of the epidemic had passed or the protective measures, including cleanliness campaigns and quarantines, were sufficient to arrest the spread of disease. Furthermore, although some Long Island Italian enclaves were seriously affected, others seem to have escaped unscathed. In any event, the problems hardly made a dent in the continuing influx of immigrants to the established Little Italies of Long Island which grew impressively.

THE EMERGENCE OF WESTBURY'S LITTLE ITALY

Although precise figures regarding the number of Italians in Westbury in 1900 are not available, there could not have been more than a few dozen. Yet, growth was monumental and in 1915 the New York State Census showed 492 first and second generation Italians out of a total Westbury population of 3,176, or slightly less than one out of six. While the state census listed eighteen as boarder/lodgers, the more revealing statistic is the much larger figure—94—who lived in their own households either as renters or home-owners. In other words, by 1915 the typical Italian immigrant lived in the characteristic nuclear family setting. To a considerable extent demographic characteristics of an ethnic group provide a mirror of past historical tendencies. The New York State Manuscript Census of 1915 is useful in this regard because it reflects the influence of the then recent migration from Italy to Long Island. When an analysis of the age structure of Westbury's Italian-descended population is undertaken some significant differences become immediately apparent. The youthful character of the Italian population in the village is a significant characteristic which demonstrated that at least half of the 94 heads of households were 35 years of age or younger, and that only four were over 50 years old.

With a median age of thirteen years or younger, the 252 Italian-originated inhabitants were considerably younger than other components of the United States population. The cohort through the first five years of age numbered 147 or approximately 30 percent of the total. This markedly youthful skewing of statistics means that there was a virtual absence of teenagers in the Italian enclave. Only 42 non-married teenagers were counted in the thirteen through nineteen age cohort, comprised of 30 males and twelve females. The discrepancy in sex representations is accounted for in part because some teenage females were listed as married, while several teenage males were listed as boarders. No females were listed as boarders although a fifteen year old and a nineteen year old worked as servants/cooks on estates.

TABLE 1

AGES OF HEADS OF HOUSEHOLDS BASED ON EXTRAPOLATIONS FROM NEW YORK STATE MANUSCRIPT CENSUS 1915

AGE	NUMBER
20-25	8
26-30	22
31-35	17
36-40	26
41-45	14
46-50	2
51-55	3
56-60	1
UNKNOWN	1

Source: New York State Manuscript Census, 1915.

TABLE 2

DEMOGRAPHIC PROFILE OF WESTBURY'S ITALIAN AMERICAN POPULATION BASED ON EXTRAPOLATIONS FROM NEW YORK STATE MANUSCRIPT CENSUS 1915

TOTAL POPULATION	3,176
ITALIAN AMERICANS	492
MALES	275
FEMALES	217
HEADS OF FAMILY	94
WIVES	94
WIDOWS	1
LODGERS/ BOARDERS	18
ALIENS	187

Source: New York State Manuscript Census, 1915.

Most of the aliens were from within the adult population while the younger children were more likely to have been native-born citizens.

The proletarian bent was undeniably manifest in the designations under occupation which showed that of 125 men listed, none were professionals while varieties of laborer categories numbered 69 or more than half of the

TABLE 3

OCCUPATIONS OF ITALIAN AMERICANS IN WESTBURY, NEW YORK, 1915.

OCCUPATION	NUMBER
Housekeepers	128
Auto Mechanic	1
Baker	3
Bricklayer	1
Barber	2
Butcher	3
Butler (Servant)	1
Cook (Servant)	1
Chauffeur	1
Carpenter	2
Dressmaking	1
Driver	3
Dry Goods	2
Farmer	1
Farmer Foreman	1
Gardener	9
General Store	1
Hotel	1
Laborers (General)	47
Laborers (Nursery)	20
Laborers (Mason)	2
Painting	2
Plumber	1
Poultry Man	1
Peddler	1
Plaster Man	1
Real Estate	1
Saloon	1
Stamp Binder	1
Stable Man	1
Sidewalk Foreman	1
Stationary Store	1
Tailor	3
Teamster	4
Umbrella Factory	1
Watchman	1
Waitress (Servant)	1
	254

Source: New York State Manuscript Census, 1915.

total male work force. One hundred twenty-eight women listed housekeeper as their occupation, with only one woman working as a servant/waitress, statistics which underscore domesticity. Most of the adult population were aliens who had not yet become naturalized citizens, thereby reflecting both recency of arrival and possible interest in returning to Italy.

THE FAMILY: A FLEXIBLE INSTITUTION

Having discussed the emigration process, the settlement pattern and work activities, what of the social activities, leisure-time orientation and interaction within and without the Italian ethnic community? Historians and social scientists have provided us with varying interpretations as to the degree of alienation experienced by the ethnic group in a harsh American environment. Some groups found the experience, especially in the urban centers, to be largely negative towards family life; such an interpretation is, however, not borne out by the overall greater Patchogue area experience. What emerges instead is a perception more in keeping with the view of historian Virginia Yans Mclauglin (1974). whose studies into the south Italian work experience adumbrate the family as a flexible institution capable of adjusting the traditional family structure with options available within the new environment. As such, family life among Italians in Patchogue gives ample evidence of strong blood ties. The researcher must acknowledge, however, the relative absence of perceptive and analytical published material regarding Italian family life in Patchogue in earlier periods—indeed one is impressed by the almost total neglect of the topic in the local press. Nevertheless, what emerges from the few references extrapolated, and supplemented with numerous in-depth interviews, is a suggestion of a strong attachment to family in the first generation, including that of the extended family. One example is the Fuoco family whose homestead accommodated many family members, married and single. On the other hand, within a comparatively short time period, the Fuocos, along with other traditional Italian families, adopted customs regarding separation of households more in keeping with the larger society. Residential patterns among first and second generations indicated a strikingly high degree of concentration in regions of original settlement, although considerable variation was evident among those of later generations.

First and second generations placed high priority on social interaction within the context of immediate family and relations, with older generation respondents quick to recall as the highlights of their socialization those times when the family and relatives assembled. Summertime Sundays were especially memorable as relatives and friends assembled at the home of a family member who had the means to provide suitable collation. As Elizabeth Fuoco recalled, "Our relations came out in the summertime, stayed a couple of weeks and would go to the beach. There were many hotels, but Italians did not have money for that so they stayed with relatives (Interview, Elizabeth Fuoco). When one considers that the families of the first and frequently second generations were large one can appreciate how a family get-together could readily involve upwards of 100 people.

Transplantation of family life was of paramount importance to Italian

Americans. It was the main institution that sustained the ethnic group and was one of the most characteristic features of the group's uniqueness. Family life, moreover, was experienced within the context of the larger, extended set of relationships within the community. Whether related by blood or not, Italians have always accorded a high priority to kinship based on identification with a place, a community. From the beginning Long Island Italian American communities served as matrixes which developed beyond the immediate nuclear family.

EARLY ORGANIZATIONAL LIFE: MUTUAL AID SOCIETIES

With the growth of population and staying power of Italian neighborhoods and with the establishment of large and important local families, it seemed natural for the ethnic group to create viable organizations which reflected their interests and priorities. In the pre-World War I period the first of these organizations were those of the mutual aid variety. Organized along lines of mutual background, as for example membership limited to those of a specific province or town, the society collected modest dues which served as a fund for its needy members. Thus, at times of illness or death, members and their families received some financial assistance. These societies also promoted social and cultural events, thereby serving to encourage comradery.

In 1897, the oldest of Inwood's Italian American organizations, the Stella Albanese Society, was founded. Reflecting the concentration of Albanese Italians in the community, this association served as a social and fraternal society which included the most prominent local Albanese descended families who sponsored a series of social events: dinners, dances and festivals. It also manifested a political inclination with elections for officers—frequently spirited affairs which attracted local headlines.

In other instances mutual aid societies surfaced without reference to place of Italian origination, but encompassing those in Long Island communities. The creation of the Bellport Columbus Sick and Benevolent Association and the Brothers of Columbus in 1910 and 1911, in the Bellport/Patchogue area are cases in point (*Patchogue Advance*, December 20, 1912). Mutual aid societies could also be associated with religious associations. In Inwood in 1905 the New Mutual Aid Congregation and Brotherhood of St.Cono came into existence designed to provide aid for funeral expenses. Most probably this organization led to the formation of an offshoot known as the Societa di San Cono, incorporated on September 16, 1907, whose major activity was the sponsorship of the annual St.Cono feast—the biggest festival of its kind in the area. Beginning in 1906 and continuing into the present, the feast was duly celebrated on September 26 and 27, with the full and familiar panoply of feast trappings including Italian foods, music, parades, street lights, fireworks and Mass in the Church. The eight annual feast in 1912 is typical of the early years. After the usual listing of association officers and members of the festival committee, the newspaper account told of the events surrounding the festivity: celebration of afternoon vespers, morning and afternoon Masses at Our Lady of Good Counsel Church and a beautiful electrical illumination (*Rockaway News*, September 12, 1913.

St. Rocco Society

Common place of origin and Italian gregariousness manifested itself in the formation of religious, social, cultural, political and athletic societies and organizations that flourished in Glen Cove's Little Italy in the 1900-1925 period. The St.Rocco Society, chartered under the leadership of Angelo Cocchiola in 1910, undoubtedly was the community's oldest mutual aid society, aimed at assisting members afflicted by adversity by providing sick benefits including doctors' visits at half price and money for burial expenses. As was the custom in Sturno, the society also planned and implemented celebration of the annual St.Rocco feast, while simultaneously promoting American democratic principles. Reflecting an influx of Calabrians in the area, in 1922 the St.Marino Society was formed to undertake similar activities. Members of both societies were assessed minimal dues and obtained land which was later deeded to St.Rocco's parish (*Glen Cove Echo*, May 25, 1950).

Similarly-named societies existed in adjoining Oyster Bay. Encouraged by the sympathetic pastor of St.Dominic's, Oyster Bay's Italian society preceded that of Glen Cove where Italians remained rather alienated from the pastor of St.Patrick's Church. As a consequence Oyster Bay's St.Rocco's Society was able to sponsor a feast celebration in 1910, which attracted their fellow nationals from Glen Cove who journeyed to the nearby community and enjoyed band concerts, parades, bicycle races, grand fireworks displays, and a High Mass celebrated by an Italian priest in the local church (*Glen Cove Echo*, September 2, 1910). The rather reserved natives of Oyster Bay were duly impressed by the ability of these laborer immigrants to conduct an affair of this magnitude and to follow up with grander efforts each succeeding year. These celebrations, moreover, marked the few occasions when Italians were given substantial local press coverage and one can conclude that the immigrant population left favorable imprints if the *Oyster Bay Guardian* editorial of 1911 is a guide.

> It takes the Italians to set the pace for the ordinary Oyster Bay American. For two days and two nights Italians have given the residents of Oyster Bay some food for thought. Oyster Bay is a quaint, old-fashioned

country town; its populace has been content with their lot; they do not believe in giving much toward making a show—their forte being in making a show at the bank. Not so with the Italian populace. These people are patriotic. They believe in their patriotic saint, St.Rocco, and are willing to place their earnings in support of their ideas, and as a consequence they have done things which should bring the blush of shame to the American populace, because of their liberality. "What is a dollar in comparison to the support of what we think if for our own benefit" has been their motto.

The editorial utilized the occasion to lament the miserliness with which residents supported local firemen, and remarked that they should take a hint from the Italians.

Dell' Assunta Society

The Dell' Assunta Society of Westbury is another mutual aid society created under religious auspices. Formed in 1911 to provide mutual benefits and to be an outlet for religious and social expression, it brought together Westbury Italians who immigrated from Durazzano, Nola and Saviano.

Membership is restricted to Catholic males, Italian born or sons of Italians. A dues structure of $1.00 per month entitled members to a share in sick benefits up to $10 a week and death benefits of up to $200, amounts which perhaps are insignificant by today's standards but were of some meaning in the 1910s and 1920s. A perusal of the roster of original members reveals that most of Westbury's Italian community had joined. Throughout the first two decades the society was a source of pride and identification, but its major growth came in the 1930s when it went beyond meetings in the cellars of members homes, church basements or the back room of bars. It was time for the society to acquire a home of its own and to expand the activities.

The organization persists and boasts of sponsoring the oldest and most on-going feast day in the New York metropolitan area—even older than the famed San Gennaro Feast. At its feast audiences were entertained by bands and the day's events climaxed with the largest display of fireworks on Long Island which attracted tens of thousands of people. By the end of the 1930s, crowds of 25,000 to 30,000 were not uncommon and in some years they reached 75,000.

FRATERNAL ORGANIZATIONS

Another type of social organization formed in Italian colonies on Long Island were those of a fraternal nature. The Sons of Italy, the largest local Italian fraternal order, founded the Christopher Columbus Lodge in Patchogue in 1900 and for years sponsored Italian American activities and enjoyed a membership of over 50 in 1913. Nor were activities all of a social/celebratory nature as the lodge also sponsored free evening classes in local public schools to teach English to Patchogue's Italians (*Patchogue Advance*, December 11, 1914, *Patchogue Argus*, July 12, 1918). Within a couple of years the Columbus Lodge had constructed Columbus Hall, a handsome new meeting place on Waverly Avenue, which became the scene of many dinners, dances and other activities which attracted community participation. So impressive was growth that in 1919 the larger local Knights of Columbus Hall was rented in order to initiate 46 new members. Notwithstanding this success, a rival Lincoln Lodge of the Independent Order of the Sons of Italy also came into being in Patchogue (*Patchogue Advance*, September 29, October 13, 1911).

Sons of Italy Lodge

One of Glen Cove's most eminent mutual aid societies was the Order of the Sons of Italy which was instituted in 1920 as Glen Cove Loggia 1016. It can boast of being the oldest continuously functioning lodge among dozens of lodges in Nassau and Suffolk Counties including in its membership virtually all Italian-Americans who were active in civic and political affairs locally. The opening ceremony, which was held in the Orchard House in October 1920, was indeed auspicious as it brought together the Italian ambassador and the Mayor of Glen Cove. It is interesting to note that it was the announced primary purpose of the order to promote American citizenship for Italians who had immigrated here. As it succeeded in attracting membership, it sponsored a number of social and cultural activities such as Italian classes and assistance for war-torn Italy. Giuseppe Nigro was one of the first members to become active in society affairs. His own career could well qualify him as an authentic Glen Cove Horatio Alger story; he entered the country as a young teenager from Sturno in 1911, found very humble work opportunities, and in a few years emerged as a successful and prosperous proprietor of a Glen Cove coal and lumber yard.

LABOR ORGANIZATIONS

Although not widespread, labor organizations came into being in some Long Island Italian American enclaves. What is interesting in this connection is the revelation that such types of organizations probably were among the first created within the ethnic group.

On October 4, 1891, the Italian Concordia Society, Benevolent and Political of Bellport was formed (*Patchogue Advance*, April 7, 1891). Although announced with much fanfare including a photograph of its president, little else is known beyond an assertion that, "The society has an employment office on Post Avenue, near Atlantic Avenue, one block from the old station, where all American people and others can obtain masons, carpenters, farm hands, common laborers, *etc.* No charge for furnishing the help". Listed were the names of the president and ten officers—none of which re-appeared in the subsequent development of Italian American history in that area, thus leading to speculation that this society may have been a transient one which specialized in furnishing work gangs in the general area. It is known, for example, that Italian work gangs were used extensively by the Long Island Railroad as it extended its lines at this time (LaGumina, 1985). It is also a fact that in April, 1891, Italian work gangs were employed in large numbers to clear the streets in Medford, adjoining Patchogue to the north (*Patchogue Advance*, April 29, 1891).

BAND ORGANIZATIONS

If the transient nature of the Concordia Society was true, it would indicate that the emergence of more indigenous and permanent examples of Italian organizational life would have to await the development of more permanent residential patterns—a phenomena which occurred over the next decade and a half. On August 20, 1909, there came into creation the Patchogue Italian Band, an organization made up of Italian musicians who had learned to play their instruments in the old country and who now resided in Hagerman, Bellport and Patchogue (*Patchogue Advance*, August 20, 1909). Its make-up of immigrants from the three contiguous villages constitutes proof of the close interaction between Italians in greater Patchogue early in the century. The new bandmaster was of non-Italian background and obviously chosen to coach them in the rendition of American music, and it was further stated that the band was prepared to travel all over the country to perform. There is no evidence that the band did in fact travel extensively, although at least one member, Michael Prudent, became famous throughout Long Island as the proprietor of a travelling carnival show.

Band organizations were such an attraction to Italian immigrants that astute employers sponsored them as a means of promoting good will and loyalty. For decades Italians were enlisted in industrial bands such as the Patchogue-Plymouth Lace Mill Band which was featured in numerous community events and feast celebrations.

FORESTERS OF AMERICA

Another association which attracted Italian Americans early in their Inwood history was the Foresters of America, Court Vesuvius No. 408. Organized by Vincent Zavatt on March 13, 1902, this was, strictly speaking, not an ethnic organization, but a chapter of a national American association which, for all intents and purposes, functioned locally as an Italian ethnic society. All its officers with vaunted titles such as Chief Ranger, Sub-Chief Ranger, *etc.,* were Italian Americans, and one of the major activities of the group, which in 1912 boasted of a membership of 100, was the sponsorship and coordination of an annual Columbus Day celebration. The 1912 festival, for example, celebrated with a parade through the principal streets of Inwood and Far Rockaway with colors flying and a Brooklyn band playing popular arias. The procession then returned to Inwood where members assembled in a lodge room of Vincent Zavatt's building to listen to speeches and indulge in refreshments, culminating the day with "a spledid display of fireworks witnessed by thousands of people from Far Rockaway, Inwood, Lawrence and Cedarhurst' (*Rockaway News,* October 16, 1912). In later years, Forester activities centered around recreational activities such as picnics and dances along with the celebration of national holidays like Memorial Day and Columbus Day. In 1939, a second Inwood chapter—the Court Vittoria 522 was established with the two chapters functioning independently until their merger in the 1950s.

ITALIAN WELFARE CLUB

The Italian Welfare Club of Glen Cove with Vincenzo Capobianco as president was organized May 8, 1916, when 45 members met at the Neighborhood Settlement House. Club plans called for regular meetings to discuss matters of mutual interest and to have occasional speakers. However, the main purpose was to serve as a social outlet for the exhibition of Italian plays, folk dances and music. Some of the meetings seem incredulous in retrospect. For example, one featured a recital by a Mr. Vincent, whose specialty was "Off Again, On Again, Finnegan"; one wonders how an Italian audience responded to a presentation with such a Gaelic bent. On the other hand, the club sponsored events which were undoubtedly of more intimate meaning to the Italian audience. Thus, its first dramatic program featured Eduardo Migliacco (Farfariello), universally acclaimed as one of the most outstanding performers among the repertoire of actors in Italian American theater circles of the era. Migliacco's specialty was mimicking the foibles of "greehorn" immigrants, and his performance in the Neighborhood House attracted a full and enthusiastic audience winning their plaudits for clever impersonations (*Glen Cove Echo,* May 13, July 1, 1916).

ITALIAN POLITICAL CLUB

The Italian Political Club of Port Washington, organized in 1912, was the second organization formed by Italians in that community. Although not indicated in the title, the club was Republican oriented and was designed to carve out a place for the Italian element in local politics. It, too, sponsored celebrations, particularly in honor of Christopher Columbus.

CIVIC ASSOCIATIONS

Expansion of ethnic organizational life was a concomitant of the buoyant spirit of the 1920s, a fact reflected in Long Island's Italian American enclaves. In Patchogue, for example, existing Italian American organizations continued their work, although some underwent name modifications as in the case of the Christopher Columbus Sons of Italy Lodge which henceforth became known as the Garibaldi Lodge. In addition, new Italian organizations like the Italian American Civic Club, Local No.3, were organized in Patchogue and ostensibly took in all of Suffolk County. The first meeting, held in Fr. Cioffi's rectory, claimed a membership of 75 under the presidency of Pasquale Felice. Its stated objectives were:

> To unite all Americans of Italian descent to preserve loyalty to the United States of America, to encourage cordial relationships with native-born Americans, to foster civic pride throughout all of Suffolk County. All Italian Americans of good character are eligible for membership (*Patchogue Advance*, July 12, 1928).

The organization also emphasized the importance of learning English by encouraging residents to attend evening school where English language classes were available.

Organizational life in Copiague during the expansionist decade of the 1920s manifested revealing insights about participation in community activities. A time of heightened awareness of the need to create organizations conversant with local issues, the atmosphere found residents south of the railroad track forming the Copiague Civic Association which, despite its concern for the community, continued to maintain a distance from the Italian Americans north of the tracks. The deep-seated animosity harbored by old-time Copiaguers virtually excluded membership of the Latin element and thereby proved to be a stumbling block for both continued growth of the association and true cooperation. Oldtimers recalled the snobbish attitude of southern Copiaguers whose penchant for ridicule rankled the Italian community.

The ability of Italian newcomers to organize themselves in the midst of their suburban/ rival environment soon after arrival to this country is important to note. It is a revelation that whatever else the immigrant experience may have been in terms of turmoil in the sense of being uprooted, there was sufficient dynamism within the group to form organizations of their own to improve their condition and foster their ethnic aspirations.

Italian American organizational life is the history of a plethora of organizations formed at the end of the nineteenth century and were primarily of an ethnic/ social variety although some were militant (*See,* S. Tomasi, 1975 and Giovanetti, 1979). Within several years of their settlement—as soon as numbers rendered it feasible—Italians participated in fraternal, social, civic and religious organizations to such an extent that it would seem to contradict the prevailing view of Italians as so staunchly individualistic and so family-oriented so as to preclude cooperation in joint ventures. Italian Americans were indeed joiners of many ethnic organizations and were destined to play integral roles in the wider sphere of Long Island community life.

It can be seen that the embryonic Italian enclaves which had come into existence in the late nineteenth century had, by the outbreak of World War I, become functioning vital centers of social and cultural life. Still in their infancy they were, nevertheless, well-positioned for the type of growth and evolution which would render their presence vital not only to the inhabitants of these neighborhoods, but also to the wider community. Before embarking on that history, however, it is necessary to relate the ways by which the outbreak of war affected Long Island's Little Italies.

CHAPTER EIGHT
THE FIRST WORLD WAR

In April, 1914, Europe became engulfed in a war whose length and furiosity stunned observers. The full realization of the cost of the war in human life would be realized only after it was over. Certainly during the early phases, the United States had not yet become fully aware of its devastation. The fact that the United States did not enter the conflict until 1917, one year before its conclusion, further influenced the relatively casual attitude then prevailing. For Italy and its people living in America, however, the perils of the conflagration came much sooner because in 1915, after a protracted period of hesitation, Italy entered the war as an Allied partner. By entering the war against Austria-Hungary and Germany in May 1915, Italy was constrained to assemble all her resources, including Italians who had emigrated. Now the war in all its somberness came to Italy as well as to Italian American communities.

TO FIGHT FOR THE FATHERLAND

The outbreak of World War I impinged on the Italian population in America to the extent that it served as a catalyst causing a number of immigrants to heed the calls of the fatherland, return to Italy and don uniforms to defend their native country. For Port Washington this development was not surprising in view of the recency of immigration and the realization that so many Port Washingtonians had families in Italy or actually still retained Italian citizenship. At least one local Italian, James Villani, enlisted in the Italian army in 1915 and was twice wounded before he returned to Long Island at the conclusion of the war (*Port Washington News*, December 26, 1916). Within Westbury's Italian population, which was small, a few took this path, while others became engaged almost by accident. Humbert Ianucci was on a return visit to Durazzano when the war broke out, requiring him to enter the Italian Army; subsequently he was killed in action (Interview, Frank Ciardullo). Many young Westbury Italians chose to avoid military service by remaining in the United States, a strategy which worked until April, 1917, when the nation began a call-up of men for its armed forces.

Although specific figures are lacking there is evidence that Italians from the Orchard responded by joining Italian regiments in such considerable numbers that one apparently overeager correspondent described the volume of enlistments as "...not one or two at a time, but in the twenty-fives and hundreds at a time". In 1917, when America went to war, Italians responded even more enthusiastically.

Many Italians were to serve and in the Westbury community there is reason to believe that they may have been a disproportionate number of the complement drafted when compared to other groups. Anthony Razzano (Tony Anel) recalled that when the draft was instituted, the local draft board, was bereft of Italian Americans when it began its registration operation of the young men in the community. Anthony's bilingual abilities enabled him to assist the draft board with respect to local Italians, most of whom were unable to read English. For a week, he was on hand helping young Italian Americans complete government forms. He was surprised to learn that his own name had come before the local board because he had been assured that everything was "taken care of"—which Razzano interpreted as meaning he would be granted a deferral classification due to his noncitizen status. Much to his astonishment he learned that he was liable to be called up immediately. Concerned, he approached a local judge who agreed that noncitizenship entitled him to reclassification and deferral. Clearly Razzano is of the opinion that many local Italians were exploited and probably received improper classifications thereby resulting in their induction into the service in disproportionate numbers. The problems resulting from carelessness were to have long-lasting effects on some. Thus, when Westburyite Rocco Buffalino was drafted the inducting officer, unable to pronounce his name, recorded it as "Buffalo". Being illiterate, Rocco did not consider this a serious matter at the time but came to regret it many years later when he encountered immense difficulties as he tried to obtain his Social Security and Veterans Benefits (Interview, Tet Zaino Razzano).

Some Italian immigrants became American citizens through their wartime service. Such was the case with Aniello Piscitelli who arrived in Westbury in 1907. He returned to Italy a few years later, served in the Italian Army during a war against Turkey and then came back to Westbury. In 1917 he was inducted into the American Army in which he served for thirteen months. At the time it was army policy not to send noncitizens on overseas duties unless they volunteered. Impervious to exhortations that he do so, Aniello refused to volunteer resisting the type of intense pressure which was so effective among so many others (Interview, Aniello Piscitelli).

Once the American draft began, Port Washington's Italian Americans became full participants, accounting for 47 of 309 servicemen from that community, a 15.2 percentage of the total and slightly more than their proportion of the population (*Port Washington News*, December 17, 1918). More than carrying their share of the burden of the war, they were, furthermore, imbued with a high degree of patriotic enthusiasm as revealed in a front-line letter written by Frank Polizzi which so impressed the *Port Washington News* that it decided to print the letter from an "Italian boy". It read in part "...I was very glad to hear that the folks at home are doing all they can to win the war. That's the spirit. We will show the world that Americans can do wonders before this war is over..." (*Port Washington News*, August 23, 1918).

No Long Island Italian community responded with the kind of enthusiasm as that was exhibited in Glen Cove. Some, like Patrick Maccarone, enlisted immediately, while others were drafted. In a remarkable outpouring of immigrant patriotism approximately ten percent of Glen Cove's male Italian element, some not yet American citizens, became members of the American armed services. One account put the figure of Glen Cove Italian Americans who went to war at 106, with the Orchard alone supplying 47 (*Glen Cove Echo*, February 2, 1920).

Nor were these men forgotten by the folks back home. Mothers and sisters in the Orchard knitted sweaters, scarfs, wristlets and socks for them even though they were not quite sure how these garments would reach their boys (*Glen Cove Echo*, November 17, 1917). Participation in the war effort won for Italians in Glen Cove a degree of respect otherwise lacking as local press readers became acquainted with news items which stressed their contribution in stories of general human interest, but which were of special meaning to local Italians, such as an account of Red Cross officials distributing ambulances to Italian forces in Italy and meeting many Italian soldiers who had previously lived in the United States.

Glen Cove's upper classes also contributed to Italian war relief. In June, 1918, the famous Pratt Killenworth Estate was the setting for a fund-raising effort which attracted numerous local residents. Guests met the Italian ambassador, saw authentic war films, heard an address by an Italian Naval captain and were treated to appropriate music (*Glen Cove Echo*, May 22, 1918). The close relationship between Italian Americans in Glen Cove and Italy was evident in the appearance of the famous Italian Bersiglieri fighting unit which visited the Orchard and participated in a program in which the residents sang the Italian national anthem followed by the Star Spangled Banner (*Glen Cove Echo*, November 2, 1918).

WAR CASUALTIES

War casualties to the local Italian community included those who suffered grievous wounds or were victims of gas attacks. Solicitous about their worrying parents, wounded soldiers on the front lines wrote to their folks back home in efforts to allay their feelings. The following excerpt from a letter by Private Frank Giordano to this mother in Glen Cove is an example.

Meanwhile, I don't want you to worry in the least, as I am well taken care of. Can you imagine sleeping in a bed between white sheets and with pillows, with a beautiful nurse feeding me four times a day. No doubt my name will appear in the casualty list in the papers, and I know you will be greatly alarmed. I hope this letter reaches you before you have any time to worry (*Glen Cove Echo*, September 28, 1918).

Others like Private Aniello Stanco and Private Luigi Capobianco of Glen Cove were less fortunate, paying the supreme sacrifice with their lives, sacrifices which the community honored by inscribing their names on the Roll of Honor tablet of the Soldiers Monument erected in 1926 and naming two streets in the Orchard after them.

Honors were heaped on the casualties and the entire contingent of Italian American Glen Cove heroes in a fitting and heralded celebration featuring a parade of 48 veterans marching from Orchard House through the main thoroughfares of the city to Schultz's grounds where refreshments were served. Italian Americans, headed by Rocco Cerullo, president of the Italian Political Club, were prominent in the ceremonies along with Glen Cove Mayor Burns and other officials. "The Italian people of Glen Cove did themselves proud on Sunday September 7th on the occasion of their welcome celebration to the returned soldiers of Italian extraction in Glen Cove", stated the mayor to the happy audience (*Glen Cove Echo*, September 13, 1919).

PERSISTENT LOYALTY

While the spectre of disaster visited some Port Washington Italian American families via the First World War, the same cataclysm served as a transmorgrifying event for others as the story of Nicola Sica demonstrates. Born in Torelli Lombardo in 1890, Nicola emigrated to Port Washington in 1907 as a young man of seventeen, went to work as a laborer in the sand pits for meager wages and boarded in various homes on Avenue A in the village. The outbreak of war found him entering the army and seeing front line duty with the famous Lost Battalion of the 77th Division. While serving as a stretcher bearer he sustained gas wounds which adversely affected his eyesight and won him the Purple Heart. Unable to return to the sand pits because of his physical condition, he earned a living selling refreshments by peddling them through the streets of Port Washington in a horse and buggy.

Nicola exhibited a fierce devotion to his adopted country—a ringing confirmation that an immigrant could demonstrate his patriotism by an undiluted loyalty which went hand in hand with fighting on behalf of the country. Every November 11 afforded an unmistakable example of Nicola's love of country. As his daughter Virginia Galasieski described it:

Armistice Day was his day—a holiday like you wouldn't believe. He threw a party for fifty or sixty of his friends including musicians which he organized into the Nicola Sica band which provided entertainment by playing music from the rear of a rented truck which was decorated with American flags and traversed the neighborhood. He also put on his own fireworks. That was his day and when the holiday was changed to Veterans Day we did not tell so that until the day he died he continued to believe that it was still Armistice Day (Interview, Virginia Sica Galasieski).

His patriotism was well-acknowledged within the community and well into his senior years he continued to serve as grand marshall for Memorial Day parades.

MARCONIVILLE PARTICIPANTS

The outbreak of the First World War found Marconiville, like other Italian American communities, ready to make its contribution. Ironically the local press was virtually silent on the subject aside from the mention of three Italian Americans who served in the United States Army—a number which in reality represented only a small measure of its role. Sensitive to the desireability of highlighting Italian American participation in the war effort, John Campagnoli commissioned the erection of a 24' high 6' thick concrete plaque honoring Italian American servicemen. This grey stone monument contains letters carved in English and Italian on both sides of the plaque indicating that no less than twenty-one Marconiville inhabitants served "their adopted country" in its armed forces. Even making allowances for some who were undoubtedly summer residents, the list is impressive. Proud of this contribution on the part of the small Italian population, Campagnoli placed the monument in front of his home on Great Neck Avenue, where it remained until the 1950s when it was removed to a new location in Veterans Memorial Park—a small park-like setting near the Copiague Railroad Station.

INWOOD COMMUNITY SUPPORT

As it did with communities all over the United States, the First World War intruded into the private life of Inwood. Regarding the bellicose activity at first as an unwelcome visitor, the community transformed itself into a vigorous enthusiast within a few months of entry, supporting the purchase of war bonds and Red Cross drives (*Rockaway News*, February 27, 1918). In the spring of 1917, Inwood demonstrated remarkable cooperation in a countywide effort to attract volunteers into the Home Defense Corps, an organization expected to replace the now-activated National Guard. The first quota of 100 men was filled so quickly that another company was recruited entirely from the Italian district. By July, 1917, the latter's 40 members met for weekly drills and on one occasion broke up an anti-draft meeting led by an outside agitator (*Rockaway News*, July 21, August 1, 1917).

Father Mahon, pastor of Our Lady of Good Counsel proved a strong supporter of the war effort including the publication of the *Interparish Monthly*, for distribution in parishes where there was a large concentration of Italians and which featured exhortations "...toward their brethren who have dedicated themselves to the work in which the United States is now engaged" (*Rockway News*, November 28, 1917). Italian Americans responded by generously supporting the Red Cross drive which was intended to aid forces in Italy. A description of some activities in April 1918 manifests an ethnic community thoroughly engrossed in wartime activities. Thus, a meeting for Inwood's Italians held in Public School 4 to rally support for the purchase of war bonds saw prominent New York City Italian American leaders present such as Coroner Antonio Zucca, Judge John Freschi and Frank Frugone, editor of the *Italian Evening Bulletin*. The "Italian" church also promoted the effort by hosting a rally which featured three girls from the Blessed Virgin Sodality who sang "An Ode to Liberty" along with addresses in English and Italian, and the St.Cono Society band playing the national anthem in behalf of the drive (*Rockaway News*, April 13, 20, 1983).

Emulating a pattern of other Long Island Italian communities, eleven Italians from Inwood left Long Island for their native land to join the armed forces (*Rockaway News*, July 17, 1918). Although exact statistics are not available. A memorial to servicemen sponsored by Our Lady of Good Counsel Church showed that out of 105 parishioner soldiers or sailors, 53—slightly more than half—were of Italian extraction and of eight fatalities five possessed identifiable Italian names (*Rockaway News*, January 31, 1920).

The most celebrated Inwood war hero was an unlikely dark-haired, diminutive barber named Fudie (Fiorentino) Nuzzolo, whose heroics received belatedly recognition—sixteen years after the war ended—in 1934. But the story of Fudie Nuzzolo is fascinating not only because of his war service, but also because his life history so exemplified that which was typical of the Italian immigrant of yesteryear—hope, ambition, sacrifice, hard-work, religious devotion, aesthetic sense and steadfastness. Furthermore, he was most unique in that he wrote his life story in a very sensitive manuscript of hundreds of pages allowing the reader to share in his experiences, his joys and his disappointments as he recounted the cycles of his life. Born in Tufo, near Avellino in 1895, as a young boy he recalled, "I used to hear folks tell about America and how wonderful life was in America. I used to hear them say: 'Blessed is he who finds work in the wonderful land of America'". Coming to the United States as a teenager in pursuit of that "pot of gold" which served as a beacon for so many, his words reveal his youthful thoughts while reading letters of his three older brothers who had already emigrated.

> When their letters came, I was so eager to read them. They stated that they were getting along quite well and the entire family was happy to hear this. When a townsmen came to our town from America, we noted he was well-dressed, looking like a millionaire—everyone thought, and so did I. I too began to dream about going to America. I too, would become a millionaire (Interview, Ferdinand Nuzzolo).

In an attempt to assuage his saddened mother who realized that she might never see her youngest son again, Fudie was cheerful upon his departure from Italy telling her "Fear Not", and that he had faith in God that he would succeed. On board the immigrant ship and out of sight of his mother, he wept for two consecutive days in the knowledge that he might never see her again. Arriving in New York City in 1913, he soon relocated with a brother in Cedarhurst. In time he became a barber in Inwood where his aunt lived and it was from that town that he was drafted in 1917—one of the first from the Italian community to enter the army. Stationed in nearby Camp Upton during his rookie tenure, he was anxious to get home on leave for the annual September St.Cono Feast and to see his fiancee. Thanks to "my *compare* Mr. Zavatto" (Vincent Zavatt), he was granted his wish.

His unit was subsequently assigned to the Argonne Forest in France, where during a particular skirmish, his lieutenant was severely wounded on the battlefield he had been surveying. Nuzzolo voluntarily left his place of shelter and ventured out under heavy fire, located the lieutenant, administered first aid to his wounded leg, and then carried the officer to a place of comparative safety. For his gallantry in action he eventually was awarded the Silver Cross and the Distinguished Service Cross in impressive ceremonies at a banquet held in his honor in a major New York City hotel. Nuzzolo's heroics did not fail to escape the attention of Italian officials as well as Italian media sources. The Italian counsul in New York City made a special trip to the Nuzzolo household to praise him in the presence of Mrs. Nuzzolo who was then gravely ill and unable to travel. The *Corriere D'America*, covered the event with a three column banner headline "The Heroism of An Italian in War, Obscured for 16 Years, Today Shines in N.Y." (*Corriere D'America*, November 13, 1934).

WAR'S IMPACT ON COMMUNITY

The outbreak of World War I had an immediate effect upon Italian organization activity in the Patchogue vicinity, one of the most obvious being the decision to forego the usual celebrations such as Columbus Day parades; instead they confined their national festivities to private social affairs.

It is not known whether any Patchoguer actually left Long Island to return to Italy and don the uniform of the mother country during the war. However, when the United States entered the fray in 1917, participation of Americans of Italian descent was at least proportionate to their numbers of the population. Five with identifiable Italian names were mustered into the service as 86 Patchoguers made up the contingent of the Patchogue Home Guard, while many of the nationality left Bellport to serve in the Army and Navy (*Patchogue Advance*, July 20, 27, 1917).

The location of Camp Upton in nearby Yaphank brought the reality of war closer home to the entire Patchogue region. Since the camp site was covered with a growth of scrub oak and pine, the government gladly paid high wages to laborers, including local Italian hands, carpenters and taxi drivers hired to clear and service the area.

That the existence of a large number of men at the camp was a boon to Patchogue businessmen was evident in the increase in the volume of business activity by liquor and saloon establishments and purveyors of transportation.

Much of the benefit was of short duration, however, as drunkeness and rowdyism was apparent on the streets of Patchogue and an atmosphere of sacrifice and intolerance soon rend the air. In July, 1918, Camp Upton officials placed a ban on Patchogue establishments which sold liquor to soldiers.

A number of activities such as featured articles on Red Cross assistance to the Italian forces and the exhibition of movies like "The Italian Battlefront" served to bring the relevance of war even closer (*Patchogue Advance*, December 7, 1917, March 1, 1918). Naturally, the most sober reminder of the war was manifested through the call up of young men into the armed forces. While no single source indicates the total of Italian Americans who answered the call, one reference shows thirteen Italian American Patchoguers were in the armed services, three from the Sacco family. One of the seven fatalities was Carl Sandomenico. Furthermore, others of Italian ancestry from Hagerman and Bellport also contributed to the war effort with their lives.

Still other Italian Americans performed their duty in Italy before coming to the United States as in the case of Avellino resident Peter Chiuchiolo. In the course of his military career, Peter, who was wounded, also served with fiery Italian patriot/ poet D'Annunzio who led his countrymen in the takeover of Fiume and Trieste. In 1923 Peter immigrated to the United States where he joined his two brothers in Patchogue and worked as a barber (*Patchogue Advance*, August 18, 1931).

Thus it transpired that the war years affected suburban Italian Americans. Those were years of greater acceptance in appreciation of the contribution Italian Americans were making toward the war effort, a fact that became increasingly important when the United States became a belligerent on the same side. For their part Italian immigrants and their progeny, even while continuing to be heavily involved in their own subculture, nevertheless, became more confident of their place in American society. They had previously demonstrated their value as indispensable laborers in the development of the land and of industry on Long Island and they had just recently shown their loyalty as soldiers and sailors prepared to fight and die in behalf of their adopted land. This would seem a strong argument to begin their climb from their almost exclusive proletarianism to the bourgeoise rungs of the economic and social ladder. The fact of the matter is that Italian communities were undergoing change even before the war, a phenomenon which moved into faster pace with the onset of the immediate post war period.

CHAPTER NINE
SLOWLY CHANGING

There is little question that the massive Italian immigration which began in the 1880s was essentially a movement of poor, hard-working toilers. Ditch-diggers, seamstresses, handymen and factory hands, they could be regarded as the turn-of-the-century's archetypical proletarian immigrants. This background not withstanding, by the 1910s and 1920s significant movement beyond the humble entry stage was already self-evident in suburbia as Italian Americans began a slow but perceptible climb up the economic and social ladder, one which witnessed them attending schools, moving into better jobs, becoming entrepreneurs and expanding their social and cultural organizations.

1920s: BOOM TIMES

Government records showed that in the post World War I period Italian-descended stock in Westbury continued to grow reaching 949, or one out of six, of a total village population of 5,785 in 1925. The youthful orientation persisted with 505 aged twenty years of age or younger. Further analysis reveals a continuing proletarian predominance although a greater variety of jobs and refinements of positions was evident. New nomenclatures which appeared in the 1925 Census included: printer, painter, American Express employee, musician, *etc.* Approximately one-third were listed under various laborer categories in 1925 compared to over fifty percent in 1915. After housework and/or housewives, which totalled 157, gardeners, laborer gardeners and nurserymen formed the largest group of workers accounting for about 80. In addition, to the latter could be included some listed under the manual laborer category which would then bring the grouping to approximately one-third of the New York male work force.

The service sector grew with at least 25 Italian Americans gainfully employed as barbers, bootblacks, clerks, chauffeurs, florists and golf link, restaurant, sales and stationery personnel. Those employed in skilled trades such as auto mechanic, baker, barber, carpenter, printer, painter, plasterer, mason, seamstress, tailor and stableman totalled 39, and if one includes nursery workers, who, possessed a degree of horticultural expertise, the number could conceivably increase by 87. Italian American representation in the professions, nevertheless, remained extremely small, limited to two teachers and a musician. One is struck by the conspicuousness of their absences in fields such as bankers, lawyers, dentists, doctors, pharmacists, engineers, executives, *etc.* On the other hand there were optimistic signs when it came to the number [22] of self-employed: five tailors, five shoemaker/shopowners, four barbers, two fruit dealers, one each in dry goods, stationery, bootblack, mason and real estate business owners.

By 1925 the Italian descended population was dispersed into basically three election districts showing concentrations of 102 on Union Avenue and 202 on Taylor Hill. That there was an informal family/*paesani* migration pattern seems evident when one notices the large numbers holding the same family surnames. Thus, the 47 and 41 people who bore the names of Lagnese and Zaino respectively, probably were the largest Italian families in Westbury, accounting for approximately ten percent of all local Italian Americans.

The growth phenomenon which impacted Westbury also affected other Long Island enclaves in the 1920s, particularly Glen Cove. In 1925, out of 10,769 Glen Covites, Americans of Italian descent comprised 2,254 or twenty percent of the city population compared to sixteen percent in 1915 (*New York State Manuscript Census*, Nassau County, 1925). They were more likely to become permanent residents and were well on their way as an emerging force in social, cultural, economic and political life.

BOOSTERISM IMPACTS LITTLE ITALIES

The 1920s found Port Washington engaged in the same kind of "boosterism" which characterized other Long Island communities. With dogmatic confidence in the future, local promoters declared that Port Washington was the ideal place for home seekers, touting it as the fastest growing village on the North Shore, only 19.6 miles from Penn Station, served by 28 trains daily, possessing a high school, two banks, one loan association, four fire companies, five churches, trolley service to the county seat in Mineola and other points of merit including a beautiful harbor and lighted streets (*Port Washington News*, July 25, 1919). A narrow nationalism pervaded the era as groups such as the American Legion exhorted one hundred percent Americanism in the selection of town officials, and the Ku Klux Klan expanded its activity even if in milder form. In an unlikely gesture on one occasion a Klan official visited the local black Baptist Church and presented the pastor with a monetary gift ostensibly to promote Americanism. Nor did Italian American organizations fail to promote American nationalism. The formation of the Sons of Italy lodge in 1925 was regarded as such an opportunity. 'The Order of the Sons of Italy in Port Washington, will undoubtedly cement the mass in one harmonious, all American unit working hard for a better understanding of

TABLE 1
COMPARISONS BETWEEN THE NEW YORK STATE MANUSCRIPT CENSUS OF 1915 AND 1925, WESTBURY

	1915	1925
TOTAL WESTBURY POPULATION	3,176	5,785
ITALIAN AMERICAN POPULATION	492	949
MALES	275	543
FEMALES	217	406
BOARDERS/LODGERS	18	25
HEADS OF FAMILY	94	
WIVES	94	
GAINFULLY EMPLOYED	126	254
HOUSEWORK (MOSTLY WIVES OF ALL AGES AND DAUGHTERS FROM 16 TO MID-TWENTIES)	128	157

what America first means" reported the local newspaper (*Port Washington News*, October 9, 1925).

By 1925 the Italian American population of the village had reached 1,171 or 13.7 percent of a total populace of 8,503—a slight increase over the 1915 figure (*New York State Manuscript Census*, Nassau County, 1925). Port Washington Americans of Italian descent were also branching out into various businesses and a few professions. Several became contractors. Others opened barber shops, while one operated a real estate firm. Guy DeFeo, one of the most popular men in the community, opened a garage and service station while another member of the DeFeo clan opened an ambitious Italian American grocery store which required the help of six assistants.

Albert DeMeo, the son of one of the oldest Italian families in Port Washington, would make his name in the field of law, first practicing in the town in the early 1920s, then becoming the first Italian American assistant district attorney of Nassau County (*Port Washington News*, September 22, 1919).

GROWTH IN COPIAGUE

Like many another Long Island community, Copiague experienced growth in the prosperous 1920s and optimistically looked forward to still further expansion. Boosters from the hamlet as well as from adjoining communities embarked upon advertising programs promoting the region as a desirable area in which to purchase real estate. Typical was the Long Island Railroad which joined in heralding an invitation to these suburbs as a summons to "sane" living alongside an ocean which brought assurance of felicitous weather. "Because of this position it is cooler in the summer and warmer in the winter than any other neighboring region, the waters surrounding it tempering the heat and the cold" (*Long Island, The Sunrise Homeland*, 1924:18). Local newspaper advertisements featured the natural attractions which abounded: nearby salt water, abundant fishing, fine bathing beaches, convenient railroad transportation, relaxing tranquility and that elusive privacy which escaped their city counterparts. One of the more interesting projects in the area during the heady prosperous climate of the 1920s was the development of "Little Venice", a project intended to occupy 365 acres and designed on the model of the famed Italian city. Upon completion, "Little Venice" was to contain 2,000 homes engulfed by numerous lagoons and waterways. To add "color" the real estate promoters provided gondolas and bands to regale prospects who visited the site on weekends. However, the Great Depression put an abrupt end to the grandiose idea.

THE CONFIDENT TWENTIES

Although the Branch area of Long Island, in which Inwood was located, witnessed a degree of resurgent nativism during the turbulent 1920s, what was even more pronounced was an atmosphere of optimism and prosperity. Thus, while one could find notice of Inwood meetings of the Immigration Restriction League, one found greater evidence of a community preoccupied with growth and expansion. Article after article referred to real estate booms under way, with editorials joining the upbeat tempo by frequently commenting on the advantages of suburban life. The suburbs, it was maintained, were becoming increasingly preferable to the crowded city, and furthermore offered the advantages of home ownership, healthful atmosphere, community life and civic pride. With its churches and clubhouses serving as centers of social activity, the suburbs were held out as unresistable magnets to city people (*Rockaway News*, May 1, 1929). Accordingly, the citizenry in the Five Towns were instructed to prepare for a large influx of people who were seeking "...to live and bring up their children in God's sunshine and fresh air, surrounded by flowers and freedom of nature" (*Rockaway News*, February 20, 1926). With 8,250 inhabitants in 1928, Inwood was considered the fastest growing community in the area.

Growth of Inwood's population and the prevailing spirit of optimism set the stage for a flourishing of Italian activities and prominence in the period between the two World Wars. Recognition, it seems, was finally coming to the otherwise neglected group. One example of this is the rise to esteem accorded the Barbuti family. Immigrant Thomas V. Barbuti became a local figure of influence because of his position as Italian court interpreter for Nassau County. However, it was his son Raymond who was destined to make international headlines when he won two gold medals in the 1928 Olympics (*Far Rockaway Journal*, January 27, 1933; *Corriere D'America*, August 27, 1928). Other expressions of Italian ascendacy were evident in emergence and activities of new ethnic organizations. Inwood's Circolo Italiano, for example, was most active during the 1930s, sponsoring programs of current public issues (*Nassau Herald*, July 3, October 9, December 31, 1934).

SPORTS AND RECREATIONAL ACTIVITIES

Sports and recreational clubs attracted many Inwood Italian Americans throughout the 1920-50 period, and although not exclusively ethnic clubs, virtually all the officers of some clubs possessed Italian names. These clubs included social clubs like the Jolly Gang Club and St.George Athletic Association which came into existence in 1927 and also sponsored a number of athletic teams.

Perhaps the most interesting and unique athletic club founded by Italian Americans in this era was the Peninsula Golf Club which came into being in 1920. The existence of the club in reality reflected a remarkable tendency to develop a proficiency on the links which undoubtedly was related to the experiences of so many of Inwood's Italian American youths who served as caddies in nearby exclusive golf courses. The young men learned the sport so well that they regularly won caddy tournaments in the area. In contradistinction to the golf clubs already functioning, and which normally did not have many members of Italian extraction, Inwood's Italians organized their own. By the 1930s, the Peninsula Golf Club had matured to a level of activity which included participation in golf matches with other golf clubs, the sponsorship of a ladies auxiliary and the hosting of memorable tournaments. It subsequently purchased its own private golf course.

SOCIALIZING IMMIGRANTS

Growth, confidence and prosperity which were experienced in a substantial way on Long Island brought opportunities for advancement for the immigrant generation. The recounting of the growth of Italian neighborhoods, accompanied by greater visibility and prominence, illustrates that many mature Italian immigrants and their children were able to make positive strides towards advancement. As important as these times were for adult immigrants, they were vital, formative years for the younger generation whose upbringing would take place in their adopted land.

The increased presence of Italian Americans in the midst of an expanding suburban populace would tax the ingenuity of the custodians of local service institutions which were charged with coping with the needs of the newcomers. Having had little experience of this nature compared with their counterparts in the large cities, these socializing institutions would be presented with novel challenges in attempting the daunting tasks of assimilation and integration.

Accommodation to the needs of the younger Italian newcomers formed the principal tasks of indigenous socializing institutions. The public school, the ethnic theater and the community social service agency were cases in point. Accordingly, the impact of the rapid population increase in Westbury's public schools was immediate, Ina Wickey, hired as an elementary school teacher in 1918, was so struck by the sudden influx of Italian children in her class that 45 years later she remembered the number exceeded the alloted spaces in the official roster book requiring attendance records to be kept in ordinary notebooks (Interview, Ina Wickey).

The school experience presented a dual challenge for immigrant children. Not only were they required to perform at a satisfactory level in their school subjects, but also they were expected to make the difficult transition from one culture to another. For Italians, on Long Island, just as in the enclaves in major cities, language was the major problem since immigrant parents spoke English poorly, if at all. It was not uncommon for an Italian immigrant to reside in the United States for many decades and still be barely able to speak a sentence in English. Younger children entering kindergarten and the early grades were more fortunate because the mother tongue had not been planted so firmly and because their initial school experience began in English. Indeed, they frequently served as the immigrant family's main interpreters.

Traditional family mores from the old country further affected immigrant Italian children's educational development in Westbury with sometimes detrimental consequences for females. It was a widely-held belief among Italians that formal education, especially on a more advanced level, was a goal reserved primarily for boys. Few girls were to have such aspirations, and even if they did, custom compelled them to defer to their brothers. Established priorities and limited family resources meant that many a young Italian girl with superior scholastic ability and interest did not pursue advanced education. Another problem facing immigrant children in American schools was that of improper diagnosis of physical handicaps. Thus, it happened that a child with an artificial eye was listed by the school health office as having 20/20 vision in both eyes. Because of a traditional reverence southern Italians felt regarding teachers and because of the difficult language problem, little contact existed between parents and the school. This is probably one reason why corrective steps were not always taken in the early years of massive immigration. In the later years, as more Italian children attended Westbury schools and as they tended to remain in the system for longer durations, conditions improved. In this respect there was similarity with the large city Italian American experience. One significant difference, however, is that the suburbs offered a much more limited vocational education curriculum.

Although the opening of St.Brigid's parochial school in the 1920s saw a number of Italian students transfer from the public school to the church school, Italian enrollment in the Westbury school system continued high in the period between the two World Wars and the immediate post-World War II period.

Ethnic Theater

Students of immigration have shown what an important socializing institution the ethnic theater was for the transplanted. Considered a vital institution in the congested city neighborhoods, it was less prominent, but nevertheless, a vivid feature of social life in Italian suburban sections. Frequently, theaters in such neighborhoods featured well-known actors and actresses in the Italian ethnic repertoire, while on occasion they exhibited the works of home-grown products. For years the ethnic theater was an important part of Westbury social activity. Enjoying its local heyday in the 1930s, Westbury's Italian community enjoyed a number of plays in the Italian language, especially those revolving around religious themes such as "The Life of St.Anthony", and "A Figlia d'a Madonna", the latter featuring Rea Rosa, well-known New York City actress. Another play performed locally was "The Man Without a Face", a drama about a pioneer Italian in the mining region of the United States. Dramas based on the immigrant experience were quite popular staples and also served as inspiration for a play written by Westburyite John Monteforte who, in 1934, wrote "The Emigrant", in Neopolitan dialect. A two-act play, it revolved around the tragedy which befell a young Italian immigrant whose solitary sojourn was interrupted by World War I. He became an American soldier and participated in front-line combat in France where he was wounded and lost his eyesight. Unaware of what had befallen her son, his anxious mother back in Italy sensed some terrible news and prevailed upon her husband to go to America to find their son—a task which would prove difficult because of newly-enacted United States restrictive immigration laws. In his desperation the father became a stowaway in an unsuccessful ploy to enter the country undetected. Brought before an American immigration official, the grieving father sincerely recounted his sorrowful story which elicited sympathy and assistance in locating his son then reduced to selling shoelaces on the sidewalks of New York City. The play was performed briefly in Westbury where local Italian Americans played the various acting roles (*Westbury Times*, February 2, April, 15, December 10, 1943).

Biaggio Siano proved to be another key proponent of the ethnic theater. Having lived and worked in Brooklyn for many years, he was a character actor in the Italian American theater, and in addition wrote verses and music. Relocating in Westbury in 1924, he became a factor in the production of local plays in the 1930s and he also wrote Neapolitan dialect songs.

Plays were held in the Dell' Assunta Hall and St.Brigid's Hall, and on occasions, when the audiences were expected to be large, the huge Westbury theater was rented.

Social Service Agencies

Another community institution with which the local Italian community interacted were settlement houses such as Westbury's Neighborhood House which opened under Episcopalian Church auspices in 1916. Concerned about the need to bring social services to the community's indigent, particularly the Italians, the Neighborhood House hired a nurse whose background included knowledge of the Italian language. Westbury's Italian population received some important social services and reciprocated by contributing to the institution.

Another settlement house was the Orchard House, which opened in Glen

Cove May, 1917, as the principal settlement facility exclusively for Italians in the heart of the ethnic enclave. Over the years it strove to meet the specific needs of the immigrant populace thereby confirming the view of social scientists who have demonstrated that adjustment and integration of European immigrants into American society underwent a filter of the historical process shaped by such social institutions as the settlement house. Although there is some dissent, most historians affirm the validity of the positive impact these institutions had upon the community and credit them with offering a more humane alternative to the harsh Americanization of that era by promoting self-respect, encouraging cultural pluralism, fostering opportunities for upward mobility and advancing public amity. As John Higham (1971) stated:

> On the whole they did more to sustain the immigrant's respect for his old culture than to urge him forward into the new one. One of the great lessons the settlements discovered was that the normal, assimilative influences in America often worked too harshly. Immigrant families were divided; the children developed brassy, swaggering Americanism in their yearning for acceptance. The settlements, therefore, sought to temper as well as to improve the ordinary course of assimilation by providing a receptive environment for Old World heritages...(p. 236).

Organizers of the Orchard were public-spirited ladies of the estates motivated by a determination to attack the filth, squalor, disintegration and despair they saw in the poorer sections of town. They procured a building on Hazel Street in the heart of the Orchard as the center of their activities and assigned Grace Simpson, an experienced Chicago social worker, to organize the center. Upon receiving her assignment Miss Simpson rented an apartment in the Orchard to be able to study the problems of the neighborhood personally. The New Orchard House was formally opened with appropriate ceremonies on April 24, 1920, and was described as a roomy two-story building "whose windows gave forth hospitable light" on the street, "formerly dark and dreary, exemplifying cleanliness and cheer; a real inspiration for better things". The first floor contained a spacious hall with a small stage and a modern kitchen, while the second floor included a men's club, a library, and a district nurse's room equipped with neat beds and fresh linens. Opening ceremonies emphasized the optimism prevailing among those in attendance and the delightful surprise over the melodic singing of three Italian girls accompanied by a young mandolin player named Maccarone (*Glen Cove Record-Advance*, September 14, 1933; *Sea Cliff News*, May 1, 1920).

Among the first services rendered by the Orchard House was a kindergarden class, soon supplemented by classes in shorthand, typing, cooking, needlecraft, dramatics, sewing and handicrafts—activities which were attended by hundreds of community residents. The institution sponsored athletic clubs whose prowess was regularly cited by Glen Cove newspapers under headlines like: "Calabrians win snappy victory from Hawkins at Orchard House basketball". It also sponsored boy and girl scout troops and a variety of games and made meeting rooms available for local social, civic, cultural and political groups. The number of residents who used the facilities per year ran into the thousands.

Orchard House was to serve the ethnic enclave very well for over thirty years, periodically adjusting to meet community needs as a result of changing times. It was clear that the community was, in fact, in the state of flux with respect to upward mobility in the 1920s and 1930s. One indication of this movement was the growing presence of Italian Americans as entrepreneurs.

ITALIAN ENTREPRENEURS HELP GLEN COVE GROW

Some Glen Cove contractors of Italian descent in the period under consideration included L.M. Privati, Paul S. Dioguardi, J. Pascucci and Famiglietti, Michael Abbondondolo, Pasquale Izzo and Sons, Ralph Janotta, Rocco Grella and Angelo Martone. Collectively they built sidewalks, sewers, and roads. They constructed homes, stores, factories, schools and other structures not only within Glen Cove, but also in the surrounding community.

A number of Italian American restaurants came into being in Glen Cove with more than a few becoming widely-known for their cuisine as well as their hospitality. Marafioti's, for example, which was decorated with murals depicting scenes from Naples, Rome, Venice and Trieste, featured pure white chandeliers, and established itself as the most unique restaurant of its kind on the north shore. Its decor and superior quality cooking earned it a reputation as a genuine Italian rendezvous. The eating place that holds the record for durability and satisfaction is Stango's Restaurant, begun by Concetta and Frank Stango in the Orchard in 1919. A small restaurant, at first it provided no menu, but simply served Concetta's preferences, which more than pleased the clientele. After her husband died in 1926, Concetta continued running the business, now aided by her children and other relations. In the early years local customers, frequently boarders, delighted with the opportunity to enjoy meals with that home-made quality, would bring in their own pots to carry home food cooked in the restaurant. Currently, more than 65 years later, retaining the original old-world recipes of Concetta, her daughter Stella along with her husband Gabriel Cocchiola, continues to run the restaurant (*Glen Cove Record*, October 26, 1979).

Italian Americans also entered the newer fields of the industrial age such as the automobile industry. Born in 1882, Ralph A. Cavalieri came to the United States as a young man who thrust himself into the fledging field of automotives, working in automobile manufacturing plants in various states, including the Peerless Factory, a pioneer in the industry. This background allowed him to delve into every aspect of the business and consequently become so proficient so that motors had no secrets that he had not investigated. In 1922 he decided to branch out for himself and started a small automobile repair business in Glen Cove which he soon outgrew, compelling him to open larger quarters in 1926 which he again outgrew. In 1934 he took over a larger building on Glen Cove Road, remodeled it and created an establishment which was advertised as without peer in its line (*Glen Cove Record*, September 13, 1934; May 11, 1944).

Another interesting example of Italian American entrepreneurship impacting Glen Cove was Sicilian-born Salvatore Calderone, who emigrated in 1896, residing for a time in New Orleans and then in New York City where he was engaged in newspaper work. In 1907, he opened a motion picture theater in New York City and then moved to Hempstead where, in 1917, he opened the first theater in that village. Bolstered by that success which tapped a ready market within the village proper and the surrounding hamlets and farm communities, he was prepared to branch out and start other movie houses. Calderone's business peaked in 1927 with his most ambitious screen emporium in Glen Cove, spending much time, effort and money supervising the construction of the theater which housed one of the first air-cooled premises of its kind in the vicinity. A keen showman, he attracted considerable publicity which served to assure that this new movie house would enjoy large attendances. His son Frank managed the Glen Cove theater. In 1929 Salvatore Calderone sold his chain of six vaudeville and movie theaters to the Fox Movie interests for approximately $3,000,000.00 (*Glen Cove Record*, August 4, 1927, February 14, 1929).

ITALIAN ENTREPRENEURS IN PATCHOGUE

Patchogue benefited from the post-war boom of the 1920s—its growth evident in population increase. By 1923 greater Patchogue's population was 9,000, with that figure jumping to 9,500 in 1925. This prompted local real estate boosters to tout the town as the most desireable place to live with its impressive Carnegie Library, its fine fire company, its outstanding police department, its convenient bus service and pleasant paved streets—it boasted of more paved streets than any community between New York City and Montauk Point (*Patchogue Advance*, October 16, 1925). Business grew apace of the population as some older establishments expanded and new entrepreneurs entered the field. While no attempt at comprehensiveness will be made here, a sampling is in order. With his two sons, Pasquale Felice opened a grocery store in Patchogue in the spring of 1920, the same time that Charles Pollizzi and Richard Follini started a garage business. In North Bellport, Sullivan, Ralph and Louis Gallo began a duck farm. Michael Aviano, in the meantime, commenced a Ford Auto Agency enjoying as one of his first customers contractor Frank Romeo, who purchased two trucks for his expanding business (*Patchogue Advance*, April 16, May, 21, 1920; January 28, 1921). James Fiala was operator of a successful retail paint and wallpaper store, and Dan Gabarino operated a clean and freshly-stocked grocery and vegetable store on East Main Street. In East Patchogue Icilio W. Bianchi attracted attention for his flourishing floral enterprise. Coming to Patchogue many years before as a successful businessman in paper products, in 1929, Bianchi began a floral business which concentrated on growing orchids, a business so successful that it required the services of nine people. As in other Italian neighborhoods, midwifery was a special branch of business during this era and one could read Italian language advertisements of Mrs. Carmela Russo who advised prospective clients of her availability at the special time of childbirth (*Patchogue Advance*, November 19, 1915). Similarly Mrs. A. Palermo advertised her services in English.

Organizing and controlling transportation systems proved to be lucrative enterprises in which Patchogue area Italian Americans participated in the post World War I era. Both the Ferlazzo and the Fuoco families operated bus lines in the region and overcame obstacles including ethnic bigotry on their way to success.

The Fuoco entry into the world of business began with the remarkable immigrant Antonio Fuoco whose large house and store became the heart of the Italian colony in North Bellport. His illiteracy notwithstanding, he was regarded as the unofficial leader of the area, and possessor of a natural extraordinary business sense which impelled him to move in several directions simultaneously and inspire his offspring to go into business for themselves. Antonio's main activity was to store and sell grain and feed supplies to local farmers. In 1923 he expanded his business by purchasing Joseph Villano's coal and feed business (Interview, Louis Fuoco; *Patchogue Advance*, June 15, 1923). His wife operated the small general store until her death in 1916. His oldest daughter, Elizabeth, only eleven, was then entrusted with that task. By the 1930s, Antonio Fuoco expanded his operations into real estate, sometimes leasing large buildings for business purposes; other times purchasing huge acreage in the area. His purchase in 1926 of 57 lots in East Patchogue previously owned by John N. Stephani, for a cost of $8,980, earned front page coverage. Louis started a bus line which bore his name and initially consisted of a tiny one-bus line which he operated out of his father's garage. Within months, two other buses were added and routes were established between Bellport, Hagerman, East Patchogue and Patchogue. A year later the line began serving LaSalle Military Academy in Oakdale and subsequently acquired as clients several school districts. In 1940 the buses were moved to a new garage in East Patchogue. In due course, Louis's sons Louis Jr. (Buddy) and Anthony joined the enterprise, and subsequently operated a fleet of 34 buses (*Patchogue Advance*, May 17, 1956).

A 1926 directory published by the Patchogue Chamber of Commerce provides another measure of involvement in commercial activity. Out of Patchogue's 250 retail stores, perhaps two dozen owners possessed Italian names, *i.e.,* seven of twelve barbers, two of eight beauty parlors, one of seven coal dealers, six of 38 builders and contractors and one of eight electricians. In addition, Italian-run grocery stores were operated by Musso, Lunati, Scarpia, J. Cardamone and P. Felice (*Directory of Patchogue, Long Island, New York*, 1926). Consequently, although far from the preponderant ethnic group among local entrepreneurs, Italians were emerging as business factors thereby commencing a trend which continues to the present.

Italian immigrants to Long Island entered suburbia as poor people anxious to exploit whatever opportunities for employment and advancement that the area had to offer. Bereft of much formal education, lacking in sufficient capital and without meaningful influence, they nevertheless found the suburban environment much preferred as a place of residence. They soon came to realize that no matter how lowly their status as newcomers, it was possible to alter and improve their lot in this nationalistic but otherwise congenial atmosphere. They shared in the prevailing optimism of the early 1920s and, by participation in the educational and other service systems available, their children took in stride the quintessential steps toward acceptance and accommodation. Complete assimilation, however, would have to await the future as Long Island Italian Americans strove to create their own ethnic institutions which provided the solace of their old world culture. Perhaps the most visible expressions of ethnic group life was that exemplified by religious activity—the topic of the following chapter.

CHAPTER TEN
RELIGIOUS PERSUASION

Italian immigrants entered Long Island during the "Americanist" phase of Catholic Church history—a time characterized by vigorous church leadership determined to assimilate the multiple strains of the European Catholic diaspora. American Church leadership believed it was necessary for new Catholic immigrants to shed their language and culture as quickly as possible because it appeared so alien to Americans as to constitute a threat. To divest themselves of their foreign characteristics would endear them to their adopted country and deflect un-American charges. In such an atmosphere there was little room for religious expressions of a distinctive ethnic background. To become American as rapidly as possible was the message. Although a homogeneous, unitary institutional model was held out as the most desirable way to achieve the goal, in fact what emerged were ethnic enclaves within the Church replete with the creation of national parishes generously sprinkled throughout the ethnic neighborhoods of northeastern cities.

This delineation of Italian immigrants and the Church had applicability to those who settled in suburbia either because of prior residence in the Little Italies of New York City, or because of the evolution of Italian enclaves in Long Island towns. Three models of integrating Italian Catholics developed on Long Island: 1) acccommodation and assimilation into existing Irish-oriented parishes; 2) creation of defacto "Italian" national parishes; and 3) official national parishes functioning outside of traditional geographic boundaries. Whatever the form of parish involved, it can be seen that from the outset religion held a paramount place in the lives of Long Island Italian Americans. "A man holds dear what is left. When much is lost, there is no risking the remainder", was the way historian Oscar Handlin explained the attachment of immigrant peoples to the familiar religious heritages of their ancestors. This truism applied to Glen Cove's Italian immigrants whose ancestor/peasant culture revolved around Catholic religious customs and traditions.

ST. ROCCO

To transplant the religious traditions of their ancestors became a constant refrain among Glen Cove Italians. Accordingly, they formed a religious society in remembrance of their patron saint in Sturno and attended St.Patrick's, the local Catholic church. Because St.Hyacinth, the other Catholic church in Glen Cove, was a Polish national/ethnic church, it attracted few Italian congregants. One of the oldest parishes on Long Island, Irish-run St.Patrick's did not always convey feelings of hospitality to Italians. Not all Irish Churchmen were anti-Italian; indeed some, like Monsignor Canivan of St.Dominic's Church in nearby Oyster Bay were most sympathetic and supportive.

Nevertheless, for years Italians desired their own church, one which would utilize the language of their forbears and respect their traditions and customs. Not understanding English well the immigrants found St.Patrick's too unaccommodating, failing, for example, to obtain an Italian speaking priest with whom they could identify. There was, besides, an ethnic competitive element in that the Irish and Polish people in town had their own churches while the Italians did not. Years were spent in frustrating efforts to ameliorate conditions in St.Patrick's or at least gain the pastor's backing for a new national Italian parish. Some aver that the pastor's resistance was due in part to a perceived ethnic bias as well as his reluctance to lose parishioners. It was said that he offered stiff opposition, even utilizing the threat of excommunication to those in the forefront of the new parish drive. Undeterred, the Italian element, led by Angelo Cocchiola, persisted in its course, and circulated a petition in Italian which proclaimed that thousands of faithful Catholic Italian residents in Glen Cove and surrounding communities were uniting behind a drive to establish an Italian church to be named after St.Rocco, one which would have an Italian pastor.

In 1932 the bishop of Brooklyn sent Father Ciccio to serve Glen Cove's Italians by offering Mass in the Orchard House. Shortly afterwards, the St.Rocco and St.Marino Societies jointly built a temporary chapel on their own grounds, the future site for the permanent church. St.Rocco Society then obtained the services of Father Luigi Guiment, a French priest, to celebrate Mass. Since the priest lacked authorization from the diocese, the society then brought in Father John. The upshot of these steps was to produce a situation in which there were three priests, each with his own following, thereby raising disturbing possibilities of factionalism within the community. Although this is not to suggest that Glen Cove's Italians were on the verge of establishing a schismatic church, that possibility undoubtedly entered the mind of Bishop Thomas Molloy who had experienced a trying period in the early 1930s as several Italian priests had indeed set up "independent" churches in other parts of the diocese (S. Tomasi, 1975). With little movement toward the resolution of potential schism, leaders within Glen Cove's Italian enclave took matters into their own hands. Learning that Cardinal Eugenio Pacelli, Vatican Secretary of State (and future Pope), was visiting with a Long

Island family, Angelo Cocchiola, president of the committee to build St.Rocco, and members of his committee met the Cardinal and informed him of their difficulties. The Cardinal was sufficiently impressed with the presentation. He interceded in behalf of the committee writing a letter endorsing the request to Bishop Molloy which apparently had the desired effect as a new parish was officially born (*St.Rocco Anniversary Booklet*, 1937).

In January, 1937, Bishop Molloy announced the establishment of a new Mission in Glen Cove to be headed by Father Eliodoro Capobianco, former pastor of Our Lady of the Assumption in Copiague. An enthusiastic crowd gave their new pastor a hearty welcome when he was introduced by Father Dante Fiorentino, Assistant Pastor of St.Dominic Church in Oyster Bay. Father Capobianco scheduled four Sunday Masses in the little chapel. Anxious to obtain better accommodations, on January 31, 1,200 Italians met in a school auditorium in order to raise funds by subscription for the erection of a new church. An indication of the importance attached to this effort can easily be gleaned by the realization that present in the audience were the pastors of St.Patrick and St.Dominic Churches, and the much-respected Italian Catholic leader Monsignor Arcese of Brooklyn and other Italian American diocesan clergy (*Il Crociato*, February 23, 1937). Led by several societies which immediately pledged moral and financial support, the meeting enthusiastically endorsed the formation of a fund-raising committee composed of leading local Italian families—a remarkable demonstration of solidarity considering it was the height of the Great Depression. In Father Capobianco, the local populace possessed a dedicated priest who was untiring in assisting the people to their lifelong dream of a Parish of their own.

BUILDING THE CHURCH

It was now time to see whether the fierceness with which Italian immigrants demanded their own church would be matched by the prosaic but pragmatic steps necessary to transform the dream into reality—a test which they passed admirably by dint of hard work and effort. Young Michael Pascucci, a Pratt Institute architectural student, was at chapel Mass early in 1937 when he was startled by Father Capobianco who, after completing his sermon from the pulpit, asked him to stop by to talk to him after Mass. Michael was further surprised when the pastor sought his assistance in designing plans for the new church. A novice in the field, but with exposure to carpentry and in the process of completing architectural studies, he had never before tackled a project of this magnitude. Quickly getting over his initial shock, he eagerly accepted both the opportunity and the challenge. "I was 26 years old. That's how old Michelangelo was when he was commissioned by the Pope to do the Sistine Chapel", is the way Michael describes accepting the assignment. He agreed to undertake the job free of charge. Father Capobianco selected the right man—one who in his young life had already demonstrated a fidelity and a steadfastness which would serve him well in the task ahead.

Beginning with an understanding that the newly-contemplated religious structure be an improvised gothic, the pastor and Michael took many an automobile ride throughout Long Island, seeking out churches with design features they liked, and which Michael sketched. The result was the drawing of plans for a handsome eclectic gothic church. Bishop Molloy approved on condition that the parish raise its own funds—which indeed it did as virtually the entire local Italian American community contributed (Interview, Michael Pascucci). The names of the contributors, which encompassed the few major contributors and the predominantly minor one—those who donated as little as 25 cents—reads like a who's who of the area's Italian Americans. A number of local contractors further donated goods and services, such as Patsy Izzo who provided gravel, bricks and fine stone for the front of the church. Using his own equipment, Rocco Grella personally spent ten days excavating the basement for church and rectory. Michael Stanco provided machinery to be used in mixing the cement (*First Souvenir Journal of St.Rocco's Parish*, 1937). Unable to make money pledges, many gladly donated labor, working as carpenters, bricklayers and laborers, continuing their activities long after they had satisfied their work pledges (Interview, Michael Pascucci).

It was, moreover, arduous work in the days before large transit mixers—men labored for hours and days with little hand mixers to prepare enough concrete to pour into the sixteen inch basement walls which stood sixteen feet high. "We had masons in their seventies cutting stone for the front of the church so precisely that you could not get a piece of paper in the joints. They were so meticulous that they might spend a whole day on two pieces of stone". These craftsmen worked on the impressive church frontispiece while regular bricklayers worked on the sides. In a matter of several months the building that in the 1980s would cost $2,000,000.00 was completed at a cost of $40,000.00. Commencing construction in the spring, the new St.Rocco Church was ready for Midnight Christmas services in 1937—a celebration for which the church was packed to overflowing and an occasion that those who were there would never forget.

> Father Capobianco, a short, portly man got into the pulpit with the church in absolute silence, you could hear a pin drop. He looked around at the packed church including the filled choir loft. I looked there also and prayed the new structure would hold them all. Father Capobianco then produced a big, broad, knowing smile as if to say "Here is your church after so many years". I never saw so many people cry and then applaud. I was gifted and blessed with the privilege of being an archi-

tect. It was a big honor. That Midnight Mass was the most impressive Mass St.Rocco's will ever have because it brought to worship all the people who built it with their own hands (Interview, Michael Pascucci).

Within a very short time St.Rocco's Parish became a source of pride and a vital institution in the wider life of the entire diocese.

ITALIAN AMERICAN PASTORS

While it is not possible to detail the work of all the pastors who served the parish, it would be of some interest to recount the unique career of the opera-loving and dynamic Father Dante Fiorentino who, even before the parish was established, had demonstrated his support by acting as ombudsman between the Italian community and the Bishop's office. A refined and cultured man who became pastor in February, 1940, Father Fiorentino had previously served as a curate in an Italian village where he met and developed a strong friendship with the great opera composer Giacomo Puccini, eventually writing a biography of the opera luminary. During his tenure at St.Rocco's he succeeded in bringing to the community such outstanding operas as "La Traviata", "Barber of Seville" and "Don Pasquale". The prelate also fashioned a deep friendship with Salvatore Baccaloni of Sea Cliff who was a famous bassa buffo in the Metropolitan Opera House and who attended Mass at St.Rocco during the summer. Prevailed upon occasionally to sing a Gregorian Chant or a litany of Ave Maria, the singer would sometimes take things into his own hands with astonishing results. One Midnight Mass Baccaloni surprised a girls' choir by quietly entering the choir, remaining undetected until he joined in the chorus with his booming voice virtually overwhelming the rest. Baccaloni, furthermore, generously performed in behalf of fund-raising benefits for the parish (Zolotow, 1947).

Others who served as pastors of St.Rocco included Father DiLiberte, Monsignors Balbo and DeLaura and Father Della Rosa, the current pastor. Under Father Della Rosa an Italian Mass complete with music is offered every Sunday and weddings with Italian liturgy are available. As pastor he is accessible to his people and encourages them to administer many on-going activities of parish life such as the St.Vincent De Paul Society which provides assistance to the local indigent. Perhaps the biggest event of the year is the annual St.Rocco Feast which involves many parishioners. Unique among Long Island Italian American communities, St.Rocco is the only on-going national parish. Other modes of meeting religious needs characterized the other Italian enclaves, as shall now be discussed.

OTHER ITALIAN PARISHES

The communities of Inwood, Patchogue and Copiague offer examples of defacto "Italian" parishes established in the heavily Italian areas and which reflected Italian culture. In addition, the clergy of these parishes were in the main Italian Americans, although not exclusively. Notwithstanding their origins and development, these parishes were never officially designated as national churches operating outside of traditional parish boundaries. They served, in fact, as parishes for given geographic boundaries serving those within parish lines who, although mainly of Italian descent, were not exclusively so. In time these parishes were merged into the more traditional parish boundary structure thereby losing their unique Italian identity.

Our Lady of the Assumption

The genesis of Our Lady of the Assumption in Copiague clearly can be traced to a determination on the part of Marconiville's Italians to create an ethnic-oriented parish even while they imbibed in the culture of the larger society. Unlike Westbury which already had a Catholic church of long standing, Copiague was without one. St.Martin's Catholic Church, located a couple of miles away in Amityville, was nonetheless too distant for active participation for many Marconiville residents. As long-time resident Renato Giorgini put it, "To go to Mass meant going to another town, either Lindenhurst or Amityville. People did not have cars in those days and were not likely to walk to church. I belonged to the Knights of Columbus and if I was at a meeting I would go to Mass while I was there, but not every Sunday like now". St.Martin's, moreover, presented a Hibernicized colorization not always hospitable to Italians in that era. Accordingly, local Italians determined that they should have their own parish which would reflect their indigenous culture.

Since the potential congregation was small, they proceeded slowly, beginning first with the formation of Our Lady of the Assumption Society, a laymen's group. In 1927, this society began to celebrate the feast of Our Lady of the Assumption, marking it a mainstay annual event which was a distinctive feature of the community for decades. A happy festival, it featured a band, electric street decorations, and loud fireworks including fire bombs whose thunder startled residents who were unaware of the celebration. On that Sunday in 1927, 200 Marconiville residents marched to Mass at St.Martin's (*Amityville Record*, June 26, 1927).

Because Copiague was then located within the diocese of Brooklyn it was necessary to convince the bishop that a new church was indeed a necessity—a task which proved to be difficult. Local Italians, however, had an ally in John Campagnoli who endorsed the idea because of community support and because the creation of the religious institution would benefit his real estate business. It seemed that many potential home buyers—southern Italians—resisted moving into the community due to the absence of an Italian parish. The well-connected Campagnoli was said to have contacts in the Vatican who were instrumental in obtaining Brooklyn Archbishop Molloy's consent to the concept of the ethnic parish (Interview, Reverend Francis Dell Vecchio). This incident demonstrated that it could make a difference to an otherwise impoverished immigrant community to have leadership of the kind provided by Campagnoli. The enterpreneur accordingly donated some expendable land for the church grounds and community members began the actual labor in 1929. While many were poor and thus unable to contribute much money, they helped in other ways. Given the title of Our Lady of the Assumption, the new parish was aided by a $40,000.00 loan from the diocese in the hopes that the new church structure would be built rapidly. These were Depression years, however, and progress was slow; after a decade it still remained only a basement church, its vulnerability evident during inclement weather. "That basement roof—oh, did it leak. On rainy Sundays, people brought umbrellas and attended Mass with open umbrellas over their heads", recalled a former parishioner. Not an affluent parish it tended to rely on summer visitors to augment the limited local contributions. The church, nevertheless, was utilized as the center of worship and veteran Copiaguers still recall the Italian women who attended Mass on a daily basis.

In the early years a number of Italian priests served as administrators including Reverend John F. Bruno (1928-29), Reverend Pasquale Roberto (1929), Reverend Santo Privatera (1929-33), Reverend Henry Parascandola, the first resident pastor, (1933-34), Reverend Eliodoro M. Capobianco (1934-37), Reverend Joseph F. Fusco (1937) and Reverend Gaetano Sabia (1937-40). In 1940 Reverend Francis Dell Vecchio, an Italian-born priest of the Brooklyn Diocese, was named pastor. An alert enthusiastic young clergyman, he energized the community to complete the construction of the church donning overalls, mixing cement, sawing wood and pounding nails himself in a determination to see it come into being. In July, 1941, work was begun on a new 350 seat church to replace the old, partly underground structure whose seating capacity was only 220. The new parish plant would also have a rectory on the grounds and a hall for parish functions. Italian Americans were involved in the project from the outset: Joseph DeMarco of Farmingdale was the architect, Michael Pascucci of Glen Cove was the designer and the Pagliarulo Brothers of Copiague, the contractors. It took years before the church was completed and in the interim Father Dell Vecchio succeeded in effecting a fine rapport with members of the congregation. Angelo Vacca, a member of an old Copiague family, is most emphatic in crediting Father Dell Vecchio with inspiring the parish.

The creation of the Italian parish was of interest not only to residents of Marconiville, but also to Italian and non-Italian non-Copiaguers who were predisposed to help. Father James F. Irwin, pastor of St.Martin's in Amityville, sponsored Our Lady of the Assumption as a mission of his parish. One of his parishioners, Naples-born Almerinda Esposito, made a contribution by setting up "...a fund from her personal savings toward a building many years before the plan could be executed" (*Amityville Record*, June 11, 1943). Thus, even while it functioned as a defacto ethnic parish, the terminology ought not gloss over the fact that Our Lady of the Assumption served the wider community, including a considerable number of parishioners who were not of Italian heritage. The Barry family is a case in point. Of Irish descent the Barry family moved into Copiague in 1939 at a time when Italian ethnic characteristics were still pronounced. A young teenager at the time, Ronald Barry recalls the impression the Italian flavor of the neighborhood made on him.

> Many of the old Italian people, because of the language factor, were very tight-knitted groups who could be seen growing grapes and other fruits and vegetables pretty much as they did in the old country...I remember the big Our Lady of the Assumption feasts which were very impressive. It was like the St.Gennaro's feast in New York City. It was strange to a kid like me because I had never experienced things like the parading of a statue and the big fireworks, the good odors from the cooking stands with all the Italian food. I had never seen anything like that. It was entrenched there when our family moved in. It was novel to me and I came to enjoy it a great deal. When we would go across the tracks it was like being in a different world. There were people who cultivated their gardens. I always remember the times when grapes ripened. You were entering a different kind of world, yet we lived only a couple of blocks south of the railroad tracks in a totally different environment (Interview, Reverend Ronald Barry).

Ronald Barry became the first priest to be ordained from Our Lady of the Assumption and subsequently became pastor of St.Rose of Lima in Massapequa, two towns to the west. Reverend Barry remembers the distinctive Italian demeanor which permeated the community and the church in particular. "When I first went there even the sermons were in Italian". As a consequence he gravitated to St.Martin's in Amityville although his family remained and continues to remain parishioners of Our Lady of the Assumption. Two of his brothers married young ladies of Italian descent from Copiague—developments which had a major effect on his family life.

> I'll never forget the first Thanksgiving Day Dinner, my sisters-in-laws' families and ours. Right next to Turkey there was this large bowl of ravioli and pretty soon there were Thanksgiving Days when there was no turkey; it was just ravioli. So Caesar has conquered not only all Gaul but the Barry family (*Amityville Record*, January 20, 1942, June 11, 1943).

Father Scipio Iacini pastor of Our Lady of the Assumption from 1950-53 was noted for his interest in sponsoring social/cultural activities such as grand operas, as well as for expanding the parish plant by purchasing the vacant Campagnoli home on Great Neck Road in 1952. The builder of Marconiville and his wife had returned to Italy in 1948 to live their remaining days, which for John came in 1950 at the age of 85, and for his wife shortly afterwards. The parish used the old house as a convent for nuns who had been brought in to teach catechism—an arrangement which lasted only a short period.

Father Iacini had difficulty with the community concerning church sponsorship of the Feast of Our Lady of the Assumption. While neighbors could accept the tradition of colorful streamers, lights, booths and bands, they complained bitterly about the use of fireworks which had caused numerous fires in nearby residential areas—even rocking homes two miles away. One civic association even tried to get the town to place a ban on fireworks. Father Iacini maintained, however, that the complainants exaggerated the problems and insisted on displaying the fireworks, apparently convincing the vexed authorities to refrain from placing a ban on their use. This temporary victory notwithstanding, objections persisted, in time constituting a growing chorus of complaints resulting in a diminution of extravagant feast celebrations in recent years, until currently they have been discontinued (*Amityville Record*, June 21, July 12, 1951).

In 1953, Father Anthony DeLaura replaced Father Iacini as pastor, remaining in that post until 1965. Born in New York City in 1906 of Abruzzi parentage, he was a warm, friendly and holy man who in the course of his career served in many Brooklyn Diocesan Italian parishes. Father DeLaura showed strong interest in expanding facilities of the Catholic Youth Organization (CYO) program and in creating a School of Religion. However, the bishop directed him to commence a building drive for the erection of a regular parochial school, as in other parishes. The task proved too difficult in view of people with limited finances and an identity problem. Unlike Lindenhurst and Amityville which had been well-established communities for many years, Copiague presented an anomolous image; it seemed to be "just there" without a strong sense of its own identity. Although he did not dissuade the bishop of the unfairness of comparing Copiague to these other villages, Father DeLaura's reservations about the project proved to be valid—a point that was demonstrated by his inability to accumulate sufficient funds from his flock to build the parish school (Interview, Monsignor Anthony DeLaura). Ironically, his successor, settled for a School of Religion. During his long tenure, DeLaura, who was named domestic prelate and accorded the title of Monsignor, saw the community undergoing significant change. Although still predominantly Italian in the 1950s, the composition of the population was changing in the 1960s—so even Italian Masses elicited little interest.

OUR LADY OF GOOD COUNSEL

The increase in Inwood's Catholic population vigorously augmented by large-scale Italian immigration in the early 1900s, which witnessed the 204 Italians of 1900 grow to 752 in 1910, exerted pressure for the establishment of a Catholic church in the community (*United States Census, Street Schedules*, Nassau County, 1910). Acknowledging the growth, Father Herbert F. Farrell, pastor of St.Mary Star-of-the-Sea in Far Rockaway, secured a store in Inwood where he proposed to start a Sunday school for the instruction of the town's Italian children (Bellot, 1918). Sunday catechism classes were soon supplemented by Saturday morning sewing classes—thus the humble beginning of what was destined to become basically an Italian parish. This was not a national parish in the traditional sense of an ethnically exclusive institution outside of the typical geographic-based parish to be sure—indeed a considerable number of the original parishioners were of non-Italian background—nor was it staffed exclusively by priests of Italian heritage, but rather by regular diocesan clergy. However, the popular perception was that Our Lady of Good Counsel was designed for and considered to be an "Italian parish". It is important to note that the mother church and sponsor, St.Mary Star-of-the-Sea, was predominantly an Irish American parish, but was remarkably unstinting in its efforts to enable the new, largely Italian parish get off to a good start. The contrast of ethnic names joining in the common effort is most revealing. Thus St. Mary Star-of-the-Sea contributors for the tabernacle, vestments, and other furnishings included names such as Healy, Morris, Brennan, Shanley, Dowling, Castle, Desmond, Cunningham and O'Rourke, while Inwood parishioners who provided gifts possessed names like Provenzano, D'Agostino, Capobianco, D'Elia, DiCroce, Catroppa and an O'Rourke (*Rockaway News*, April 28, 1910).

In 1909 Father Farrell purchased six lots on Henry and Madison Streets where Our Lady of Good Counsel Chapel (*La Capella della Madonna del Buon Consiglio*) was erected utilizing lumber from the first Catholic church in Far Rockaway. Reverend Luigi Salmoni, S.M.M., celebrated the first Mass in the chapel in that year and in 1910 the bishop of Brooklyn dedicated it. Irish-descended Father John J. Mahon was named the first pastor of the newly-formed parish and within a few years it became evident that the little chapel had become inadequate to accommodate the growing congregation necessitating the erection of a new building in 1914. In an elaborate ceremony in September 1915, with numerous church dignitaries from Brooklyn and nearby parishes present and with several Italian organizations participating, the formal dedication of the parish took place. At the time it was estimated that there were 1,300 parishioners, over half of whom were Italian either by birth or descent. In recognition of the preponderant Italian element, Father Mahon offered a special discourse in Italian, as did visiting Bishop Mundelein. That the parish grew rapidly was manifest from another source which indicated that in 1918 the institution was accommodating 1,800 Catholics of whom at least 1,000 were Albano-Italians. Although developments did not always proceed without difficulty, nevertheless, despite certain privations, obstacles were overcome prompting one historian to describe the evolution as follows:

> On the other hand, there will be found few places where a larger amount of good will, cooperation, zeal and sacrifice have been displayed, although the people of the locality are not favored with a superfluity of worldly possessions...The church settlement school for Italian children at St.George's place is doing excellent work under the superintendency of Miss Irene Slachta. The usual societies have strong branches at Good Counsel Church and have done much to live down and overcome the former unenviable reputation possessed by this village (Bellot, 1918:56).

The establishment of Our Lady of Good Counsel was an event of particular import to Catholics in Inwood of course, but it was also of great interest to the wider community which saw the religious development, among other things, as a desirable antidote to the violent and criminal aspects of Italians in its midst.

> That the establishment of Our Lady of Good Counsel Church has been a benediction to the neighborhood none would deny. Whatever good may have been accomplished under the settlement system, it could have been at most only desultory and inadequate. To accomplish results among any class of people, a clergyman must be very near to his flock, must come to actual touch with them daily, his administration must be part of their every day life, and this particularly so in regard to the Italian people, who are accustomed to have the offices of religion in their very doors. While several uplifting agencies have been projected...were socially handicapped because there was no great moral agency to quicken the consciences and mould the hearts of so many budding Americans of Italian birth or descent. The easterly section of Inwood was almost left to itself, bereft of those benign and sympathetic influences which gave a transplanted population a foot to stand on. The result was that the place had attained a distressing notoriety for all kinds of rascality and crime, a condition that could not fail to have a disastrous effect on the neighboring villages. Once, however, the church organization was perfected, the place took on a decided improvement. Shooting and stabbing affrays became most exceptional; one could visit any part of the neighborhood day or night

without molestation; evildoers were speedily brought to see that this is a land of law and order; children became more polite, tractable and appreciative of the advantages offered for their betterment; parents were delighted to see the interest taken in their children and a general improvement became evident on all sides. And there are few who will deny that such assimilation is the result of bringing divine influence into the hearts of the people...(Bellot, 1918:56).

Although the first pastor was of non-Italian heritage, at least one successor, Father Francis Agius, was Italian as were many assistant pastors including Fathers Vincent Margiotta, Scipio Iacino, Pasquale Spina, Marcellus Pagano, Rocco Gallitelli, Joseph Cannizaro, Edward Shillitto and Tabona. Perhaps the priest with the longest tenure in the parish was Malta born Father Francis Agius who was ordained in 1917 and who emigrated in 1921 upon the call of Bishop McDonnell of Brooklyn who was searching for Italian speaking priests. Father Agius served in several Brooklyn parishes until 1934 when he was promoted to pastor of the Inwood church. He was said to take great pride in helping poor people and was also known for his paintings as well as his art collection (*Rockaway News*, January 31, 1958). He also gave evidence of a rigidity regarding correct and acceptable behavior by his parishioners—in one instance reprimanding the widowed president of a church society for participating in a civil marriage with a non-Catholic before obtaining consent for a regularized church wedding (Interview, Ferdinand Nuzzolo).

Clearing the Italian hue from the beginning of the parish increased over the early decades, an observation gleaned from a perusal of church records. The following table indicates the preponderant Italianness of the parish.

TABLE 1

MATRIMONIAL RECORDS OF OUR LADY OF GOOD COUNSEL (71)
(Matrimonial Register, Our Lady of Good Counsel)

ITALIAN AMERICAN MARRIAGES YEAR	ITALIAN AMERICANS NUMBER	NON-ITALIAN AMERICANS
1910	11	0
1920	20	1
1930	20	4
1940	26	16

The baptism records likewise confirm the Italian emphasis as they reveal that the first 30 names in the baptism register were Italian. A non-Italian name appears as the thirty-first name, but Italian nomenclatures continue to appear regularly afterwards (*Baptism Record of Our Lady of Good Counsel, Inwood, New York*, 1910).

Similarly, the confirmation class of 1938 may be taken as a further instance of the continued Italian presence. Of the 139 confirmants, 112 possessed identifiable Italian names (*Rockaway News*, May 31, 1938). Moreover, the parish sponsored a number of ethnic societies such as the Italian Holy Name Society which functioned alongside the American Holy Name Society, with the former resting on a more solid financial basis and even boasting of its own clubrooms.

Another church-sponsored activity which became an Inwood fixture for years was the St.Cono Band. Organized in 1920, the band was to play an important part in enriching community life in the years to follow. From 1925 to 1950 the guiding spirit behind the band was Nicholas Mazza, who with his brother Ralph proved unflagging in his efforts to enlist 40 to 50 young Italian American musicians, organizing them into a harmonious entity and turning them out *en masse* for feasts and other occasions. They were the indispensable musical accompaniment for the celebration of St.Cono's Feast. By the 1960s the feast celebration experienced a decline, eventually tapering off to a minor event.

ST.JOSEPH MISSION CHAPEL

Of all the organizations formed by Italian immigrants in Patchogue and East Patchogue none was as important as the establishment of Catholic churches. The origin of these churches revert to an earlier period wherein the spiritual needs of Catholics in the greater Patchogue area were regarded as the responsibilities of missions of existing older parishes such as St.Francis DeSales and Mary Immaculate in Patchogue and Bellport respectively. The start of St.Joseph the Worker Parish in East Patchogue (Hagerman) dates to 1892 when Mr. and Mrs. Frank Saponaro donated a six foot square building for the small Italian community of eleven families which then comprised the "Boomertown" ethnic enclave. Aware they were isolated islands of immigrants in the midst of a rural setting with the nearest Catholic church miles away, Italians took it upon themselves to provide for their spiritual needs until a Catholic priest would be assigned to them. For years Frank Saponaro led daily prayers at the "chapel" until about 1900 when the community had grown to a point where larger facilities were required. Accordingly, they shared in the use of Hagerman Hall which was a combination civic center, catering hall, theater and clinic. Built by the local Sons of Italy Lodge, this hall eventually became the Hagerman Firehouse; Saponaro's chapel sits on the grounds of the Hagerman Fire Department. In the beginning Father John J. Robinson of Mary Immaculate Church in Bellport used to ride on horseback to Hagerman to say Mass for the small congregation (*Long Island Catholic*, March 18, 1965, January 6, 1980).

Just prior to World War I Hagerman Hall was superceded by St.Joseph's mission church which was intended to serve the largely Italian populace, and whose national background was manifest in many ways in the early period. It was shown in the names and customs of the congregation as, for example, March 19 when the parish made a major celebration of St.Joseph's Day, replete with housewives baking St.Joseph's bread, having them blessed in the church and sharing them with friends as in the old country. Another parish custom was a celebration of the feast of the Blessed Mother, with a procession in which a statue of the Blessed Mother was carried from house to house through the streets of the village. A newspaper account of this festival in July, 1910, describes the meaning of the event to the Italians in the area.

> A number of Patchoguers drove to Hagerman last Sunday, which was St.Mary's Holiday, and intermingled with other visitors representing New York and neighboring villages. The observance of the day was under the direction of Frank Saponaro and the expenses were met by subscription. In the morning the Hagerman band marched about the villages, visiting every residence therein, and races were held by the children, many of whom, attired in white, also took part in the parade. In the afternoon, a large altar, erected outside, was occupied by the Reverend Father Robinson of Mary Immaculate R.C. Church of Bellport who gave an address. Visitors to this little village brought their luncheons and the highways and byways, at noon time were lined with parties of merry picknickers. In the evening $150.00 worth of fireworks were set off. It was a great day for Hagerman (*Patchogue Advance*, July 22, 1910).

The Church of SS Felicitas and Perpetua

When several Italian families came to settle in the village at the turn of the century, St.Frances DeSales was the only Catholic church in Patchogue; a parish whose reflection of Hibernian hue could be seen in a 1912 program which featured an Irish priest speaking on the subject "The Irish Influence in the Church" (*Patchogue Advance*, March 22, 1912). The Irish background was also manifest in the names of the children making their First Communion and in the Confirmation classes. By May, 1915, St.Frances DeSales experienced such a growth that it announced its confirmation class of 200, the largest the parish had ever seen. A change, however, was already discernible as a reading of 100 published confirmands indicated that 31 possessed Italian surnames (*Patchogue Advance*, May 11, 1915). Thus, what was once a trickle had now become a significant stream—surely it would not be too long before the special needs of these newcomers would call for an extension of pastoral services—a development not lost on St.Francis' pastor, Father James J. Cronin. A builder in the traditional sense of shepherds of the old school, Father Cronin had not only taken over and expanded the little parish of St.Francis, but also had organized two other parishes: Mary Immaculate in Bellport in 1905, and Our Lady of the Snows in Blue Point in 1917 (*Patchogue Advance*, July 7, 1922). He responded to the challenge of increased Italian parishioners in West Patchogue by placing their needs in the hands of Father A.R. Cioffi. By May, 1918, Father Cioffi was already being referred to as the vicar of the as yet unnamed new parish, and simultaneously presided over the mission church of St.Joseph in North Bellport. By 1919, Father Cioffi was called the official pastor of SS. Felicitas and Perpetua. Although Father Cronin gave his blessings to the new parish, the Italians would have to build it with their own financing. A builder in his own right Father Cioffi expended much energy in missionary efforts at fund-raising in Brooklyn and Long Island City where he had served previously as assistant pastor (*Patchogue Advance*, August 4, 1922).

Until 1922, Father Cioffi offered masses for West Patchogue Italians in an auditorium, a makeshift arrangement that made a regular church all the more desirable. Eager to get his church underway he announced the signing of a contract for a pure Gothic-style frame and stucco edifice, 35 by 97 feet.

Father Cioffi launched many fund-raising activities to demonstrate that the Italian element could indeed support its own church. In July, 1922, the new parish sponsored what was felt to be one of the most successful fund-raising bazaars ever held in the town. Hundreds of prizes were donated by people of various religions and nationalities—indeed so many prizes that quite a few were left over for another function. On the final night over 2,000 people brought the bazaar to a successful conclusion (*Patchogue Advance*, May 19, August 4, 1922). On December 31, 1922, in solemn ceremonies over which Bishop Molloy of Brooklyn presided and which 700 people attended, crowding every inch of space, the Church of SS. Felicitas and Perpetua was formally dedicated. The new church, whose seating capacity of 400 plus 200 in the balconies, had cost $40,000 of which amount $32,000 was already on hand (*Patchogue Advance*, October 29, 1922, January 5, 1923).

In rapid fashion Father Cioffi had won the confidence of Italians in West Patchogue, not merely with regard to the erection of a church building, but also because of his role as a spiritual leader. His remarkable record of constructing a church so quickly did not go unnoticed, however, and in September 1923, the bishop called on him to become pastor of the large St.Rosalie parish in Brooklyn. Although it was abundantly apparent that what Father Cioffi had wrought was an Italian national parish, it was never exclusively of that nationality as is evident from a review of church records. For example, church Confirmation records for four terminal points from the beginning of the parish into the 1950s indicate that while the percentage of Italians confirmed in 1922 constituted 88.1 percent, they constituted only 67.8 percent in 1951. Baptism records likewise showed a dwindling of Italian names over a similar period, and marriage records illustrate the same tendency.

Reverend Anthony Manno succeeded Father Cioffi as pastor and immediately set about performing priestly functions in the parish. His tenure, however, was even shorter than his predecessor's, remaining in Patchogue only eighteen months before being transferred (*Patchogue Advance*, September 28, 1923, March 19, 1925).

Sicilian-born Father Stephan Cottone became the next pastor of the church, and it was during his tenure 1925-30 that the name of the church was changed to the Church of Our Lady of Mount Carmel in 1925; an alteration attributed to the need for a less confusing title. Thus, SS. Perpetua and Felicitas was the church's official name for less than four years—a period so brief that currently even active church parishioners are unaware of the original name. After Father Cottone, the following served as pastors: Father Joseph Della Pietra (1930-31), Father Joseph Schiano (1931-34), Father Henry Parascandola (1934-43), Father Cyrus Tortora (1943-53), Father Raphael Monteleone (1953-75), Father Alexander L. Sledzaus (1975-present).

Father Tortora made the deepest impression on the community both Catholic and non-Catholic. A veritable dynamo he strove to provide recreational facilities for young people in the area, organized low-cost housing, interacted in a spirit of ecumenism with other religious area leaders, served as chaplain for a nearby Army camp and was a dedicated community promoter. An indication of the mark he made in Patchogue is evident in a village decision to build a memorial park in his honor (Interviews with Marie Contino and Ralph Tommassone).

In addition to religious-directed activities within the confines of the church, Italian immigrants also manifested a religiosity which reflected their cultural heritage in the celebration of feasts—events which were frequently initiated and prompted by laymen even while beneficiaries often were the local parishes. Thus, beginning in 1895 in Hagerman, it was laymen like Frank Saponaro and Antonio Fuoco who were instrumental in putting on the feast of Our Lady of Mount Carmel. Their counterparts in West Patchogue was Carmine Bianco and Joseph F. Cardamone. The tradition of laymen initiative in spiritual matters was to be a singular mark of Italian American religious activity in the area. One more notable instance of this deserves to be recounted if only briefly. Italian-born Crescenzo Vigliotta, who came as a poor teenager, eventually purchased extensive property in Suffolk County, much of which he donated to the Diocese of Rockville Centre. This expansive seventy-acre land parcel in Eastport presently stands as the site of the beautiful shrine of Our Lady of the Island. Thousands of believers make pilgrimages to the shrine annually.

Westbury and Port Washington Parishes

Italian Americans in Westbury and Port Washington formed neither formal national Italian parishes nor defacto ethnic ones. Instead they were accommodated into the existing Catholic churches in their communities, content, in the main, that these institutions satisfied their religious needs.

Catholic roots of Westbury can be traced to the 1830s when Irish immigrants offered their homes as a place to worship; in 1856, these people created St.Brigid's Church, the first Catholic parish in Nassau County. The predominantly Catholic Italian immigrants, therefore, found a thriving parish, one which accommodated them sufficiently to preclude the establishment of their own parish, as was the case for Italian immigrants elsewhere. The Hibernicization of the parish was manifest in the names of its pastors, assistant pastors, active church members and activities from the early days of the past. Nevertheless, Italian parishioners emerged as active participants via the Italian societies. The absence of Italian American curates always rankled, however, becoming a pronounced sore point in the 1940s when Italian-descended parishioners complained to the Bishop of the diocese. The pastor, Father Sullivan, apparently lacked insight in dealing with congregation members of different ethnic backgrounds, especially the Italian element.

In 1946, Father Sullivan importuned Father Anthony DeLaura, a descendant of Italian immigrants, to accept assignment as assistant pastor at St.Brigid's specifically to accommodate its parishioners of Italian descent.

In courting the Italian American priest, the pastor made it clear, however, that what he had in mind for him was a narrow assignment designed to render pastoral service almost exclusively to the Italians. "Father Sullivan, I have to repeat I just came back from the war. I was in the regiment as a chaplain. I took care of Italians, Jews, Poles, everybody. I'll take care of all the people here and the Italians too" was Father DeLaura's answer. For the next seven years Father DeLaura remained as assistant pastor, until in 1952 he was assigned as pastor of Our Lady of the Assumption parish in Copiague. Even in the latter capacity he frequently returned to Westbury where he continued to serve as chaplain of the Durazzano Society; he also served as a liaison with Italian speaking priests to St.Brigid's for special occasions such as feasts because, as he put it, the Westbury people "...needed somebody in their style" (Interview, Monsignor Anthony DeLaura).

In their religious orientation, Port Washington Italian Americans for the most part maintained their adherence to Catholicism, apparently satisfied with the services and hospitality rendered them at St.Peter of Alcantara Church. Consequently the result was that, unlike the road traversed by Italian immigrants in Copiague, Glen Cove, Patchogue or Inwood, who manifested their religiosity through the creation of an ethnic parish within their communities, no such interest seemed to be manifested in Port Washington.

This conclusion is borne out by the absence of any reference to the idea of an ethnic parish in the local newspapers, as well as interviews which revealed that Italian immigrants readily contributed to the building of St.Peter's Church (Interviews, Ralph Lamberti; Helen Dejanna). This is not to be interpreted to mean that there was complete harmony, because in fact there was bias against Italian immigrants from the Irish Americans in the area, but of such a relatively minor degree that it did not produce animosity. It was the view of some that Italian Americans were not consistent churchgoers, especially in the absence of an Italian clergy. More faithful church attendance followed the addition of Father Rosario Pitrone in 1938—a curate with whom the Italian parishioners could identify. Father Pitrone remained at St.Peter's until 1946 (Interview, Jennie DeMeo). Father Mariani was another American of Italian descent to be assigned to St.Peter's. There were numerous instances of mutual support and involvement by Italian Americans within parish societies and activities. For example, the Italian Mutual Aid Society, along with a cross-section of the Italian community, contributed to fundraising drives and more than a few Italian Americans became officers of church organizations such as the Holy Name Society (*Port Washington News*, October 25, 1940; September 12, 1948).

Interestingly, it was in the post-World War II period that a latent ethnic interest in relation to the church was detected. As a result of a spectacular growth in population in the 1940s and 1950s, the Manorhaven area of old Port Washington, which had received incorporation as a separate village, came to have its own Catholic parish of Our Lady of Fatima in the early 1950s. By 1953 Reverend Leonard Pavone and Reverend Saporito had become pastor and assistant pastor respectively. Thus, while technically not an ethnic parish, Italian Americans were extremely involved in the activities of Our Lady of Fatima. The catalyst for much of this energy was the pastor, Father Pavone, an uncommon leader who was born in Bari, where he received extensive training not only in theology but also in music, especially the piano and Gregorian Chant. Upon coming to America in 1928, he was assigned to various Italian American parishes where he combined religious duties with musical activities, achieving notable success in the formation of musical companies and the production of operas. With asperity, he delved into the task of building facilities for the parish upon his appointment as pastor of Our Lady of Fatima, utilizing his musical background as a means of raising funds.

FROM CATHOLICISM TO PROTESTANTISM

The history of Italian American Catholic life in suburbia offers evidence that the overwhelming majority adhered to the religious faith of their fathers. Either through assimilation into existing churches or the creation of defacto or formal national parishes, Italian Americans became important factors as participants and principals in Catholic life on Long Island. For a small but distinctive minority, however, abandonment of their Catholic roots and entrance into Protestantism marked the character of their religious persuasion. The road traversed by most of the latter was involvement with Pentecostalism. The movement to Pentecostalism could be attributed to the attraction that the denomination had for immigrants who desired more intimate relationships, less formalism and structure, while simultaneously providing outlets for emotional releases. Furthermore, allowance must be made for the widespread growth of Twentieth Century Pentecostalism which contained provisions for the ethnic group to give substantial rein to its nationality as reflected in Italian titles for the Pentecostal Churches and Italian-speaking services.

In Glen Cove a very small number broke with their religious heritage and embraced Pentecostalism. Led by Domenico Buffa, a native of Pioppo, Sicily, who founded the Glen Cove Pentecostal Church in 1930, a few of Glen Cove Italian Americans joined that denomination. Able to convert only a small portion of his fellow Italian-Americans locally, Buffa had some following without the community and even succeeded in converting his family in Sicily who founded a Pentecostal church of their own in the old country. After he moved away from Glen Cove in 1957, Buffa remained active in his ministry as a lay preacher in the Christian Church of God in Elmont (Interview, Mary LaGumina, *Glen Cove Record*, February 8, 1968).

While the majority of Copiague Italians remained Catholic, a few identified with Protestantism beginning in the early 1930s. The tiny band formed an informal congregation largely through the efforts of Jim Gorgolione and his sister who offered their home for meetings. Known among local Italian Americans as "Holy Rollers", the group adopted the name of the Italian Pentecostal Church of Copiague, and was under the auspices of the Christian Church of North America which assigned Reverend Dominick Guido as pastor. His leadership and the generosity of Sabina Malvella, whose husband donated land, enabled the congregation to build its first cottage meeting house. A small congregation with an unpretentious meeting house, the group evoked some ridicule. In 1959 Reverend Guido was succeeded by Reverend Joseph Calella, under whose direction the cottage was expanded into a more commodious structure. Reverend Calella remained as pastor until 1969 when a non-Italian, Reverend Ross Davi was appointed pastor. Once again the church was expanded and now can accommodate a few hundred. While not exclusively Italian any longer, its membership has a sprinkling of Italian names (*Newsday*, January 3, 1984).

In the Patchogue area, a small but significant minority exercised their religious options outside of the church of their fathers and adopted instead one of the prevailing Protestant forms. For example, in May, 1922, a Brooklyn Italian Baptist minister spoke in the Patchogue Baptist Church on the subject "The New Americans from Sunny Italy" (*Patchogue Advance*, May 12, 1922). In November, 1941, the Manorville Bible Protestant Church, several miles away, featured an Italian gospel. In 1951, Reverend Dominick Cianella became rector of St.Paul's Episcopal Church in Patchogue (*Patchogue Advance*, November 21, 1944; May 24, 1951). However, the foremost example of Protestant activity among Italians in the area revolved around the Assembly of God congregation in East Patchogue. Opened in April 1938, this organization was under the direction of Pastor Nunzio Vitalone and featured services in English and Italian. In March 1940 this church was incorporated as the Italian Affiliated Church of God in Christ of the Christian Assembly in North America (*Patchogue Advance*, April 2, 1938; March 5, 1940). However, few Italians from the greater Patchogue area actually became members.

CONCLUSION

The Italian element in the majority stayed close to their Catholic roots. An examination of the interaction between newly-arrived immigrants and the religious institutions demonstrates the staying power of religious heritage, at least nominally, even while accommodation and adjustment to American social religious norms developed. Some slippage towards Protestantism was discernible, as recounted above, however, a reading of items on religious matters over the course of a century confirms a Catholic loyalty, albeit in modified form, compared to the style of worship of the first generation. Thus the immigrant generation retained a religious heritage explicable within their transplanted definitions of Catholicism which included minimum scrupulosity for dogma and rules—attitudes which cast them as poorly practicing exemplars of the faith when compared to the predominantly Irish Catholics in their midst. Nevertheless, their attachments to their religious roots encouraged them to stay within the fold either by absorption in extant Catholic parishes when local pastors were understanding and accommodating, or by creating their own defacto ethnic parishes or actual non-territorial national parishes. Based on the Long Island communities examined, it can therefore be said that thus, whereas ethnic/ religious cultural patterns persist in some locales, in most places they have been diluted and integration into the mainstream pattern of Catholicism has occurred.

CHAPTER ELEVEN
THE DEPRESSION YEARS

The Great Depression saw immigrants confronted with some of the grimmest years yet to be endured in their adopted land. The concomitant effects of a wrecked economy, huge business failures and massive unemployment did not spare the Italian enclaves. Feeding a family for a few cents a day, walking to work to save a few pennies, taking in "homework" or piecework in the garment trade were recurring and familiar scenarios in many Italian American households. Despite almost impossible odds, nevertheless, these kinds of sacrifices enabled the family to remain intact and less subject to the disorganization characteristic of some other ethnic groups. Although suffering and deprivation were perhaps not as severe as that experienced by their counterparts in city neighborhoods, Long Island Italian American communities had to deal with strains and shocks to their subculture. At the same time, their indigenous culture, including the acknowledged strength of their families and the comfort of other social institutions, enabled them to survive.

CAUGHT UP IN THE ANTI-ALIEN CAMPAIGN

As severe economic conditions wreaked havoc with the nation in the 1930s, concern over employment of Glen Cove aliens prompted a lengthy and devastating article against aliens in America's midst, charging them with lowering standards of living because they enjoyed most of the benefits of citizenship yet used the country's resources to benefit other nations. It is significant that in this tongue-in-cheek article a fictitious Italian immigrant named "Tony Alienetti" is used as the foil who enjoys the benefits of an American job.

> Certainly I should like to be a citizen. I have lived here since I was a little boy. Never been further away than Montauk Point one Sunday. But citizenship costs too much. Altogether it costs me $10 for my first papers, if I went on I figure it would cost me $50...And so what would I gain by becoming a citizen. I have a good job. If not I could get home relief. What should I care (*Glen Cove Record*, July 28, 1938).

The reporter then went on to inform his readers that people like "Italian Tony, represents about seven-tenths of the Nassau alien population".

Fortunately aliens had their defenders such as the son of an Italian alien who rebuked the insulting reporter:

> Let it be remembered these same aliens were once freely encouraged to come to America and were greatly welcomed to undertake the lowly but never-the-less necessary tasks involved in the building of this nation from 1900 on. Menial jobs on the railroads, in the mines, on the farms and in the factories were cheerfully taken and well done. Now that this nation has slowed down we have had time to look around and wonder at what these "foreigners" are doing here. They are here to stay and become assimilated in the so-called "melting pot"...Let the writer, if he will, redeem himself by writing another article on the subject of how the alien has been trying to surmount numerous obstacles of a foreign language, a strange land with its entirely different customs and ideals and how he has met these difficulties in most instances to succeed in improving and in doing so he has contributed his share to the building of this great land of ours (*Glen Cove Record*, August 4, 1938).

The Anti-alien campaigns of the 1930s in essence reflected economic hardships bearing upon Glen Cove which resulted in increased unemployment and a riot by frustrated jobless people. In this atmosphere it is not surprising to learn that aliens became scapegoats whom local politicians were only too quick to denounce. In 1931, Long Island Congressman Robert L. Bacon advocated that federally funded government projects in Long Island villages restrict employment to citizens (*See,* LaGumina, 1970). One village passed a local ordinance requiring the licensing of boarding houses occupied by foreign laborers. Although there is no evidence that Glen Cove enacted such an ordinance, there were indications that economic conditions for its alien population would be grim, and that some would need government relief.

SURVIVAL TECHNIQUES

Because they were inured to slim incomes and because of their peasant background which taught them to survive despite adversities, the Italian Americans in Glen Cove weathered the storm. They did it by making do with what little they had, by adjusting and improvising, by sacrificing and helping one another. Above all, mothers learned to be even more frugal and practice old ways of supplying edible and nutritious meals on meager budgets, or find new ways to survive within their limited means, depending on store-bought finished products as little as possible. They made their own macaroni and bread and, in short, learned the fine art of improvisation as they salvaged all kinds of usable and re-usable items and in the process acquired a keen sense of humor. Feedbags with company labels made wonderful curtains and cement bags brought home by construction workers were bleached and re-bleached soon to appear as clothing for youngsters.

But the contribution of Italian women was even more pervasive—with many of the men now out of work, women supplemented the family income by finding remunerative occupations often in the numerous small clothing factories located in their own city. Such enterprises manufactured dresses, jackets, skirts and other garments, and employed large numbers of people, in some cases up to 100 in one plant. Attempts by outside organizers to unionize the factories met resistance not only from the employers, the expected source, but also, surprisingly, from workers who based their opposition on preconceived negative views of unions. Henry's factory, manufacturer of women's suits, became a particular target of the union organizers.

> The employers hired some men from the Orchard; my brother was one of them, whose job it was to stay at the station and be on the lookout for trains coming from New York and if they spotted guys that looked like they were from the union, they used to put them back on the next train that came from Oyster Bay and send them back. They did not hurt them but they wouldn't allow them to come into town. They used to get paid good from the shopowners (Interview, Mary Renaldo).

Thus, the initial efforts were frustrated. However, by the mid-1930s, unions began to break through and eventually succeeded in organizing virtually all of the factories.

Grit and perseverance enabled Italian Americans to endure the hard depression years as they obtained adequate, if low-paying, employment. They also relied on a measure of self-sufficiency by growing their own food in backyard plots.

It is also understandable that in group socialization, where reciprocity was given such high priority, absorbed most of their leisure time. Moreover, Italian Americans worked together with relatives and neighbors for pragmatic objectives which, nevertheless, were conducted in a social context. Bread-baking in outdoor furnaces is a case in point. Baking bread in the community hearth continued until the end of World War II. Ralph Tomassone of Patchogue reminisced about going into the woods with other youngsters to collect branches to feed a large hearth—as large as the size of a room—in a neighbor's backyard which neighborhood people used to bake their bread (Interview, Ralph Tomassone).

For Patchogue Italians, living close to the land meant growing their own fruits and vegetables, and raising their own livestock, primarily cows, goats and pigs. Bascially without sufficient funds to purchase these products commercially, the self-reliant immigrants grew their own food, made their own sausages, hams, pepper and capicol. Every fall slaughtering crews went about the neighborhood in a ritual which involved cutting the dead pigs into sections, placing them in large barrels filled with hot water, scraping off hair with broken pieces of glass, cooking, smoking, and hanging in cellars for later use. Growing fruits and vegetables served the basic culinary and gustatory needs of Italian Americans and it likewise engendered a kind of competition to see which Patchoguer could surpass his neighbors by growing larger and larger crops.

COPING WITH THE DEPRESSION IN PORT WASHINGTON

Although specific figures elude us, it is clear that Port Washington's Italian American population grew in the 1920s and 1930s, especially with the influx of Sardinians into the community. Compared to other regions of Italy, Sardinia sent few immigrants to the United States. However, a number of them did come in the first decade of the century. Natives of an Italian island which had been infested with malaria for centuries, Sardinians had built up a certain immunity to the dread disease and were thus enlisted to construct the Panama Canal where similar malarial conditions prevailed. Inured to rough living conditions, they adjusted to the hardships of life in Panama where they lived in tents amidst tropical heat and humidity. After completing the project in Panama some returned to their homeland, while a number went to Western Pennsylvania, lured by the prospects of working in coal mines. Spending some years in this activity they learned of work opportunities in the sandbanks of Port Washington, the Long Island destination which became their objective in the 1920s and 1930s. While there were possibly a few dozen Sardinian families in Port Washington during this period, a considerable number left for their homeland in the wake of the Great Depression, expecting a later return, a plan which would be frustrated for the most part because most had failed to take steps to become American citizens.

Privation was the difficult lot for Sardinians in Port Washington and for their families back in their home island. For many, residency in the Long Island village meant long separations from home and family, with years unfolding before they could be rejoined. Port Washington's Sardinians maintained close ties to their homeland, making frequent trips to the towns of their birth and welcoming new arrivals from Sardinia.

INTER-ETHNIC DISCORD IN INWOOD

In November, 1932, a vicious race riot disrupted Inwood. Actually the second major altercation between Inwood Italian Americans and blacks that year, it was described as an "old feud", although the genesis of the riot was unknown. The police reported that the fracas might have started over ongoing unfriendly feelings existing in the section since an earlier riot several weeks prior. The account cited numerous calls to police headquarters. Several people were injured and several were arrested. The absence of references to further racial disturbances in 1932 suggests that they subsided. However, the local papers provided no additional enlightenment as to the causes of the altercations. With the benefit of hindsight one could speculate that they may have had their origins in economic factors—namely the frustration of two ethnic groups taking their grievances out on their nearest neighbors in a time of Depression. There is little question that Inwood was the hardest hit of all the Five Towns during this time of economic hardship resulting in many of its inhabitants becoming idle through unemployment—the breeding ground for major disturbances in the social order. It is significant to note that a perceptive analysis of the unemployment problems in the area earlier that year had predicted serious trouble for the community at large unless greater attention was paid to the victims of the Great Depression. Describing the terrible feelings of men seeing their families, which were frequently large "...practically starving and without adequate clothing and heat, those men, I say are going to be serious problem cases...", warned the report. To local people oblivious of the acute destitution of their neighbors, this report further remonstrated:

> There seems to be a lamentable lack of understanding of the conditions confronting us among the residents of the five villages. To those who know only the road on the railroad station and the shops in the village, life seems to go on just as usual. But in every one of the villages there is the most abject poverty, with heads of families who in a great many cases have been without work for over a year and willing and desperately anxious for jobs that will enable them to keep their self-respect and keep their families not only from starving and seeking aid, but also to keep their children from being institutionalized. During the past week it has become necessary to ask for police aid at the places where these jobless congregate when asking for assistance (*Rockaway News*, January 13, 1932).

PROMOTING THE ITALIAN LANGUAGE

As Italian immigrant families began to assimilate, parents feared their children would never learn or forget to speak Italian. Therefore, more than one community organization was created to promote teaching of the Italian language. One was the Circolo Independente Italiano in Inwood, spearheaded by Patsy Alfano who, in January, 1935, announced the establishment of an Italian school. Many Inwoodite Italian Americans saw this as a desirable goal and joined in the effort. A few years later the Circolo Piero Parino appeared on the scene, also promoting Italian language classes (*Port Washington News*, June 23, 1933).

There seems little doubt that the subject of the Italian language was a burning issue in the Inwood area during the 1930s as several Italian American organizations urged its inclusion in the regular school curriculum, in addition to promoting private instruction in the subject. In July, 1933, John Schettino, Jr. of Lawrence led a movement to include Italian among the languages taught in the Lawrence High School arguing:

> Although a fair percentage of students at the high school are of Italian born parents, they do not speak Italian fluently and in addition to these students, there are many others who would want to take up the study (*Port Washington News*, June 28, 1933).

The *Rockaway News* concurred with Schettino in a lengthy and well-reasoned editorial in which it cited the educational history of the New York Public School system in accommodating German immigrants by acknowledging and offering German language classes.

The cause of the Italian language constituted a true rallying point for the Italian citizenry of Inwood as 500 of its leading residents signed a petition asking for instruction in the language at the Lawrence High School.

Happily the concerted effort by Inwood's Italians, assisted by other sympathetic parties, proved victorious with the announcement in 1934 that Italian was to be incorporated into the language instruction program at Lawrence High School.

Strenuous efforts to promote Italian language study in local schools also surfaced in Port Washington during the Depression years. Boasting of the existence of so many overlapping Italian American organizations that clamored for unification, the ethnic organizations were most successful in efforts to promote local education. The result of the cooperative effort provides further reflection of the high priority accorded to this commodity by the Italian American community. Gradually, as the numbers of Italian American graduates of Port Washington's schools increased, collective efforts were made to introduce the study of Italian. One hundred twenty-five residents signed a petition calling upon the Port Washington School Board to offer Italian among foreign language options in the district. John Jenkins, spokesman for the Italian community, went before the board. He maintained that in view of the vast sums being expended for things of lasting value, it would be desirable to improve the education of young people by offering the

Italian language, pointing out that the language was already being taught in many city and state colleges.

Despite the unanimity within the Italian community over this issue and the validity of the cause, the Italians were to be denied by the school board. In covering this episode the *Port Washington News* printed the remarks of an opponent of Italian language study which is revealing about the bias with which the Italian population had to contend. "If people adopt this country they should be taught our language, and if they desire another language, it should be learned at their own expense", observed the myopic letter writer who simultaneously possessed a convenient blind spot in his thinking since in fact the school district did offer foreign language studies in French and Spanish. In rendering its negative decision the School Board cited additional costs of $500 for new personnel and voted unanimously to reject the request to include Italian as a foreign language offering stating that it "...was not essential at this time" (*Port Washington News*, April 12, 1935).

Understandably rankled by the decision, the Italian community did not, however, seem to be able to marshall its forces in an effort to alter it. For example, Italian Americans failed to coalesce for the election of Italian Americans or others sympathetic to their cause to the school board where they could have a voice in policymaking decisions—in fact Italian Americans were conspicuous by their absence on the board throughout this entire era.

Failure to obtain school board approval for Italian in 1935 did not prevent the Italian community from implementing its own programs for encouraging Italian culture among the second and third generation. In August, 1935, the John Marino Sons of Italy Lodge and the Italian Mutual Aid Society sponsored a dinner for eighteen Italian American Port Washington High School graduates. One speaker was the same John Jenkins of the class of 1926, who argued the case for the Italian language before the school board and whose speech at the dinner rang with chauvinistic pride.

> To all you people here this evening, let me say that the Italian people are in the process of a new era. We have been given a flaming torch by our ancestors and fathers, so let us carry on and feed this torch with that spirit which will always stamp us the premier Americans of the United States (*Port Washington News*, June 20, 1974).

Charles Hyde, publisher of the *Port Washington News*, who was described as "...a friend of every Italian in Port Washington", also addressed the graduates as did Albert DeMeo, who in 1916 became the first Italian American graduate of the local high school and who then held a position as an assistant district attorney. Finally, Professor Medici spoke to the audience in such forcible Italian that his oration impressed even the staid reporter who, not possessing knowledge of the Italian language, nevertheless reported,

"His audience was held spellbound by the silvery and smooth oratory that flowed so easily from his lips" (*Port Washington News*, August 23, 1935).

If the Italian community could not obtain cooperation for the study of Italian from the public school board authorities, it could and did make language study available on a private basis for a period of time in the mid-1930s. During the heyday of the course offerings, students of the Italian language classes rendered public the fruits of their learning and won the acclaim of the community.

IN BEHALF OF EDUCATION

Language instruction was not the extent of education interest on the part of Inwood's Italian population. It was important to evaluate the wider scope of the educational service system offered to the children with respect to both extant official and voluntary educational institutions. Fortunately there were philanthropic-minded individuals who took an interest in the plight of the immigrant population early in the century and who accordingly developed programs designed to assist them through a settlement house project. Mrs. Lord's Trade School, created in February, 1907, for the purpose of aiding the immigrants in Inwood and surrounding areas, apparently made such an immediate impact that within weeks of its debut it enrolled over 100 young boys and girls for afterschool programs in carpentry and sewing.

The institution soon changed its name to the Nassau Industrial School, an appellation somewhat misleading since in reality it was more accurately a settlement house located in North Lawrence, close to Crow's Hill and therefore of particular importance to Inwood Italian Americans who utilized its classrooms, gymnasium, auditorium, meeting rooms and office facilities. Settlement house support was evident in its sponsorship of Il Circolo, an organization for young adult Italian Americans to facilitate a better understanding between parents and the schools. To promote this praiseworthy objective the Nassau Industrial School offered Italian language classes with the following justification:

> To some this may seem like "bringing coal to Newcastle" but to anyone with an understanding of the problems of the foreign-born and their offspring it is easily understood. In many of the families where the foreign-born parents have never learned their foster country's mother tongue the relationships between them and the American second generation is quite a problem. The children lose respect for the standards and demands of the old-fashioned parents. They drift away and lose the desirable home influences. To cement the bonds between the younger generation and their parents, to bring about relationship based upon mutual sympathy and understanding, these Italian lessons have gone a far way (*Nassau Herald*, October 25, 1938).

Adult middle and upper class Italian Americans also manifested an interest in their cultural heritage, as a report of the Italian Civic Center of Inwood, Inc. indicated. Meeting in facilities of the Nassau Industrial school, the group, which was headed by Dr. Pumilia, presented suitable prizes to students attaining honors. In addition, the club debated the wisdom of forming a parent-teacher association of persons of Italian extraction as a kind of pressure group and considered a scholarship fund for Italian American students. The inclusion of many prominent community leaders such as Michael C. Mazza, Vincent Zavatt and Joseph Zavatt, rendered this an important undertaking in ethnic consciousness-raising.

The pre-World War II generation of Inwood Italian Americans attained a level of maturity with respect to playing a meaningful role in determining future development of school policies by inclusion on policymaking school boards. Two public school districts, 14 and 15, encompass the Five Towns area with Inwood falling largely into the latter, although even District 14 contained a considerable number of Italian Americans. By the late 1930s the ethnic group actually gained positions on these boards beginning with prominent contractor Vincent Provenzano. Although originally an Inwood resident, he now lived in Hewlett and thus was elected to the District 14 School Board in 1939, the first of his national background to be elevated to such a position in either district.

SUCCEEDING IN A DIFFICULT ATMOSPHERE

It is of interest to note the role played in promoting education on the part of local Italian Americans who had or were achieving middle class status. Attainment of positions beyond the proletarian stage in the midst of unfavorable times came in a variety of ways. One of the more curious paths to economic success was to take advantage of the opportunities afforded them as a result of the national experiment to rid the country of alcohol.

During the era of Prohibition, a few resourceful Westbury Italians resorted to bootlegging and thereby improved their financial postures. This phenomenon was not peculiar to Westbury, of course, as the entire nation wrestled with the "noble" experiment. For others in Westbury these were the years to try to establish themselves in small businesses leading to an increased presence of Italian-owned barber shops, shoe stores, butchers, restaurants, etc.

Because economic opportunity constituted the single most important reason for Italian immigration into Glen Cove, it is useful to inquire into the degree of achievement in the two decades following World War I. As has already been made manifest, Italian immigrants could well serve as the archetypes of mass immigration—humble, docile, hard-working men and women with few marketable skills fending for themselves in a country which was prepared to exploit their muscles. As noted earlier, state records for 1915 and 1925 readily bear out this stereotype, although some significant changes should be cited. For one, although married women remained exclusively at home, an increased number of unmarried women were gainfully employed outside the home. Some were not really mature women but rather thirteen or fourteen year old girls (*Glen Cove Record*, October 15, 22, 1953). The following figures, extrapolated from the 1925 census, reveals that two-thirds of young women from early teenage through their twenties were in the workforce outside the home, surely an impact of assimilation forces as well as the need to supplement family income and take advantage of the American economic system.

TABLE 1

YOUNG WOMEN AT WORK IN GLEN COVE IN 1925[a]
(*New York Manuscript Census,* Nassau County 1925)

Type of Occupation	Number
Shirt factory	32
Needleworker	2
Dressmaker	2
Milliner	1
Factory worker	1
Stenographer	1
Packing concern	1
Business school	1
Operator: sewing machine	2
Housework	21

Note:
   a. Includes females from age 14 through their twenties, unmarried and not in school.

Source: *New York Manuscript Census,* Nassau County 1925

While overall Italian immigrants continued to appear primarily as manual and unskilled workers, they nevertheless were also entering new job categories: letter carrier, hair dresser, plasterer, house painter, police officer, stenographer, jeweler, blacksmith. There was a sizeable increase in such occupations as carpenter, junk businessman, and contractor. Even the laborer category was subject to refinement as indicated by the following categories: golf course laborer, gardener, farm and road construction laborers. Only one Italian immigrant was attending college. The other difference between the 1915 and 1925 statistics is the greater number in business enterprises in 1925, some in rather prosperous businesses. (*New York Manuscript Census,* Nassau County 1915 and 1925).

While it is impossible to be encyclopedic, a sampling of a cross-section of businesses is in order. Practically from the beginning of Italian settlement in Glen Cove, members of the ethnic group engaged in fruit and vegetable and grocery enterprises. One of the earliest of such stores was started by Mr. Muzante who emigrated in 1881 and settled in Glen Cove in 1892. He is credited with originating the first fruit store in Port Washington, an establishment he operated for 25 years. (*Glen Cove Echo*, February 5, 1942; *Glen Cove Record*, March 16, 1967). Mr. and Mrs. Maccarone came to live in Glen Cove in 1902 where they subsequently opened a grocery store which they operated together until Mr. Maccarone's death in 1938. The widow continued to run the store alone and for many in the Italian neighborhood this was the place to purchase cheese supplies and loose macaroni which was stored in large bins. In 1970, at the age of 90, she was still operating the venture, although by this time it was a place where people in the neighborhood shopped for last minute items. (*Glen Cove Record*, August 8, 1970; December 21, 1972).

Small enterprises such as shoemaker shops were operated by DiPietrantonio and Manfredo, among others, while Gaetano DiGiovanni became well-known as the barbershop proprietor begun in 1897 and stretching well into the twentieth century. Other types of small enterprises included junk shops as one operated by the Mike Trotta family, a furniture store owned by V. Capobianco and a flooring store owned by Fred Capobianco. Other individuals operated small gardening businesses.

Entrepreneurial success was not the only reflection of Italian visibility in Westbury. By creating ethnic institutions the newcomers sought to provide a modicum of security against family disasters while enriching their social and cultural lives. Presently, the village houses three Italian societies the oldest of which is the Dell' Assunta Society formed in 1911 as an organization which could provide mutual benefits, religious and social expression.

SURGE OF ITALIANITÁ

The Durazzano Society of Westbury became the community's second oldest Italian organization, the Dell' Assunta Society, previously discussed, being the oldest. Chartered in 1929, its constitution limits membership to Durazzano-born males, their sons and those who marry into a Durazzanesi family. In addition, there is no constitutional insistence on adherence to the Catholic Church, although that is the religion of virtually all its members and the highlight of the year's activities is a feast in honor of St.Anthony. Although it's beginnings reflected a rift within the older Dell' Assunta Society, it also was a reflection of the increased numbers of Durazzano immigrants who wanted their exclusive organization.

In actuality, although different in some respects the Dell' Assunta and the

Durazzano societies have overlapping membership with many individuals belonging to both organizations while others are intertwined by virtue of membership of relations and friends. A look at the membership names and officers is a revealing comment on the persistency of ethnicity. Guiseppe Abbatiello, who was a recent immigrant was the president of the Durazzano Society in 1979 is related to one of the oldest and best-known Westbury Italian families whose descendants are to be found in both organizations. Frances Juliano, president of the Women's Auxiliary of the Dell' Assunta Society, is the granddaughter of Nicola Piscitelli, the society's first president, and daughter of Mayor Dominick Piscitelli, who himself had served as that organization's president for many years. Indeed a Piscitelli name has been at the helm of the organization throughout a majority of its history.

The surge of Italianitá, reflecting a more active populace, was especially pronounced in Port Washington during the 1930s as new Italian American organizations were founded and older ones expanded. By the late 1930s the local ethnic group was represented by at least four organizations: the Italian Mutual Aid Society, the Order of the Sons of Italy, the Italian American Republican Club and the Italian American Civic Association. On occasion they worked together harmoniously as in endorsing an American Legion convention or in calling for the supply of more information regarding unemployment benefits for the community. In other instances the organizations went their separate ways. The newly-formed Italian American Civic Association made front page headlines for its energetic advocacy of a new community public school, despite the fact that like propositions had been defeated previously several times. This demonstration of support also revealed a strong Italian American committment in favor of educational opportunities for their children and indeed the children of the entire district, even if it meant higher local taxes (*Port Washington News*, June 10, 21, August 15, September 23, 1938).

The Depression years of the 1930s were years of staggering economic setbacks for the nation as a whole as well as for individual families. For many the strain of unemployment, absence of income and dissipation of existing resources proved overwhelming and accordingly created severe emotional problems and intra-family tensions. While not entirely absent among Italian Americans, the economically-induced malaise was not such a devastating experience that it produced paralysis. For suburban Italian Americans, these were years of belt-tightening, however, not a time of suspension of group activity. Indeed, in many respects ethnic group activity flourished within Long Island's Italian enclaves thereby revealing an ethnic group dynamism determined to articulate their needs and desires, unfavorable economic conditions notwithstanding.

CHAPTER TWELVE
SEEDS OF DISTRUST

Over the course of history, leadership miscalculations have been responsible for the horrors of war which severely impacted frontline combatants and also have affected the community back home. This was true for the United States during the years of World War II as the seriousness of the conflagration was brought home to civilians. Caught up in the inflamed rhetoric and hoary propaganda of the period, the public became intolerant of residents who were associated with enemy nations. United States entry into the war proved, therefore, to be a wrenching experience for all Americans, but even more traumatic for those whose ethnic background linked them to one of the "enemy" nations. One need only recall the harsh treatment meted out to Japanese Americans who were rounded up and placed in detention camps.

While Italian Americans were spared this kind of degradation, leading a normal life became increasingly difficult once Italy joined the Axis powers and thereby became a United States enemy. Even before America's entry into the war questions of loyalty surfaced and suspicions were voiced over the enthusiastic manner in which Italian Americans openly and chauvinistically celebrated the heritage of an aggressor nation. Thus, the embracing of fascism and Hitler by Italian dictator Benito Mussolini placed many Italian American organizations in such awkward positions that they were constrained to curtail their activities. For its part, the Mussolini government sought to promote its cause in the Little Italies of the United States through the formation of fascist-sponsored organizations. Although most of these activities were evident in the large urban centers, they were also pursued in suburbia on a smaller scale as fascist-sponsored organizations appeared in some communities.

CLOUDS ON THE HORIZON

The deterioration of international events following Italy's invasion of Ethiopia in 1936 is a case in point. Condemned by many in democratic countries, the act of aggression was defended by Italian authorities. For Inwood's Italians the incident generated spirited reaction including one occasion when over 1,000 turned out for a mass meeting to subscribe $1,000.00 to the Italian

Red Cross. Every Italian American organization was represented amidst reports that there might be disturbances because of the presence of twelve anti-Fascists and Communists marching before Sacco's hall where the meeting took place. Also in attendance was an Italian vice-consul and Dominick Trombetta, editor of one of the most strident Italian language fascist newspapers in New York City (*Nassau Herald*, December 24, 1935). The meeting adopted a resolution urging President Franklin D. Roosevelt to exercise strict neutrality *vis-à-vis* the Italian-Ethiopian situation.

In an effort to counter unfavorable public opinion, the Italian government sponsored propaganda within Italian colonies in America through various channels such as the Italian Education Society of Inwood which in 1937 presented three sound films concerning the African war, followed with a talk by an American representative of the Red Cross in Ethiopia (*Nassau Herald*, April 27, 1937). The newspaper account made no reference as to the size of the turnout for these showings, but there is evidence that for a few years, at least, this society functioned locally. Aside from these few instances in the 1930s, there does not seem to have been other activities of a fascist nature within Inwood's Italian enclave.

The invasion of Ethiopia stirred the Italian American community of Port Washington also. For one of the town's newspapers the incident was of such import it was emblazoned on the front page in a feature article which related an almost unanimous chorus of public opinion for the United States to "Keep Out of It."

> That, according to prominent Port Washington people interviewed yesterday by a *Times* representative, should be Uncle Sam's attitude toward the Italo-Ethiopian controversy which not only makes war between these two nations a certainty, but also threatens to embroil the entire world in a bloody and costly struggle (*Port Washington Times*, August 23, 1935).

The aforementioned sentiments by various non-Italian public officials were echoed by Italian community leaders such as Albert DeMeo who saw war as inevitable because Italy's efforts to acquire colonies peacefully had been frustrated. Other Italian American leaders joined in the defense of Italy's aggression. "Italy has been denied the right of expansion for 50 years and there can be no further delay", opined Pasquale Petito. James J. Jenkins was just as resolute in his comments.

> Il Duce has pledged to the conquest of Ethiopia and his action is justified, it was perfectly all right for England, France, Germany and other nations to have an expansionist policy, but when their imperialism is threatened, it is a different story. I do not believe in war, but if Italy finds

it necessary for self-preservation, then she has no choice (*Port Washington Times*, August 23, 1935).

An intriguing aspect of the episode is that while the *Port Washington Times* provided extensive coverage of the topic in its August 23, 1935, edition, there were no follow-up stories in that newspaper, while neither of the other two town newspapers covered it at all.

FASCIST ACTIVITY

The ascendancy of fascism in Italy produced a dilemma for democratic Italian Americans who struggled to retain a love for the old country. Although minimal, a fascist presence in Glen Cove was not entirely absent. Italian fascist government representatives were conspicuous on the occasion of a celebration of the Italian School in Glen Cove.

> At 8:45 p.m. the representatives of the Italian consul, Commissioner Vichiotti entered the auditorium where they were enthusiastically received by more than five hundred people, whose ovation was increased by cheers which were well-known to every Italian such as "Viva il duce", "Viva the king, Emperor of Ethiopia". The orchestra played "Giovanezza" and the "Star Spangled Banner" and the Italian national anthem...Mr. Percivalli introduced the Italian Vice Consul, Dr. Branucci, as the first speaker, who thanked as real Fascista soldiers the Italy colony of Glen Cove for the solid front the latter presented during the seven months of the Italo-Ethiopian conflict. He urged that the Italians here continue the same feelings for Italy, but he further stressed that Italians living in America obey and continue to respect the laws of the country of their adoption...(*Glen Cove Echo*, August 20, 1936).

The absence of similar incidents in the local press as well as responses from interviewees corroborate an impression that fascism in Glen Cove was of minor influence.

In the 1940s, as the war then engulfing the globe spread, the Italian colony of Patchogue was affected. In contrast to other suburban communities, here there was an absence of pro-fascist political activity, save for some women who donated their gold rings in support of Italy's invasion of Ethiopia. As a result there would be no severe backlash against Italians. However, there were instances in which local Italians were incarcerated. In October, 1941, Pupino Pietro Carbonelli, an Italian newsman of East Patchogue, was held by American authorities for overstaying his visa time. Francesco Panciatichi, an Italian newsman working for *Corriere d'America* and an East Patchogue resident, was held as an enemy alien (*Patchogue Advance*, April 2, 1942; October

24, 1951).

THE CALL TO COLORS

The declaration of war between the United States and Italy following the attack on Pearl Harbor in December, 1941, escalated tensions in the nation's Little Italies. Now, formally and officially, Italian names, words, and culture were the marks of the enemy; now perhaps it would be wise for Italian Americans to register low profiles and to demonstrate unstinting loyalty. There could be no better demonstration of devotion to the country than by bearing arms to defend it against its enemies.

The outbreak of the Second World War was clearly heard in Glen Cove where Italians along with other Americans took to the colors, whatever regard they may have had for the land of their forebears. They entered the armed services by the hundreds once the conflict began. The rate of participation can be gleaned from a 1942 Honor Roll which listed six Nigros, six Capobiancos, six Dileos, five Pascuccis, four Abbondondolos among a long list of Glen Cove servicemen—this, only a few months into the war. In December, 1942, the Honor Roll unveiled at St.Rocco's Church revealed over 300 names, a further indication of support for the war effort on the part of the Italian community. Nor was it only the young who were involved. Peter Lado, whose military experience included service in the British Navy in World War I and service in the Italian Navy in the 1930s, was prepared to enlist in the American Army in the latest conflagration. Denied admission because of his age—he was 65 —he appealed to President Roosevelt who responded by suggesting that he try the Coast Guard. Accepted into that branch, he was shipped out and saw combat twice, for which he was awarded a Marine Combat Bar (*Glen Cove Record*, November 25, December 3, 1942).

In a conflagration of such proportions it was inevitable that many would die. According to one count fifteen of the 70 Glen Cove residents to die in the war were of Italian descent (*Glen Cove Guardian*, May 25, 1979). Friends and relatives remember their willingness to serve, even at the risk of life itself. When Salvatore Marafioti was drafted, for instance, it was common knowledge that although he could have received an assignment exclusively in the United States, thereby precluding service to a high-risk overseas war zone, he was emphatic in rejecting any such consideration. Many years later his sister Rose recalled that he could have gone to West Point (Interview, Rose Marafioti).

Surely no survey of military heroes in Glen Cove would be complete without mention of Ralph A. Mastalio, known to all his friends as "Big Ralph". A legend in his time, he exemplified the guileless character of the unlettered but courageous immigrant who exhibited unbounded loyalty to his adopted land. A sixteen year old emigrant from Salerno, he boarded with the Capobianco family until he enlisted in the American Army at the outbreak of World War I. Following the war, he joined the Nassau County Police Force. With the coming of World War II, although 52 years of age and therefore beyond the acceptable enlistment age of 39, he was so determined to be in the army that he dyed his hair and managed to convince the draft board that he was still a young man.

Assigned to duty in Asia, he was the oldest man in the regiment where he served as a source of inspiration and encouragement to the younger men. Wounded in action, he received the Bronze Star, Purple Heart and several citations for bravery.

The heroism and sacrifice of Glen Cove's Italian Americans would not be forgotten quickly. In this regard there exists in the city of Glen Cove something unique: a military historian in the person of detective Angelo Capobianco who writes regularly about the contribution of his city's servicemen in various wars. Published locally around national holidays such as Memorial Day, these articles are a font of information and serve as useful reminders that the Long Island city furnished an ample number of Italian Americans who came to the aid of their country (*Glen Cove Guardian*, July 21, 1978; May 25, 1979; May 22, 1980; November 12, 1981).

Americans of Italian descent in Port Washington came through the ordeal with heads held high as some of its sons were among the first to be drafted and listed among the casualties. The first Port Washington to pay the supreme sacrifice was Anthony Fasano, who lost his life in the crash of a Navy bomber plane months before the bombing of Pearl Harbor. Other indications that the ethnic group was carrying its share of the burden of war included a March, 1942, listing of 278 Port Washington residents in the service, 38 of whom had recognizable Italian names. The July, 1942, Honor Roll of the servicemen from the parish of St.Peter Alcantara, to which most Port Washington Italian Americans belonged, demonstrated that Catholic participants in the armed forces were in excess of their percentage of the population (*Port Washington News*, April 11, 1941; July 10, 1942).

A number of Port Washington families could proudly boast of multiple members fighting for their nation. Those who paid with their lives included members of the Caruso, Fasano, Porcella, Salerno and Yorio families.

BACK HOME

In the aftermath of Pearl Harbor, Patchogue quickly took on a wartime atmosphere. The announcement that lace mill workers had to be American citizens and subject to fingerprinting found local photographers doing a brisk business snapping alien identity photos. In addition, enemy aliens (Italian and German nationals) were required to surrender their short wave reception sets—orders with which they complied. Italian Americans, in fact, assumed their share of the war burden as exemplified by serving on the home front as air raid wardens: seven of ten in East Patchogue and thirteen of fifty-one in West Patchogue were so identified by April, 1942.

If the litmus test of ethnic group loyalty is measured by duty in the armed forces, in Patchogue and its vicinity it is apparent that Italian American participation registered as a ringing endorsement of patriotism to the United States. A perusal of the local press during the war years evidenced a constant parade of Americans of Italian extraction either volunteering or being drafted in various branches of the armed services.

Although no accurate record of the number of servicemen of Italian ancestry from the greater Patchogue area is available, one source shows 276 of 1,153 had Italian names, including 240 of 789 in the army. Anthony Bugala, of East Patchogue, Leonard Salvatore and Armand Serrabella of Patchogue and Anthony J. Iaracci of North Bellport paid with their lives. Many were wounded and received Purple Hearts. The number of Italian families with multiple members in the armed forces were legion. Clearly Italians in the vicinity produced many a medal winner and hero.

OVERCOMING THE AMBIVALENT ATMOSPHERE

The war contained its share of irony for suburban Italian Americans as they witnessed the ambivalence of their neighbors. Thus, Westbury, as already described, opposed Italian feast celebrations as tantamount to anti-American expressions. The irony was readily apparent in the realization that young men of the ethnic group comprised a major portion of Westbury's servicemen. The irony was further compounded when Italian aliens, whose sons were in the service, were required to register as enemy aliens. The drive to register aliens in Westbury was perhaps one of the most intense of its kind in the county as between 250-300 were registered, most of them long-time residents who had neglected to obtain citizenship.

One factor which helped to alter the atmosphere was the willingness with which local Italian Americans supported the war effort. The Dell' Assunta Society, for example, held War Bond Drives and proudly presented checks to the local banks for the amounts purchased by its members. Such cooperation earned the respect of Nassau District Attorney Edward J. Neary who, in his Columbus Day address in 1942, praised the society as an "...essentially patriotic group, thoroughly imbued with the American spirit". Neary reminded the Italians that they had overcome criticism and prejudice and proved themselves completely behind the United States. "Many of their sons are now far afield in battle lines. What greater sacrifice can anyone give?

Who can question that you are making your contribution to the service of your country".

LOYALTY AFFIRMED

The war was a terrible ordeal for Americans of Italian descent. There was no question of loyalty to their adopted land—the large number of Italian Americans in the various branches of the armed services provided a ringing affirmation of their committment. But there was an understandable pathos in the realization that they were cut off and without news from their close relatives and friends in the old country. Even more incomprehensible was the knowledge that in some cases their children would be fighting their own relatives. Indeed there were several instances of Westbury Italian American soldiers running across relatives in Italy while serving in the Army, including one occasion in which Private Louis Pascucci met his grandmother and cousin in a town south of Naples (*Westbury Times*, February 25, 1944).

One can only imagine the anguish of a family whose members served with opposing belligerent powers. This dilemma of fighting against one's own ancestral country with the knowledge that they might well be killing their own flesh and blood could not help but produce a sense of melancholy or fatalism; but it did not overcome the sense of American patriotism which was shared by Italian American soldiers.

Although the question of having men of Italian descent take up arms against Italy appeared to be a minor concern, and indeed because so many were so engaged in such actions during the war, it would seem to render it a moot point. Nevertheless, the prospect of fighting against Italy served to make for some discomfort, if not present an outright dilemma.

Italian Americans responded to the dilemma of taking up arms against the land of their fathers by subordinating the anguish of violence against ancestral obligations to an unabashed claim that they were Americans first and foremost and whoever was an enemy of the United States perforce was their enemy. Thus they fought unstintingly when called upon to serve in Italy. As Albert Romeo put it when questioned on the subject of bombing emeny locations.

> We were bombing South Germany, Austria, Yugoslavia, but toward the end of the war we were bombing Italy in mopping up operations. But it was still Italy and it was a mixed emotional experience. We gave it a thought but did not dwell on it. We had our mission (Interview, Albert Romeo).

While stationed in Italy Albert actually met his grandmother and other close relatives. Family meetings between Italian American soldiers and their relatives in Italy were not uncommon and were frequently the subjects of Long Island newspaper articles (*Nassau Herald*, August 11, 1944).

ETHNIC COMMUNITY RESPONSE

Italian Americans contribution to the war effort encompassed not only active military participation, but also activity on the home front. Thus, their efforts in local blackout drills won special commendation as an illustration of "...a keen interest in the affairs of the community".

The ethnic Inwood community did its share on the home front by working in war production plants, planting victory gardens, writing letters to boost morale and buying war bonds. One Italian American Inwood firm purchased full page local advertisements urging the citizenry to buy bonds. Likewise Copiague Italian Americans played meaningful roles on the home front during wartime by participating in a wide variety of civic works. For example, Anthony Curcio was chairman for the local United Service Organization (USO) which provided amenities for American servicemen. Jean Campagnoli, Ann Orlando, Mrs. LaPorte and Mrs. Anthony Curcio, were active in war bond drives, and Mrs. Roselli chaired a war relief drive (*Amityville Record*, January 20, 1942, June 11, 1943).

Italians of Westbury made the best of a tragic situation and when the fortunes of war found that Italy had wrested herself from Axis power control, and had thereby become a co-belligerent with the United States, they once again were able to make contact with their relatives who were in desperate need of food and clothing. Early in January, 1944, a local committee was formed to solicit clothing for the Italian populace. In a meeting at St.Brigid's Parish Hall, Father Thomas Brennan stressed the great needs of these people caught up in the vortex of war, and called upon Westburyites for help.

Port Washington's Italians also organized themselves in efforts to bring aid to Italy. The James Marino Lodge of the Sons of Italy, for example, sponsored a "Bundles For Italy" drive which was very successful.

Prompted by the plight of thousands of starving and destitute Italian children, the Inwood community as a whole cooperated in drives such as one which created the Italian Children's Relief Society, which was designed to aid war-ravaged Italy after it had become a co-belligerent (*Nassau Herald*, June 6, 1947).

Italians from Glen Cove remembered their relatives in Italy and, when war circumstances allowed, sent food and clothing to liberated parts of the wartorn country. Dominick Genova headed an "American Relief for Italy" committee which sponsored clothing and canned food drives in a door to door campaign. Patchogue's Knights of Mount Carmel formed a "Bundles for Italy Committee" which encouraged sending relief packages of food and clothing (*Patchogue Advance*, March 23, July 5, 1944). Italian Americans thus endured the difficult war-time experience, accepting an opportunity perhaps to assuage or alleviate their guilt by responding with asperity to succor the land of their forbears with good works.

Strong supporters of the American cause, the Italian community could not entirely forget the human and spiritual needs of Italians, especially those prisoners of war in their midst. In October 1944, 185 Italian prisoners of war, then being held in Brooklyn, were brought to St.Rocco's Church for religious services. Afterwards they were served spaghetti and refreshments at the Orchard House and enjoyed dancing (*Glen Cove Advance*, October 19, 1964).

The extraordinary war-time efforts of Italian Americans in Long Island suburbs illustrates that the suspected group had more than proven their loyalty. Their willingness to fight on the front lines, their acknowledged bravery in action, and the blood they shed in defense of the United States demonstrated a convincing, unquestionable loyalty. Theirs was a singular sacrifice experienced by few others as they sought to show that, their ethnic origins notwithstanding, they were first and foremost Americans. The supreme testing time had come and gone and their participation at home and at the fighting front, could not but elicit praise and commendation. They had earned their place of acceptance.

CHAPTER THIRTEEN
UNITY FOR ADVANCEMENT

Ethnic suburban enclaves traversed a course which saw small communities planted in the latter years of the nineteenth century and the pre-World War I period evolve from a pre-occupation with the economic struggle to a fuller participation in community life. The necessity to earn a living, together with unfamiliarity with the customs, language and laws of the new country, as well as opposition by the establishment, helped explain the immigrants' relative low profile in the early period. To the community at large they were the indispensable local work force, bereft of other significant roles. However, as the original pioneer community grew because of on-going immigration and with the emergence of the second generation, the picture began to change and Italian Americans undertook viable efforts at cooperation to advance the cause of the group. Not all of these efforts, especially in the very early years, proved successful. Nevertheless, they illustrated a willingness and a determination on the part of the ethnic group to marshal together their resources for common ends.

MEDIA COVERAGE

One of the early examples of unification for advancement of the group was to be seen in Port Washington in the 1930s. Here was one of the most significant examples of the rising importance of Italian Americans in the years prior to World War II via extensive and regular coverage accorded them by the community's main newspaper. The *Port Washington News* provided a full column to an Italian American leader to comment on issues relating to the ethnic group. The *News* selected George W. Zuccala, who by the late 1930s was emerging as a noteworthy figure in the Italian community, to write the column (*Port Washington News*, June 25, 1937). Dr. Zuccala became a strong proponent for community involvement of Italian Americans, urging their support for the Village Welfare Society, an organization engaged in bringing private assistance to those in need locally—both Italian and non-Italian. Zuccala's column, variously entitled "Italian Bulletin" or "Italian Review", appeared weekly from May 5 to July 7, 1939. The first article was a lengthy piece which touched on several subjects including politics, science and religion, but was primarily devoted to organizing Italian youth in the community, who, he believed, were in a state of bewilderment concerning their relationships with family, society and their Italian heritage.

> Italian Americans: It is my aim as well as that of many Italo-Americans to have a newspaper devoted to the Italian American element, and the *Port Washington News* has generously offered this space so we may expand in a movement which could develop into a highly efficient and recognized county organization of Italian Americans, of professionals and business men to make a group directing and advancing Italian American culture and prestige. Especially to the young Italian Americans I wish to present the idea which ought to be of vital interest to all. The idea may not be original, but I believe it has possibilities of development and expansion in every town in Nassau and Suffolk Counties. There is a crying need for a well-organized association to balance various small clubs and to meet the problems of the Italian American in the counties today. Through the means of the press devoted to Italian Americans in general those self-made or alleged leaders would be less selfish and a county-wide association will be able to do great things without submitting to the humiliation of Anti-Italian discrimination. This would be the supreme aim and goal of the Italian American Central Organization. This central committee will be formed mostly of professionals and outstanding business men, and will stimulate the desire of each Italian American to be of service to his fellow men and to society in general. It will encourage high ethical standards in business and the professions. It will quicken the interest of every Italian American youth in the public welfare of the community and cooperate with others in civic, social, commercial, political and industrial development. This central committee will also sponsor civic programs...It should be the ambition, as good Americans of Italian origin, to break down the barriers which exist between other races and to show that we Italians are worthy of the great American hospitality, ideals and traditions. We aim to have this column of news in every Italian home as well as in many American families who are in sympathy with our race. Our contemplated lectures, books and lists of facts should stimulate great interest in Italian cultural contributions to America's making. The time has come when the new generations of Italians in America should become conscious of their possibilities. There is [sic] now throughout the County many Italians who should be guided by the principles of American life (*Port Washington News*, May 5, 1939).

In exhorting the organization of Italian youth, Zuccala also took a swipe at some leaders within the Italian community inferring they assumed leadership positions for purposes of self-aggrandizement.

> As a matter of fact some of our Italo-American leaders will be surprised some day when they will discover that they are no longer in power, and that their past history shows that all their effort has not been entirely for the betterment of the Italian community in general, but for themselves (*Port Washington News*, May 19, 1939).

Within a few weeks Zuccala's "Italian Review" column began generating a number of queries and observations from Italian Americans in town which elicited his response and helped provide further insight into the issues affecting the ethnic group. In one instance he advised an Italian alien to take steps to become an American citizen as soon as possible, recommending either Albert DeMeo or Alphonse Epaminonde as individuals who could be helpful in this regard. In another instance he advised a letter-writer against forming another Italian American organization for the village, suggesting that the man join the extant organizations depending upon his interests. Without apology, he advised anyone whose bent was toward politics that there was the Italian American Republican Club. If one was interested in mutual aid, there was the Italian Mutual Aid Society and the Order of the Sons of Italy; if the penchant was towards religion, one could join the Holy Name Society of St.Peter Alcantara Church. In still another instance Zuccala concurred with a correspondent about his assessment of certain Italian American leaders whom they mutually deemed undesirable. "Yes, you are right. If Italians of Port Washington would get rid of a couple of so-called leaders, it would do the community some good..." (*Port Washington News*, June 7, 1939).

DISSENSION WITHIN THE COMMUNITY

Zuccala's articles appeared at a time of considerable dissension within the local Italian ethnic community, which was clearly reflected in a number of references calling for ethnic unity. Although it would be an exaggeration to charge Zuccala with instigating the controversy, his vehement cynicism and categorical castigation of certain individuals clearly contributed to the promotion of intra-ethnic discord. In retrospect, Zuccala animadversions reflected a myopic inconsistency. Thus, while on the one hand he called for unity and harmony within the Italian American community, on the other hand the manner in which he assailed some individuals—calling for their ouster as leaders in the ethnic community—precluded true concord.

> I have tried to build up courage, and bring forth ability and sincerity and also prove to the American people that we also have a place in the

American sun. I am trying to show you that your leaders are keeping you in the dark and are making it very difficult for the younger generation to follow the path. I could write a book on the poor impression that the leaders have built up among the people of other nationalities (*Port Washington News*, June 13, 1939).

While Zuccala did not mention the objects of his tirades by name, the men could be identified by inference and by those who became conspicuous in publicly counterattacking and criticizing him. They could be inferred also by the statements of Italian American leaders who supported him as well. Alfonse Epaminonde, president of Port Washington's Italian American Republican Club and the head of the Italian Central Committee, was lavish in his praise of the columnist, calling his pieces, "...the finest thing that could happen for the greater consideration and unity of the vote of the Italian American citizen". Epaminonde also cited two Italian American leaders as harmful to the cause of the group charging one "...who was ashamed to call himself an Italian born until he realized materially from that distinction" (*Port Washington News*, September 6, 1939). This could have been a reference to either of two men: Joseph Dell, Jr., secretary of the Italian American Republican Club, or Michael G. Marion, president of the North Shore Italians American Civic Association. Both of these men wrote letters, critical of Zuccala, to the editor of the *Port Washington News* and applied further pressure by submitting formal resolutions whereby each organization went on record condemning Zuccala for casting reflections on Italian American leaders (*Port Washington News*, June 23, 1939).

Zuccala maintained that he had been misunderstood and that indeed he did have the interest of the Italian community uppermost in his mind. Interestingly, even though he had steadfastly refrained from mentioning specific targets of his criticism in his column, he diverged from that pattern and explicitly cited Dell and Marion in his final piece. Refusing to answer their letters specifically, Zuccala became philosophic saying that "...since they feel that I express the view of myself personally and not of the Italo-Americans, I shall leave this entirely to the march of time...time will tell, they may be right, they may be wrong" (*Port Washington News*, July 1, 1939). He then informed his readership that the column would be discontinued during the summer months—implying the resumption in the fall. In fact, Zuccala's column never again appeared in the paper—apparently the division with Port Washington's Italian American community was of such a nature that it could bring an end to a unique and remarkable instance of utilizing the American press to discuss Italian American issues.

DISTRICT COURTS

One of the burning issues in the late 1930s concerned the judicial structure in Nassau County which was then undergoing a reorganization wherein district courts were established in place of the antiquated justice of the peace system. Generally speaking, communities which previously were served by a justice of the peace would now have a district court to dispense justice—except Port Washington—a decision which prompted a vigorous protest on the part of Italian Americans. Commanding front page headlines the North Shore Italian American Civic Association denounced the decision and insisted that Port Washington be given its own district court.

> ...We know of no reason why this community, one of the largest in the county, should be so singled out from all other communities and be deprived of this most necessary branch of our judicial government...It is not our purpose to say that we alone, this community, be the only community graced with a District Court, but it is our purpose and our duty to our community and its people to insist for our best interests and for the best interests of the District in general (*Port Washington News*, January 2, 1938).

Although other local civic groups engaged in similar protests on the matter, the North Shore Italian American Civic Association was the acknowledged leader in the fight which was concluded successfully earning it praise as an organization "...rapidly becoming one of the strongest in the community..." (*Port Washington News*, January 2, February 25, 1938).

ITALO BALBO VISIT

The visit of an Italian air armada in 1933 was the occasion of an unusual instance of a shared solidarity which brought a sense of pride to those of Italian blood. Coming as it did during a time of economic duress in the Great Depression, the visit of General Italo Balbo, who had led a fleet of Italian war planes in a recordbreaking flight across the ocean, served to divert suburban Italians from their economic woes and personal tragedies. Truly a chauvanistic experience, the triumphant trans-Atlantic flight of Italian planes was an event which electrified Italian colonies throughout the United States; it energized Italian residents in the Five Towns area who could not fail to be impressed by the aeronautical feat in view of the fact that the fleet rested in the nearby Rockaway waters. Exuberant in its praise, the *Rockaway News* saw Balbo's feat as the culmination of a long line of discoveries pioneered by Italians from the time of Christopher Columbus. It described the adventure as a thrill "...which holds captive the wonder and imagination of the American people must be traced to the undaunted and gifted Italians of the latter part of the XVth and early part of the XVIth Centuries" (*Rockaway News*, July 22, 1933). Surely such acclaim could not fail to warm the cockles of Italian American hearts. Judge Frank Giorgio of Far Rockaway declared a five minute recess of his Rockaway courtroom in order to witness the departure of the Italian armada late in July 1933. "As the planes approached the courthouse, Magistrate Giorgio, himself an Italian, ordered the recess and the throng of people hurried from the courthouse and stood outside waving to General Balbo's fliers". The magistrate got even closer to the armada by ascending to the roof of the courthouse where he "waved vigorously" at the passing planes (*Rockaway News*, July 29, 1933).

For Port Washington Italian Americans the Balbo flight contained an additional element of excitement because of an announced visit to the community in conjunction with proposals to develop a major international seaplane airport in town (Smits, 1974). Possessing a fine harbor and suitable airplace facilities, the community was stirred by reports that the Savoia-Marchetti Company, an Italian airplane manufacturer, was planning to build its aircraft in Port Washington. Production actually began in 1929, amidst optimistic forecasts that Port Washington would become one of the world's great airports —prognostications which proved to be premature as the Italian firm soon retrenched its operations. In later years Pan American Airways operated its international seaplanes flights from the village base, but with the opening of other major airports in the area, Port Washington would lose its desirability. Accordingly, in 1933, glowing news reports highlighted the flight and Balbo's impending visit to the community where he was to be honored by his fellow Italians. "Enthusiastic Welcome Will Greet Italian Fliers When They Arrive in Manorhaven", was the headline in the *Port Washington Post*, as it prophesied that the reception would be the greatest ever given to visiting notables in that village. The *Port Washington News*, was just as certain with headlines announcing that the Italian planes were indeed coming to Port Washington. These newspaper headlines notwithstanding, the visit never took place. Speculation suggested that the cancellation may have been due to local opposition, but a full explanation of the turn of events remained elusive.

> The big days which Port Washington people were looking forward to with great eagerness because they would have seen the greatest event the community ever witnessed, probably in its history—the visit of the Royal Italian Flying Squadron, in the harbor, while on their visit to the World's Fair at Chicago—in all probability will not come at all...The information received...that the Italians fliers were not coming here...as planned because they thought that the people did not want them here...(*Port Washington News*, June 23, 1933).

Disappointed community leaders unsuccessfully importuned spokesmen for the Italian colony in Port Washington to request Italian authorities to change their minds and arrange for a local visit. While Balbo and his fliers spurned requests to visit Port Washington, the Italian general did find time to meet with friends in nearby Roslyn causing a sensation among his co-nationals in the community. "Residents of a nearby Italian section, hearing of his presence, flocked to the entrance of the estate, calling for him and the distinguished guest was obliged to step out on the terrace and greet the gathering" (*Port Washington News*, July 28, 1933).

INFLUENCING ITALIAN POLITICS

Unity of action in behalf of a common effort was an important dimension of Italian American suburban life during the years of World War I and the immediate post-war period. Accordingly, although these people harbored mixed feelings about taking up arms against the land of their birth or their parents' birth, they readily responded to opportunities to assist Italy when such arose. Preparing packages to send to distressed relatives in the old country was an activity which would occupy Westbury Italians for several post World War II years as Italy strove to regain a degree of economic and political stability. Concern for relatives and friends was evident in the Long Island town as it was throughout Italian American enclaves across the country in 1948 when a major letter-writing campaign urging Italians not to vote for the Communist Party in the critical elections of that year was underway. Giuseppe Abbatiello, who was living in Italy at the time, recalls that letters arriving from America with the anti-Communist voting advice had deep impact in Durazzano (*Westbury Times*, February 25, 1944).

In the early 1950s Westburyites became interested in developments in Italy. A local women's group called Operation Democracy, whose membership was largely of non-Italian background, was ready to begin a program to aid a less fortunate town in India. Upon hearing about the group's intention, Mrs. Julia Ianucci attended the next meeting and convinced Operation Democracy sponsors that it would be more appropriate to extend aid to an Italian town in recognition of the many Italians in Westbury and because visible assistance by Americans in Italy would be instrumental in forestalling a Communist elective victory in that country. Accordingly, Operation Democracy settled on adopting the town of Coreggio in northern Italy and sent aid in the form of children's clothing and by exchanging young women "ambassadors" who visited each other's town in their respective countries. In 1952 Westburyite Anita Perotti won a contest for "ambassador" in an event which elicited numerous responses from many young Italian American women in the village, while Coreggio chose Alba Vezzani. Coming to Westbury in 1953 as Coreggio's ambassador, Vezzani met with Operation Democracy members who showed her how democracy functioned in America. Widely feted by the community at large, and the Italian American population in particular, she impressed local people by her visits to hospitals, schools and stores. Westburyites also honored her with teas, dinners and sightseeing tours. When her visit was complete the Italian woman was able to return with phonograph records made in Westbury extolling democracy which were designed for broadcast over Voice of America facilities in Italy at a later date (Interviews, Anthony Razzano; Giuseppe Abbatiello).

In Glen Cove Dominick Genova headed an "American Relief for Italy" committee which sponsored clothing and canned food drives in a door to door campaign. This assistance continued during the Cold War period, reaching extraordinary proportions in the late 1940s—a time of dramatic struggle between the Communist and non-Communist elements for control of Italy. By word and deed, Italian Americans in the Long Island community rallied resolutely behind the democratic Italian elements. In March, 1948, at a mass meeting in the local high school, the community formally endorsed Operation Democracy, a project which involved a formal obligation to adopt Ponte Corvo, a needy Italian town, and provide it with aid in the form of food and clothing. Five hundred Glen Cove Covites were present on the occasion and although somewhat disappointed at the failure of popular radio and TV star Perry Como to show up as expected, nevertheless were enthusiastic in receiving other guests who told of the plight facing Italy. Among the speakers were New York City Judge Juvenal Marchisio who for years spearheaded programs to aid Italians, opera favorite Salvatore Baccaloni, and an Italian official. The audience was informed that Father Fiorentino had recently visited Ponte Corvo confirming the desperate need for clothing, hospital and school equipment. By cooperating in this effort Glen Cove joined 200 other American communities which had also adopted needy Italian towns. For years local media detailed Glen Cove's efforts in numerous drives to accumulate school equipment. A demonstration of good will, these humanitarian and religious efforts also encompassed a political dimension (*Glen Cove Record*, March 4, 8, 25, 1948).

By March, 1948, Americans of Italian descent locally, led by the Sons of Italy Lodge 1016, became part of a nationwide campaign of letter writing to friends and relatives to influence them in the coming Italian national elections. Italians were to choose between the Christian Democratic Party and the Communist Party for their country's leadership with serious implications, it was predicted, for the rest of Western civilization. Local Italian American organizations did their utmost to mobilize a pro-Christian Democratic vote holding rallies in Glen Cove in which prominent speakers warned against the dangers of Communism and the need for local Italians to flood the mails with letters to their relatives in Italy containing the message. At an eleventh hour mass Glen Cove rally, prepared letters on the topic were supplied wanting only signatures and addresses.

The Sons of Italy proved itself to be a unifying force when it obtained the support of Glen Cove newspapers which featured the drive with front page headlines outlining the forthcoming event and opened its columns for generous coverage of related items, for example, an excerpt on the subject from House Speaker Joseph W. Martin, stated: "As individuals, the people of Italian descent living here have a great opportunity to help save the land of their fathers and prevent a catastrophe which would result from a Communist victory". Contacts with other Italian American organizations in Glen Cove and in neighborhing towns such as Oyster Bay, Greenvale, Roslyn, Westbury and Port Washington, elicited enthusiastic response (*Glen Cove Record*, March, April 1, 1948; *Glen Cove Echo*, March 18, 1948). The result of the effort proved most gratifying and Glen Covites took justifiable pride in aiding the Christian Democrats in the critical Italian elections.

> Operation democracy-Glen Cove is helping in the battle against Communism in Italy. Word has just been received from Giulio Ardreoti, Democratic deputy to the Italian Parliament from Ponte Corvo, that he personally believes that the public announcement of aid to Ponte Corvo from Glen Cove on April 16th, two days before the Italian elections, helped him immeasurably in his overwhelming election victory. He was most effusive in expressing his thanks for this assistance (*Glen Cove Echo*, May 13, 1948).

Within days of the favorable election results, local Italian Americans directed their attention to relief for Ponte Corvo sending an initial shipment of school supplies followed by more substantial aid. That the Italian town was in desperate need of help was apparent as correspondence from officials from the Catholic Committee for Relief Abroad, which were published in the Glen Cove newspapers, indicated. Some made their own visits that confirmed the need for on-going assistance for 172 Ponte Corvo families which, due to illness or war-time deaths, were without breadwinners and therefore in extreme straits (*Glen Cove Record*, June 3, October 21, 1948). Over the course of the next few years Glen Cove continued to play a meaningful aid role until at last Ponte Corvo was able to clear away the terrible wreckage of war.

EMERGENCE IN SCHOOL MATTERS

Having demonstrated their effectiveness in uniting for action of special meaning to their own ethnic group, Italian Americans also were prepared to play their part in activities which extended to the welfare of the entire community. One important example of such activity was the ability of the group to unite in behalf of proper representation on local school boards where they helped advance the cause of education for the entire community.

The significance of the school board as a key center of influence cannot be overestimated. In the absence of genuine home rule in a number of unincorporated villages, the school board served as a means of identifying the community. Accordingly, the attainment of positions on the board were estimable goals for suburban Italian Americans, goals which would not be achieved simultaneously in the several Long Island communities. With some exceptions Italian American presence on the school boards was to be a post World War II phenomenon. One exception, and undoubtedly the first instance of Italian Americans serving on a local school board, was to be found in East Patchogue where the ethnic group became conspicuous in school matters as early as 1913 when John N. Stephani was elected to the board. Indeed Stephani, who was to become famous as a law enforcement officer and who was also a factor in the community's economic and political development, altogether served at least fifteen terms as a board member including a few years as president (*Patchogue Advance*, August 9, 1929). From Stephani's time on, Italian Americans were generously represented on the East Patchogue School Board, frequently constituting the overwhelming majority as in 1938 and 1940 when four out of the five board members were of Italian extraction (*Patchogue Argus*, October 25, 1938; *Patchogue Advance*, June 25, 1940).

Italian American school board representation in East Patchogue was unusual. For other Italian American Long Island communities it would be a rarity to have members of the ethnic group entrusted with such respected community positions in the pre-World War II period. The few who did succeed in gaining school board posts prior to the 1940s were required to overcome persistent opposition. Marconiville and Inwood are cases in point.

Marconiville Italian Americans made their first important inroads in local school matters in the 1920s when they elected the first of their fellow ethnics to the three-person School Board in the person of Louis Campagnoli, son of the founder. Enlarged in 1925 to seven persons, the board soon included William Bernagazzi and Renato Giorgini. The latter's election in 1931 was reflective of political overtones. With Italian residents the largest single nationality group in the district and in the total school population, it was surely a sufficient case for educational representation.

That Giorgini's school board election reflected the wider political arena, there can be no doubt, as indicated by the following account:

> At the August meeting 231 votes were cast and Renato Giorgini and J. Robin-Smith, who were candidates received, respectively, 107 and 109, neither of which was a majority of the total. When the second meeting was held this week the total was run up to 256 votes, but Mr. Smith's vote dropped to 100 while Mr. Giorgini's increased to 130. There has been a prevailing feeling that the election in Copiague represented

contests between the older Copiague south of the railroad and the so-called Marconiville section north of it. The new member of Copiague's Board of Education is a young man who is well spoken of by the community in general (*Amityville Record*, April 25, 1931).

A friendly, personable man, Renato was fully aware of an absence of Italian Americans on the faculty, a situation which can be considered startling when one realizes that a 1933 official report showed Italian children to comprise 60 percent of the entire school population (*Amityville Record*, September 1, 1933). Overcoming resistance, he sought to correct the injustice by fighting against a school board policy which served as a pretext for prejudice. By complying with a policy which authorized the hiring of teachers with only two years of college credit, they felt absolved of any policy infraction, even while refusing to hire an Italian American candidate who had a full four year college degree. At Renato's insistence the board selected its first Italian American faculty member, thereby presaging a gradual increase of Italian Americans for district faculty and administrative posts. That progress was slow can be seen in a 1940 listing of two Italian American names out of fifteen faculty and administrators.

Italian American representation on the Copiague School Board increased. In the 1930s several Italian Americans were elected to the board and Silvio Tassinari was chosen treasurer. Old-time Copiaguers continued to resist, however. In 1934, three separate ballots for positions on the school board failed to produce a single majority, although the two candidates with the highest vote totals were of Italian descent. This prompted the press to observe that it was no longer a question of the Italian element versus the old Long Island faction (*Amityville Record*, September 21, 1934). These obvious community preferences notwithstanding, the Copiague Civic Association, which was a spokes-organization for the southern part of town, refused to endorse the leading contenders and appealed to the State Department of Education in behalf of non-Italian candidates who trailed in the balloting. These machinations eventually lead to the defeat of the two Italian American candidates: Renato Giorgini, however, was re-elected (*Amityville Record*, September 21, 1934).

For District 15, which embraced Inwood proper, Italian Americans would have to wait until after World War II, long after they were acknowledged as the district's largest single nationality before achieving school board recognition. When Dr. Alexander A. Vivona, a well-known physician and surgeon who had practiced in Inwood since 1928, was named to the board in 1946 it was regarded of major ethnic import.

> In the selection of Dr. Vivona as a member of the Board, the Italian American residents who make up the larger percentage of the popula-

tion of Inwood now have representation on the school board, something for which they have been working for the past number of years (*Nassau Herald*, February 22, 1936).

Dr. Vivona remained a board member until his death in 1963. His death set the backdrop for an interesting election to the school board in 1964 over what could be considered the "Italian seat". Four candidates, including two Italian Americans, competed for the position with Jesse Cestari emerging as victor. In announcing his candidacy, Italian-born Cestari, who had become a graduate pharmacist, evoked the memory of Dr. Vivona asserting that he always believed in the late member's ideals "...and would like to carry on in his place" (*Nassau Herald*, March 3, May 7, 1964). Peter Bertucci won a seat in 1970 thus doubling Italian American representation.

Did the presence of Italian Americans on school boards presage a trickling down of recognition on the ethnic group as a whole? This is not always easy to measure with precision. Furthermore, there is little to warrant charges of blatant anti-Italian discrimination in the local schools so far as queries of several schoolgoers of that generation can discern. Nevertheless, Italian Americans who went to the local schools during the 1920s and 1930s can recall no Italian American faculty members present; what was abundantly clear was that the ethnic group was bereft of role models of their own background within the school system of that era. The first teacher with an Italian name cited in the local Inwood press was Edith Vairo, who was appointed teacher of Italian in 1934. That the appointment was considered important to the Italian American community is easily gleaned by reference to favorable comments the move elicited. Peter Provenzano, who initiated the drive to hire her when he joined with a committee of prominent citizens to confer with the board president about the position, lauded the announcement as an affirmation that the board president,

> was making good his promise made before the election to the school board that he would recognize the large Italian colony in the district. He further shows that he is a man of his word, inasmuch as he promised before the election that Italian Americans in the district would be given recognition if they offered deserving persons for appointment in the district (*Nassau Herald*, September 11, 1934).

In the 1940s the picture began to change with the appearance of more Italian American teachers and administrators. Although not originally a resident of the Five Towns area, Nicholas Farina, who became a teacher at Lawrence High School in 1935 and served also as football coach there, became principal of P.S. 6 in Cedarhurst in 1945 (*Nassau Herald*, April 18, 1963).

As for local products, mention should be made of Inwood-born Theodore J.

Camillo who went through the local public school system including P.S. 4 and Lawrence High School and who, after military war service, began a teaching career in District 15, including five years as football coach at Lawrence High School (*Nassau Herald*, March 11, 1955, March 11, 1965).

In 1955 he served as principal of P.S. 2 in Inwood. The first Italian American to serve in the capacity of School Superintendent was Dr. Michael Santopolo (*Nassau Herald*, February 24, 1956).

The relative absence of Italian American faculty in pre-World War II Patchogue was a vivid reality. It must be pointed out, however, that the situation was not due to a dearth of qualified individuals within the community. Matilda Romeo, for example, an outstanding Middlebury College student, garnered many scholarly honors and enjoyed a successful teaching career for many years outside the district (*Patchogue Argus*, June 19, 1934). Likewise, her brother Eugene also amassed an admirable academic record. It is not to be inferred that their relative absence in village educational matters was due to formal written codes barring them, but rather that there existed an inhibiting atmosphere which perhaps discouraged ethnic group members from seeking such positions. The result was a pattern of virtual exclusion at a time when the ethnic makeup of the school district encompassed a significant number of Italian Americans, but were without teacher role models of their background.

After World War II, however, Italian names became more frequent on faculty rosters with some individuals achieving important administrative positions. Eugene Romeo, who started teaching in 1946, became School Music Director, while Michael Felice was appointed to the Patchogue School Board in 1950 (*Patchogue Advance*, May 4, 1950; August 6, 1953). Subsequently other Italian Americans ran and won school board positions but it was not to be easy, as Victor Yannacone Sr. was to find out. The son of an Italian immigrant, Victor became a lawyer during the Depression years and moved into Patchogue in 1945 quickly immersing himself in civic and church affairs, and thus becoming reasonably popular. A member of many local organizations, he ran losing races for the school board in 1957 and 1958. On the other hand, Frank Zanuzzi and Frank Scutari were winning election and re-election in approximately the same period. In the 1970s Alfred Chiuchiolo and Albert Benincase became presidents of the Board of Education (*Patchogue Advance*, August 31, 1972; February 1, 1973). Thus from the 1950s on Italian Americans played visible roles in local school affairs.

The improving role of Italian Americans in the important community endeavor of education was a meaningful development. To be entrusted to positions as teachers, administrators and educational policymakers was, in essence, a recognition of having attained a respected level of professionalism and civic responsibility. For the community at large it represented a willingness to accept a role for Italian Americans in the pursuit of education.

For Americans of Italian descent the development also conveyed the message of a growing appreciation of their professional classes as committed people who helped enrich community life. Examples of the increased role of Italian American professionals are in order.

UPWARD MOBILITY

Although the first generation of suburban Italian Americans were of the proletarian class, considerable upward mobility marked the coming of age of the second generation which was moving impressively into the professions as doctors, lawyers and bankers. Italian-born Eugene Calvelli, Sr., was the first of his nationality to practice medicine in Port Washington. Immigrating to this country as a child, he graduated from Columbia University with a degree in Pharmaceutical Chemistry and received a medical degree from New York University in 1915. Following service with the United States Army during World War I, he began practicing in the village in 1919, developed an intense interest in cardiology and was credited with being one of the first cardiologists on Long Island. He was a leader in the drive to establish cardiology units in two county hospitals and eventually became chief Cardiologist for Meadowbrook Hospital in 1935. He served as consultant in Cardiology for Mercy Hospital in Rockville Centre and St.Joseph's Hospital in Far Rockaway. A respected medical man, he served as president of the Nassau County Medical Society in 1939. Since its inception he was a devoted friend and benefactor of St.Francis Hospital in Port Washington, serving on its staff for 25 years until his death in 1962. His son, Eugene Calvelli, Jr., followed in his footsteps also becoming a medical doctor. Despite his busy schedule the senior Dr. Calvelli performed his share of community responsible endeavors and became the first Italian American to serve as a member of the Port Washington Board of Education. He never forgot his ethnic roots becoming a charter member of the John M. Marino Sons of Italy Lodge, and served as its first venerable.

A native of Italy who came to Port Washington to live in 1900, Dr. Anthony Ames Ressa attended Columbia and Fordham Universities and received his medical degree from Tufts Medical School in 1925. He opened his practice in his home town and earned renown for his work in arthritics. He also won coveted awards from civic and religious organizations (*Port Washington News*, April 4, 1962; August 25, 1966; April 5, 1971).

Albert DeMeo, the son of one of the oldest Italian families in Port Washington, would make his name in the field of law. Albert attended local schools where he excelled to such a degree that he won the Alumni Award at Port Washington High School. He then matriculated for a law degree at Fordham University and opened a law practice in the town in the early 1920s. He later became the first Italian American assistant district attorney of Nassau

County (*Port Washington News*, September 22, 1919).

A native of Italy, John Salvatore Lordi entered the United States in 1883 and in that same year began to operate a private banking establishment on Mulberry Street, the oldest "Little Italy" in New York City. In time he acquired a reputation as a major figure in the Italian colony in the city, but was also connected with Port Washington where he and his family were summer residents until his death in 1921 (*Port Washington News*, February 4, 1921).

Climbing the ladder of success in the professional and entrepreneurial worlds was a feature of both suburban and urban Italian Americans. Nevertheless, given the earlier beginnings of Italian colonies in the cities and thus their longer histories, it would seem to indicate that upward mobility was obtained more rapidly by suburban Italian Americans. Having to contend with fewer competing groups, and eliciting a somewhat less hostile response by the host communities which more readily acknowledged their contributions, Italian Americans were able to achieve positions of significance more quickly, if less conspicuously, than their counterparts in urban centers. Once the ethnic community foundations were firmly established, Italian American suburbanites were prepared to play a greater role in community affairs, becoming acknowledged indispensable factors.

CHAPTER FOURTEEN
ESTABLISHING SHOOTS

World War II constituted the watershed years for Long Island Italian Americans. Whereas prior to the conflict their visibility was limited almost exclusively to proletarian roles as laborers, handymen, factory operators, *etc.*, they now became prominent in the range of roles in the community at large. Moving beyond the lower socioeconomic class structure, Italian immigrants and their descendents achieved middle and lower-middle class statuses. They could be found increasingly in white-collar positions, in the professions and in business enterprises. They also emerged as meaningful factors in the social life of the community attaining positions in which they helped make policy for the wider community. One area where they had made only sporadic impact prior to World War II and in which they would now become firmly established was in the realm of veterans affairs.

VETERANS AFFAIRS

Having paid their dues, as it were, through their extraordinary war-time service, Italian Americans were inclined to take activist roles in the post-war agenda of veterans groups. Accordingly, they provided the leadership, for the creation of new veterans organizations and the expansion of extant veterans groups.

Their proclivity toward organizational life was a manifestation of the ebullient spirit of the times and perhaps was no better demonstrated than in the founding in Inwood of the Pfc John J. Oliveri Veterans of Foreign Wars Post, No. 158. As a veterans organization it was a non-ethnic organization no different from thousands of similar organizations throughout the country. However, in Inwood it took on a specifically Italian colorization which reflected a unique blending of ethnic roots and Americanization. In its name and composition it was for all intents and purposes an ethnic organization. Officially instituted in the spring of 1945 with six Oliveri family members among the 200 persons present, the unit swore in its first officers headed by Dominick Defalco (*Nassau Herald*, June 29, 1945). Most of the other officers had Italian names—a pattern which was to be followed in succeeding years—and the post boasted of an active Ladies Auxiliary quickly becoming one of the most successful units in the area. By August, 1945, it purchased its own building and attracted members not only from Inwood but also former community residents who, although now residing elsewhere, desired to maintain links with the old neighborhood. Outgrowing its facilities in 1952, it purchased a new clubhouse and sponsored numerous activities: visits to veterans hospitals, providing Thanksgiving baskets for the poor, Christmas parties for children, community blood banks, sending gift packages to overseas servicemen, awards to local schools. Its rate of activity was such that it earned the debt of the community and commendation from state V.F.W. officials. Accordingly, a number of Oliveri Post officers became influential community figures such as Matthew Pancia, future president of the Inwood Businessmen's Association, and Joseph T. Gumo who became County Commander and finally State Commander of the organization. For his efforts in behalf of veterans, Judge Frank Gulotta dubbed Gumo "Billy Graham Gumo" (*Nassau Herald*, March 2, July 10, 1953; January 22, 1954). In 1957, for the first time in the history of the V.F.W., three commanders of the Oliveri Post served on local, county and state levels. Notwithstanding the above-mentioned involvement with the Oliveri Post, the presence of names such as Thomas Montemarano, Joseph Calabria and George Ponte in the J. Franklin Bell American Legion Post in Inwood indicated that not all Italian American interest in veteran affairs was exhausted by that organization (*Nassau Herald*, June 2, 1953).

COMMUNITY INVOLVEMENT

Not confining their organizational interests to nationality groups, increased numbers of Italian Americans became prominent in various community wide social, fraternal and benevolent organizations such as the Odd Fellows and the Lions Club. Thus, over and beyond veterans groups local, Italian Americans assumed civic obligations in various community organizations. Some examples are cited as representative even if not comprehensive. For many years Joseph Canamare, an Inwood product who became a patrolman, served as director of the Police Boy's Club of Inwood, winning plaudits for promoting fairness and sportsmanship among community youth. In 1946 Joseph C. Zavatt became Chairman of the Board of Managers of the Five Towns YMCA which sponsored numerous youth programs in the area (*Nassau Herald,* May 3, 1946). Theodore Spania, Charles Morelli, Jack Rose, Christine Meredino and Carmella Iannarone served as officers in the Inwood Homeowners Civic Association as well as other community and choral groups. Charles Morelli, for example, a funeral director since 1933, was an activist in Community Chest, Cancer, Red Cross and Salvation Army drives, while Jack Rose was president of the Holy Name Society of Our Lady of Good Counsel as well as the Italian Republican Club. Finally, in 1963, a number of

Americans of Italian descent joined in forming the Long Island Garden Landscapers Association, which although not an ethnic organization, represented many long-time Italian American gardeners (*Nassau Herald*, December 3, 1963). Although few women of Italian background emerged as community leaders, mention should be amde of the aforementioned Christine Merendino whose work in the Five Towns Child Care Center and the Planning and Zoning Committee earned her a "Women of the Year" citation. Thelma Pacetta was for years president of the Far Rockaway Auxiliary of the Peninsula General Hospital and president of a local P.T.A.

NEW LEVELS OF ITALIAN COMMUNITY PRESENCE

Port Washington experienced its greatest population growth in 1955-65 as thousands, primarily from New York City, expanded the population from 20,000 to 30,000 (Kaplan, 1977). Italian Americans, including newly-arrived immigrants, were well-represented in this migration resulting in a consequent increase in Italian American organizational life. Their presence was reflected in the formation in 1948 of the Italian American Social Club of Manorhaven as that area of old Port Washington witnessed phenomenal development. The club was formed to unite Italian Americans for social-welfare benefits.

Italian American groups exhibited unusual degrees of cooperation as three separate entities—the Marino Lodge of the Order of the Sons of Italy, the Italian Mutual Aid Society and Ichnusa Society—joined together under an umbrella organization with the appellation of the United Italian Society of Port Washington. This collective effort saw them jointly sponsor the erection of the Villa Nova House, a meeting hall whose groundbreaking ceremonies attracted front page treatment, and further fostered the impression that the efforts represented a majority of Italians in town (*Port Washington News*, April 8, 1949). Each society continued to sponsor its own affairs such as dinners and dances, while also collaborating in functions such as fundraising bazaars and activities in behalf of the entire community (*Port Washington News*, September 11, 1953; June 11, 1954). In 1953, the United Societies of Port Washington, under the leadership of Dominick Imbese, became prominent in a local drive for Korean relief. Imbese, in explaining the interest of the Italian organizations, described their recent experiences in aiding flood victims in Italy which served to sensitize them to other unfortunate people who had been driven from their homes. In 1955 the societies held a joint dance to raise funds for cancer research (*Port Washington News*, April 24, 1953; February 3, 1955).

The active 1950s and 1960s represented the nadir of activity for many

Italian American organizations—years which were followed by decline and extinction. For instance, the Ichnusa Society found it increasingly difficult to function as its Sardinian-born founding members died. In the 1960s it was no longer a viable entity and the remaining members disbanded. On the other hand, some Italian American organizations continued to flourish. The Marino Lodge of the Order of the Sons of Italy organized the first county wide Columbus Day parade, an event which has since become an annual affair. In 1975, the lodge celebrated its fiftieth anniversary boasting of a membership of 150 as it reported ongoing activities of a social and benevolent nature (*Port Washington News*, August 4, 1966; October 23, 1975).

MANORHAVEN, POST WORLD WAR II ITALIAN ENCLAVE

Italian Americans were also beginning to surface as factors in areas surrounding Port Washington such as Manorhaven, where they formed a substantial portion of the population. Originally New York City residents, in the 1940s these newcomer Italian Americans purchased, for summer cottages, low-lying land previously spurned by old Port Washington. In the post-war period these abodes were converted to all-year round residences and Italian Americans emerged as mayors and village trustee members. The Manorhaven Italian community was to produce its own interesting figures, one of whom was an Italian-born Gregory D'Elia who emigrated to Manhattan in 1908, when he was eighteen years old, and who eventually combined a real estate career with journalism, writing a column for *Il Progresso Italo Americano*. After moving to Manorhaven in 1950 he quickly immersed himself in civic affairs, serving as village sewer inspector during the construction of sewers in 1956 and 1957. He also began to author a column in Italian for a new community newspaper, *The Post Reporter*. Although his newspaper career in Manorhaven was short-lived because of his death in 1968, his writings were nevertheless interesting because they told of the beginnings of Italian American interest in Manorhaven. According to D'Elia, Generoso Pope, who served as the catalyst for growth because of his sand and gravel operation in Port Washington, familiarized himself with the possibilities for Italian Americans to acquire land in a country setting for low cost. Thus, a community of 500 in 1937 grew in 30 years to over 10,000.

Manorhaven was to witness a plethora of civic-minded Italian Americans from the 1950s on. To inquire into the campaign of Manorhaven Italian American politicians is to glean an insight into reliance on ethnic support. Thus when "Tony" Pasquale A. Solamita ran for mayor of Manorhaven in 1964, his Fidelity Party listed 60 couples as members, 45 of whom had Italian names.

BUSINESS

The post-World War II period witnessed a further emergence of Italian Americans in the economic and civic life of Long Island. The well-known Port Washington Gildo restaurant, for example, continued to be operated even after the death of the founder in 1957. The new owner, immigrant Rico Contino, retained the Gildo name and standards and when he died in 1968, his wife and son continued to run the restaurant (*Port Washington News*, July 19, 1962). The Quality Fish Market became prosperous. The founder, "Papa" Marinello, traversed the area with a horse and wagon, peddling his products from door to door by loading fish into baskets hanging from his shoulders as he made the rounds. Seventy years later, with "Papa" Marinello's six sons as joint operators, the Quality Fish Market had become the largest seafood wholesaler on Long Island, supervising a fleet of trucks out of Port Washington which supplied the finest restaurants and clubs in the metropolitan area (*Port Washington News*, July 26, 1973).

For others this period marked the entry point into the business world. George Nuzzolese became the proprietor of the Port Washington Ice and Coal Service; Charles Murro opened a new automobile service station; and Joseph Fraumeni was the proprietor of a bowling alley. In 1954 Frank Leone opened a restaurant on Main Street, hoping to develop a brisk trade for the internationally-known continental cuisine made famous by his mother of the popular "Mama Leone's" of New York City (*Port Washington News*, August 30, 1962). In addition, a number of Italian Americans emerged as leaders in the business community. Real estate operator Albert R. Palminteri, was elected president of the newly-formed Port Washington Businessmen's Association and won renown for his energetic promotion of business. Jeweler John Marino played a leading role in community boosterism becoming district chairman of the Port Washington National Federation of Small Businessmen. In 1957, Marino was elected president of Port Washington's Chamber of Commerce, while diner owner Ben Ingoglia served as treasurer of the Nassau-Suffolk Diner-Restaurant Owners Association (*Port Washington News*, March 14, 1947).

Renato Giorgini of Copiague opened a large bowling alley in 1949. Giorgini was not the only successful Italian American entrepreneur in Copiague. The number engaged in commercial activity prior to the 1940s was substantial in the grocery field and the shoe and shoe repair business among other endeavors.

A listing of selective Copiague businesses published in the mid-1950s is revealing in that it shows that out of 37 companies advertising in the publication, ten were recognizably Italian-owned by title designation. Thus, although not an affluent community, Marconiville Italians were moving beyond the proletarian stage becoming small businessmen and gaining influence locally (*Map and Listing of Copiague,* undated and untitled publication of Copiague Chamber of Commerce). Italian American emergence in local commerce was also manifest in a listing of the officers of the Copiague Chamber of Commerce which demonstrated that four of the top six offices were held by Italian Americans as were six of the nine seats on the Board of Directors. Although most of the commercial enterprises were of a modest kind, rather than in the rich and rarified air of Fortune's 500, they were important nevertheless in that they manifested a willingness on the part of an immigrant people to work long hours and undergo huge sacrifices to reap the material rewards of the free enterprise system.

The Mid-twentieth century brought vast social changes to Westbury as reflected in demographic data. Whereas the village population stood at 4,527 in 1940, it had reached 7,055 in 1950, qualifying it for first class village status. The building boom which hit the community in 1947 would continue unimpeded for a number of years until the population exceeded the 15,000 mark in 1970 when the village also boasted of over 1,000 businesses, eight churches of various denominations, an extensive school system and a library, in addition to a number of other civic institutions (*Westbury Times,* April 26, 1946, February 6, 1947).

By 1946, there were other indications of upward mobility among the Italians of Westbury. Amelia Romano became a teller at the local bank. John V. Leonardo was elected to the school board and Mrs. T. Guidera was elected president of St.Brigid's Rosary Society, while Joseph Summa gained election as the village water commissioner. Local political parties, moreover, were now more likely to run Italian American candidates (*Westbury Times,* February 23, 1946).

The 1940s and 1950s witnessed an acceleration of Italian Americans into the realm of mid-sized businesses in the Patchogue vicinity. Even small merchants were gaining community recognition in this period. It was an extraordinary evening in December 1948 when 50 fellow townsmen honored Angelo DeSantis, "dean of the Bellport merchants", with a dinner. Born in Italy, DeSantis came to this country in 1905 with cash assets totalling 86 cents. Somehow he managed to get by and in 1908 opened a cobbler's shop in Bellport, which was still functioning 40 years later. The organizer of the affair was Frank Trotta who had received his own start in business when DeSantis taught him how to shine shoes; Trotta subsequently opened a shoe shine stand, a newstand, and a grocery in partnership with his brothers (*Patchogue Advance,* June 3, December 9, 1948).

Unmistakably the most famous name among greater Patchogue entrepreneurs is that of Felix Grucci, Sr., of the Grucci Fireworks family. Already a world-renown name by November 1983, the Grucci name became even more widely known, if not controversial, after an explosion at the Bellport fireworks plant site shattered the calm of a Saturday morning and killed two members of the Grucci family, including James, Felix's son (*New York Times*, November 27, 1983). It had been many years since such a tragedy had struck the tightly knit fireworks manufacturing family—Felix's uncle had been killed in an explosion in the pre-World War II period—and it now threatened to undermine what had become a national institution.

It is to be noted parenthetically, that the Grucci enterprise was an established venture utilizing and perfecting an Old World pyrotechnic craft, one which was acknowledged by the United States Army and Navy (*Patchogue Advance*, February 19, 1953). By the 1980s the firm had become foremost in its field and thus the November, 1983, explosion was accompanied by widespread attention.

In addition to the two deaths, the local citizenry, openly concerned with safety matters, threatened the viability of the firm, leading to speculation whether the fireworks manufacturer would be closed down or forced to move. But there were also Grucci supporters such as Ralph Tommassone who pleaded that the Gruccis remain in business in the area, reminding people how much they had enjoyed the fireworks in the past. This exteme trial by tragedy for the Gruccis truly tested their resolve. After numerous appearances before public meetings of the Brookhaven Town Board in which experts buttressed the Grucci family request that it be allowed to open a new, safe facility in barren woodlands several miles away, the Suffolk County Legislature approved a land-swap which enabled the Gruccis to build on an 86 acre county tract in Yaphank (*Newsday*, April 10, 1985).

As has been demonstrated, Long Island Italian Americans emerged as major participants in social, cultural, religious and economic life in their respective suburban communities. Although the host society tended to ignore their presence in the early part of the century, except as hired hands performing the work necessary for the enjoyment of middle class living, it was no longer possible to keep them in an inferior position. Italian American suburbanites had long demonstrated their committment to the hard work ethic, their attraction and devotion to their homes and gardens, their industriousness and reliability in business and their value in social community organizations. The host society's lingering resistance over questions of loyalty were quickly swept away by the performance of Italian Americans in behalf of the American effort during World War II in which they displayed an unstinting patriotism. Furthermore, the increase of Italian Americans in suburbia in the post-war period soon rendered them the largest of all ethnic groups in Nassau and Suffolk. Without question, they had earned their place and would have to be accorded their just desserts in suburban society.

CHAPTER FIFTEEN
THE RISE TO POWER

Having earned their places in various aspects of suburban society by the coming of age of the second generation, Italian Americans had exhibited a remarkable degree of upward mobility. Within a generation the children of the immigrants were aspiring to and in many instances achieving more respectable positions in lodges, associations, entrepreneural activities and social circles. There remained, however, the realm of politics. The supreme test of acceptance and assimilation would be in the political arena because it was there that power, which embodied instruments of control throughout the community, would be exercised. Was the community at large prepared to entrust critical policymaking decisions to this group of immigrants? For the mass of southern and eastern European immigrants participatory democracy was an endeavor with which they had little direct experience. Italian suburban immigrants, however, were to learn the lessons of power politics very quickly as a number of first generation men broke barriers to participation by pioneering efforts which forced political power brokers to heed them as viable entities. Succeeding generations of Italian Americans were to exploit these political beachheads.

REPUBLICAN INROADS IN PATCHOGUE'S LITTLE ITALY

Ever solicitous about shoring up its partisan strength, Patchogue's Republican Party assiduously cultivated the area's Italian population. Carefully and shrewdly it sought to maintain its power base by according a few local leaders recognition without, however, really relinquishing a great deal of its power to the ethnic group. The Italian American leaders involved usually were business and organization factors and pioneer settlers who had limited education but were nevertheless with substantial following in the ethnic community. This can be illustrated in the careers of a few men, although there is no pretense at exhaustiveness. Thus, in the first half of the century, the previously mentioned John N. Stephani and Antonio Fuoco, along with Joseph Cardamone and Michael Prudent, were important in the political life of Italian Americans from Patchogue to North Bellport. Republicans all, they served as local leaders who regularly turned out Italian voters for the Republican ticket. For example, Cardamone, known locally as the "Mayor of Waverly Avenue" (Patchogue's Little Italy), and therefore an indispensable key to the Italian vote, never held a position higher than Brookhaven Town Dog Warden. Hardly illustrious, it was sufficient to retain his loyalty for a lifetime. Michael Prudent, a carnival impresario with a fourth grade education, was the first of his nationality to be elected to the Patchogue Village Board in 1932. In 1952 he was chosen as the first Republican Italian American to run for Patchogue Village Mayor. He lost as have all subsequent Italian Americans who have run for that post.

Of the above-mentioned names only the Fuoco name remains active in elective politics. Antonio's grandson, Louis "Buddy" Fuoco was elected to the Suffolk County Legislature, where he remained until 1975.

This is not to be interpreted to mean that Patchogue area Italian Americans were not involved with the Democratic Party, because, in fact, several of them won election to the Patchogue Village Board as Democrats. Furthermore, Democrat Julio William Bianchi, scion of an old East Patchogue Italian family, has served as a New York State Assemblyman for many years. These examples notwithstanding, the majority of successful political activity in village and township affairs continues to be through the Republican organization. Thus, Republicans Jerome Laviano, Suffolk County Coroner, and Art Felice, Suffolk County Clerk, are examples of recent Patchogue Italian American office holders.

INWOOD REPUBLICAN MACHINE

Political participation for Inwood Italian Americans in the pre-World War I era was of minimal significance for the obvious reason that so few of them possessed citizenship and because the recency of their arrival rendered them unfamiliar with both issues and candidates for office. These conditions notwithstanding, more sagacious politicians realized that the ethnic group constituted a sleeping giant, a potentially critical, even indispensable bloc of voters in order to effect political control of the area. Republicans were the first party to recognize such possibilities in the Five Towns area, carefully cultivating the group early in the century. Wilbur G. Doughty, a major force in Nassau Republican circles because of his proximity to the new immigrants and his shrewd political sense, was astute enough to perceive in them the basis for an ongoing political power base resting on reciprocity. To extend a hand to Italian immigrants in their beginning years was to earn political loyalty for years to come. Accordingly, through his influence, Italian Americans obtained the first positions of any consequence such as official Italian interpreters in the county courts and appointments as deputy sheriffs. This was the route followed by Cosenza-born Vincent Zavatt, the first Inwood Italian to achieve a position of political prominence locally. In 1906 he was named the Italian interpreter for the Nassau County courts, starting a career which propelled him to the most important position then enjoyed by anyone of his nationality locally. His son Joseph, although not as politically active in Republican partisan politics, in the 1950s was appointed a federal judge— only the second of Italian extraction to rise to that honor (Interview, Joseph C. Zavatt).

Nomination of ambitious Italian Americans to seemingly minor government posts became a staple of political life in the Italian Inwood enclave. The position of Italian Court Interpreter for Nassau County, for example, did not appear to be an extremely prestigious title, yet it was deemed a prize so valuable that more than a few schemed and fought for it. The signficance of this position was that the nominee came to be regarded as the unofficial liaison between county political powers and the local Italian community.

Another instrument which was utilized extensively both to cultivate the Italian vote and to serve as a manipulator of power was the ethnic political club. For years the Italian American Republican Club of Inwood proved a useful vehicle for both Italian and non-Italian candidates for office. That the local populace reciprocated by voting consistently Republican was verified in the results of election after election. Sometimes, the solid Republican vote in Inwood alone kept the entire peninsula from going Democratic as the 1938 election demonstrated. When the votes were tabulated it was Inwood which proved the bulwark of the Republican Party locally (*Newsday*, July 24, 1983). The loyalty thus exhibited continued to produce government jobs, many of them of a menial nature such as public works department laborers, for Inwood's Italians. In addition, they also obtained administrative and policymaking positions such as that given to Peter DiSibio, in the supervisory level of the Hempstead Town Highway Department.

MR. REPUBLICAN OF INWOOD

Of all the products of Inwood's Italian American Republican Club none has achieved such political influence for a longer duration than Peter DiSibio. Born in Inwood in 1908, he has lived there ever since, indeed at the same address since an infant. Obtaining his start in politics through friendship with Republican power Wilbur Doughty, DiSibio became a Republican committeeman in 1938 and executive area leader in 1945, thus becoming the first Italian American in the county to join the party hierarchy of the Sprague machine. His emergence, in effect, illustrated the demographic change affecting Inwood wherein the original Protestant predominance was succumbing to weight of an increasingly Italian population (*Nassau Daily Review*, January 2, 1952). In 1947, DiSibio was appointed Hempstead Town Deputy Highway Commissioner, serving simultaneously as chairman of the Inwood Fire District Board. Subsequently he was appointed to the Atlantic Bridge Authority, becoming its chairman in the 1970s. Wearing multiple hats he exercised extraordinary political influence including control over many patronage jobs (*Newsday*, October 16, 1979). A man of immense political power, he was naturally a controversial public figure eliciting in some instances negative reactions. While on occasion individuals challenged him in intra-party fights, he always defeated his political enemies.

DiSibio has been able to make his Republicanism become remunerative primarily as a partner in a public relations firm which functions as the GOP's principal advertising contractor, receiving much work from Republican-controlled towns as well as the county government. In the mid-1980s, over 76 years of age and with over half a century in political life, he eschews retirement, preferring to remain a power in local politics.

GLEN COVE POLITICS

In Glen Cove, unlike other Long Island communities in which Americans of Italian descent formed a significant bloc, first and second generations acquired with asperity the mechanics of politics, embracing the conviction that government was susceptible to popular control in which their interests would be served. The reasons for an active involvement on the part of the ethnic group in Glen Cove was probably due to the unique political posture of the community itself. Becoming the first city chartered in Nassau County in 1917, it enjoyed a municipal form of government which was conducive to enhanced self-governing processes, enabling the community to attain a high level of political-mindedness. It would now be able to elect its own five person city council and mayor, who also sat on the Nassau Board of Supervisors. Consequently there was less recourse to surrogate forms of political power through local school boards or fire departments as was frequently the agenda in communities which lacked home rule governmental structures. A veteran Glen Cove reporter articulated the phenomena cogently as he described politics in Glen Cove.

> Politics is almost a religion with Glen Covers—and there have been years when as many as 96 percent of the registered voters turned out on Election Day. But Glen Covers don't seem to follow party lines. Although the Republicans have a greater enrollment than the Democrats for years as of now the Democrats have won more often than the Republicans. For the past twelve years only the Council has been split three to two Democrat or Republican. It makes for a great disagree-

ment at City Council meetings with Glen Cove residents enjoying it immensely, and the Council meetings are well attended. There was a time when the manager of the local theater complained that attendance at evening Council was hurting his business (*Glen Cove Record*, Community Edition, June 1961).

Until the 1930s, Italian American enrollment patterns paralleled those of the community at large, that is, greater numbers were registered Republicans than Democrats, although not overwhelmingly so. Perhaps the most accurate indications of patterns are the published enrollment statistics for Glen Cove in 1930 which revealed that for Americans of Italian extraction, there were 173 registered Republicans compared to 149 registered Democrats. In addition, a small number of blanks indicated no party affiliation, while there were a few isolated Socialists.

Proletarians Become Republicans

One might be tempted to inquire as to the reason why Italian Americans, primarily a proletarian people, were not in the majority Democrats like their counterparts in the large cities, particularly during the cataclysmic Depression. The reality of the matter was that they were not living in Democratic-controlled New York City, but rather in a county and suburban cities in which the Republicans predominated. As one veteran politician explained, "Why did they join the Republican party? Because it was well-established and controlled patronage" (Interview, John Pascucci). There were those whose initial political orientation had weaned them to Republicanism, those who had settled in the community in the pre-World War I period and had therefore seen a visible demonstration of the power and respectability accorded that party especially since the popular former Republican President Theodore Roosevelt was a resident of adjoining Oyster Bay. Thus it was that Angelo Cocchiola became a "die-hard" Republican who founded the Italian Political Club of Glen Cove in 1916, but whose seemingly non-partisan title soon gave way to the Italian Republican Club. That the Republicans were better organized is also demonstrated from another source in 1937 which listed a membership of 167 for the Italian Republican Club of Glen Cove while the Third District Regular Democratic Club, which corresponded to the Orchard, listed only 85 members. In addition, there was a 50 member Ladies Republican Victory Club, while no comparable Democratic organization seemed to be in existence (*First Souvenir Journal of St.Rocco Parish*, May 1937).

The Democratic Machine

In reality both parties in Glen Cove enlisted loyal and dedicated workers within the Italian population. Ralph "Lefty" Limongelli became a young enthusiast for the Democrats while he was hardly out of his teen years, much to the dismay of his father, who attributed an anti-Italian atmosphere to the Democratic party under President Woodrow Wilson. The elder Limongelli was aware, also, that "Republicans were the only ones who give jobs". Notwithstanding his own preferences, the father did not interfere with young Lefty, even allowing him to place lights across the house advertising Democratic candidates. For decades Lefty served as Democratic committeeman and a catalyst for much political activity in the Orchard, remaining unwavering in his party loyalty (Interview, Mary Renaldo). So pronounced was the political brew in the Italian enclave that candidates striving for national as well as local political offices regularly campaigned there. The 1934 race for a Congressional seat is a case in point. The Democratic candidate capped off his campaign with a big rally sponsored by Limongelli's Democratic Club which attracted hundreds of people. For years the Orchard provided the only bright spot for the local Democratic Party (*Glen Cove Record*, April 4, November 1, 1935).

Italian Americans became more assertive in the years between the two World Wars, partly due to a growing confidence because of the important role they had played in World War I, a significant increase in their numbers and, ironically, because of pressure tactics of nativists who promoted Americanization. That they were a force to contend with in the 1920s is evident in the realization that political figures from without the community such as Fiorello H. LaGuardia, president of the New York City Board of Aldermen, called upon Glen Cove's Italian Americans to denounce a judge who had voiced a strong anti-immigrant stance. Fraternal and mutual aid societies flourished along with specific political clubs such as the Republican-oriented Italian Political Club which held regular meetings in the Orchard House. Indeed, within a few years the partisan Italian Republican Club of Glen Cove was matched by Democratic counterparts although in smaller numbers. By the mid-1920s Italian Americans in Glen Cove had evolved into a presence which no politician could ignore. Both parties, in fact, not only strove to organize them, but also frequently entered their environs to appeal for the ethnic vote. In October, 1925, for example, all the Democrats on the ticket campaigned in the Italian section of town aided by the presence of a fellow ethnic leader from Brooklyn. Democrats were led by Glen Cove Mayor Burns, a country doctor turned politician who possessed excellent political sense. Recognizing Italians as an ascending voting bloc whose voting power could be harnessed by visible inclusion in the political process, he hired Mary Pascucci as City Clerk, a position in which she served for decades and in which she could be of particular help when Italian speaking people came into the office. Her ability to resolve their governmental problems and explain public policies rendered her invaluable to the city government while it also demonstrated inclusion for the ethnic group.

Italians in Politics

Democrats in Glen Cove officially organized a club in December, 1926, electing Giuseppe A. Nigro second vice-president, thereby establishing him as the first of his nationality to achieve an important position within Democratic ranks in the city. In 1927 Nigro ran for city bursar receiving the fewest votes among five candidates, however, running strongly in the Italian section (*Glen Cove Record*, December 9, 1926; April 27, 1939). Not one to be deterred by a setback of this kind, Nigro remained an active, partisan participant for years to come.

At the same time, Michael A. Petroccia, a young, dynamic lawyer from one of the oldest Italian families in the Orchard and a contemporary of Nigro, was beginning to assert himself politically. A graduate of Fordham Law School, he had gained a reputation as an outstanding trial lawyer, village clerk and acting counsel in nearby villages during the 1920s and 1930s (*Glen Cove Record*, April 7, 1939). Active in fraternal organizations and politically ambitious, in January, 1932, Petroccia became chairman of a proposed Oyster Bay division of the newly-organized pro-Republican Italian voters of Nassau County dedicated "...to insure the advantage accorded other citizens to Italian voters in Nassau" (*Glen Cove Record*, January 28, 1932). Although the organization was short-lived, Petroccia's political career was just beginning.

An activist lawyer, Petroccia won renown among local Italians after successfully winning reinstatement for fifteen municipal employees who had been summarily dismissed by a newly-elected Republican administration in 1934. Although a Republican himself, he did not hesitate to speak out in behalf of fairness to these Italian American employees who had been hired by the previous Democratic administration. Ironically, his stalwart defense of fellow Italians was like a two-edged sword—effective in winning the deep loyalty of the ethnic group, it also was resented by non-Italians when he ran for higher office. Nevertheless, such a record of exemplary public service clearly merited consideration for mayor of Glen Cove. Indulging himself in that ambition, he entered the race at the wrong time—he would now have to try to gain the Republican nomination against a popular incumbent, Mayor Mason, in the Republican primary. It was a formidable and ultimately futile challenge, but one in which he would show his mettle. That he had the "Italian vote" was a foregone conclusion, although he asked his fellow-ethnics to consider not the nationality but only the issues when they exercised their vote. Petroccia enlisted support other than the city's Italian Americans as indicated in his vigorous showing in the *Glen Cove Record-Advance*—a surprising result considering that he possessed neither an organization nor was a declared candidate at the time of the poll.

In addition, Petroccia gained the endorsement of the newspaper.

> Mr. Petroccia shows an unusual grasp of the affairs of the city. His platform is constructive and we believe he is sincere in his pledge to carry out its provisions if nominated and elected. He has given us his assurance that if elected he will not favor any group or individual within the city...A few of Mr. Petroccia's critics have objected to the fact that he is of Italian extraction and that he might, if elected, favor job-seekers who are of Italian extraction. He is proud of his Italian ancestry. But Mr. Petroccia is an American by birth and citizenship and proud of both. Mayor LaGuardia, of New York, a man of Italian extraction, has made a great mayor, courageous, sympathetic to the masses of people, conspicuously honest. Mr. Petroccia has expressed himself so clearly on the subject of favoritism to groups and individuals that we are convinced that no one need fear that he would favor any one section of the people more than any other (*Glen Cove Record-Advance*, August 17, 1939).

Mason won the September primary in a victory attributed to several influences including his personal popularity, the efficient Republican organizational support, incumbency, the absence of corruption and a recognizable name. Of the eight election districts in the city, Petroccia won only two, the 3rd (by 250 to 47) and the 8th (by 147 to 98), both of which were in the heart of the Italian areas (*Glen Cove Record*, September 21, 1939). Interestingly, his slate fared fairly well in an intra-party struggle for committeemen.

What they failed to gain prior to the 1940s, Glen Cove Italian Americans succeeded in attaining in the immediate post World War II period—political achievement. It began with Luke A. Mercadante, a product of the Orchard who attended St.Patrick's Elementary School, Glen Cove High School, Auburn University and the University of Georgia Law School. Admitted to the bar in 1939, he worked in the office of a Nassau County judge until he enlisted for Officer's Training School. Even while away on military assignment he maintained ties to his old neighborhood. In 1945 he was nominated to run as Democratic candidate for city judge while still on military duty in Italy. Although as an absentee candidate he lost the race, he gained increased popularity which would benefit him later. Upon discharge, he returned home and was promptly appointed to the Glen Cove School Board in 1946. His activity in a number of civic organizations and his outspoken stand on city affairs propelled him to a prominent role among city Democrats who nominated him for mayor in 1947 (*Newsday*, July 4, 1976; Interview, Joseph Suozzi). A quiet, mild-mannered and analytical man, he launched a vigorous campaign, attempting to visit all voters, and attacked his opponent for raising home assessments. He was not given much chance for victory, however, since he was facing an incumbent mayor who also possessed the advantage of Republican registration plurality. Mercadante's nineteen vote margin of victory was regarded as a signficant upset in a year in which county Republicans generally had little difficulty winning office. The victory filled Mercadante with understandable pride—he was the first Italian American nominated and elected mayor; in addition, he had defeated a man for whom he had caddied as a youngster.

One of the first actions Mercadante took upon becoming mayor was to appoint Angelo Martone to succeed him on the Board of Education. For Martone this was the beginning of a thirteen year board tenure including board president. In subsequent years Martone was to become a major factor in Democratic Party councils in Glen Cove and Nassau County. As a Democratic mayor, Mercadante engaged in a tug of war within the five member city council dominated by four Republicans.

By the summer of 1949 Glen Cove's political pot was boiling again in anticipation of the coming mayoral elections. Republicans and Democrats denounced each other in predictable fashion and rumors were rampant about the impact of the ethnic vote.

A typical Glen Cove donnybrook, Republicans and a city newspaper leveled charges of "do-nothingism" at Mercadante. All of this proved of no avail as he scored an impressive victory in leading Democrats to a sweep of the city administration. Unlike 1947, when he could count on only one council member for support, he now helped carry four Democrats into office. Almost half of his 700 vote plurality was achieved in the solidly Italian Orchard (3rd Election District) where he trounced his opponent by a 500 to 174 edge. One of those he brought in with him was Joseph Suozzi, who as city judge constituted another Italian American destined to make a major impact in local and county politics.

Mercadante's great re-election triumph had county-wide political reverberations. He was now under Democratic consideration for nomination for Congress which, however, he turned down preferring instead the Democratic nomination for Attorney General of New York State in the 1950 statewide elections. An ambitious goal indeed, he was to be disappointed and had to settle for local campaign manager for the statewide Democratic candidates. The resultant Republican victory in 1950 proved a setback for Mercadante, encouraging his critics to comment that now he would have more time to tend to his job as mayor "instead of gadding about the county, state and country in a hunt for one of the big state or national offices he appears to believe is in his grasp..." (*Glen Cove Record*, November 9, 1960).

Mercadante's decision not to run for re-election as mayor in 1951 left the field open to two other Italian Americans. The Democrats endorsed Giuseppe Nigro, the self-made businessman with a long record of community activism and then Commissioner of Public Works. Nigro brought to the fore the virtue of industriousness which led to his economic and social upward mobility. Although a previous loser in a contest for public office, his record also included tenures as City Assessor, member of the Glen Cove Zoning Board and Commissioner of Public Works. He called for modernization of the city facilities and emphasized the need to commit oneself to a hard work ethic.

Republicans nominated Joseph A. Stanco, scion of one of the oldest Italian American clans in the city, with fourteen years of government experience as Deputy Commissioner and Commissioner of Public Works and Building Inspector. Stanco was popular and, what was especially more important to the Republican leadership, his candidacy held out the promise that the party could split the Orchard, an imperative for victory. The main reservation against his nomination was that he had joined in a business partnership with Angelo J. Martone, president of the Board of Education, a leading Democrat and erstwhile advisor to Mercadante. However, concern over the business arrangement was muted by realization that Stanco and Martone were also brothers-in-law. Thus, in 1951, there occurred in the city of Glen Cove a near emulation of what transpired in New York City in 1950 when Italian-born candidates Vincent Impellitteri, Edward Corsi and Ferdinand Pecora ran for mayor. Now, one year later, two of its own Italian Americans ran for the Long Island city's highest post. But the Long Island contest was even more interesting in that Nigro and Stanco were themselves brothers-in-law. Stanco was victorious as over 90 percent of the electorate voted and endorsed him by a heavy margin of 2,720 to 1,230 for Nigro. Even the 3rd Election District, upon which Nigro harbored high hopes because of his past identification with Italian American activities, went for Stanco by a 292 to 176 margin (*Glen Cove Record*, December 1, 1951). In 1953 Stanco won re-election although by diminished margins.

Launching Pad to Higher Office

By the mid-1950s, Glen Cove Democratic Italian American leaders enlarged their political horizons. Mercadante, apparently unable to resist the excitement of political frays, waged a serious effort to become the Nassau County Democratic leader in 1952, a contest which, had it been successful, would have made him the first Italian American to hold that position. Failing in this attempt Mercadante returned to the confines of Glen Cove politics in which he remained active for a number of years.

Angelo J. Martone was next to try to gain a powerful niche in county Democratic ranks, receiving consideration for the position of delegate and party leader in 1956 (*Glen Cove Record*, June 18, July 9, 1953). Coming close, he too failed and likewise returned to the familiar terrain of Glen Cove politics (*Glen Cove Record*, May 1, 1956; January 10, 1957).

Perhaps the most brilliant of Glen Cove's political products of Italian descent was Joseph Suozzi, from Ruvo del Monte in the province of Potenza. Joseph emigrated to the United States with his family, which first settled in East Harlem. In the 1920s, the family moved to Glen Cove, where his father worked on an estate. A Harvard Law School graduate, Joseph's interest in politics was of long standing. His political orientation was fueled, no doubt, by the color and excitement of electioneering at the Orchard House and growing familiarity with local political figures.

After graduation from law school in 1949, Joseph joined a law partnership with Mercadante and one year later took the first step toward elective office by becoming the Democratic nominee for City Judge, a move which immediately raised the issue of age. Republicans considered him presumptuous because of his youth, while his supporters argued that he was indeed qualified, his youth notwithstanding (*Glen Cove Record*, November 1, 1949). Victorious by a 2,785 to 2,133 vote, he overwhelmingly defeated his opponent in the 3rd and 8th Election Districts, where he campaigned in Italian, by margins of 514 to 128 and 510 to 226, respectively, proving how decisive the "Italian vote" was (*Glen Cove Record*, November 10, 1949).

In 1955 Joseph Suozzi decided to run for mayor of Glen Cove by challenging popular incumbent Mayor Joseph Stanco. Resigning his judgeship, Suozzi won as a result of an aggressive and well-informed campaign. As mayor he championed the cause of urban renewal, a movement which was then attracting national attention as older cities strove to renew aging downtown centers. Advocating local urban renewal, Suozzi won praise for initiating the "boldest step" taken by the city in 300 years. In addition, he called for the purchase of more beachfront for recreation, a shopper's mall and new highways, among other things. His success in governing the city and in winning re-election in 1957 rendered him one of the hottest Democratic properties around. Anxious to field a County Executive candidate who enjoyed current extensive favorable notoriety, as well as a man who could hold out appeal to the increased county Italian American electorate, the Democratic Party nominated him for County Executive, the first of his nationality to be so honored. That the Italian American community was quick to recognize the development was evident in the action of one ethnic organization which readily made him a recipient of a Distinguished Citizenship Award, a distinction which it previously extended exclusively to Republican figures. It was bound to be an uphill battle, however, since a Democratic had never won the post and in view of the long-standing Republican stronghold on county politics. This indeed became the key issue Suozzi addressed during his campaign. The final results went as expected: Suozzi lost, but he surprised political pundits by his relative strength in garnering many more votes than had been predicted.

In 1959, with support from a Glen Cove daily which previously had not endorsed him, Suozzi ran for mayor the third time in a bruising race which was termed the most bitter in the history of the city. He defeated Judge Aaron Cohen, his Republican opponent, by a margin of 4,737 to 3,965—a plurality of 772 of which the Orchard supplied 333 (the 3rd Election District vote was 469 to 136 in his favor), thereby vindicating the view that the ethnic vote would be a decisive factor (*Glen Cove Record*, October 29, 1959). Suozzi did not complete the term, however, because in 1960 he was nominated for a State Supreme Court judgeship. "He topped all candidates in the race for Supreme Court and ran up the biggest vote and plurality ever received by any candidate in Glen Cove's history when he received 6,682, votes about 2,600 more votes than those of his closest competitors (*Glen Cove Record*, November 10, 1960). Upon completion of his term on the State Supreme Court he was appointed to the New York Appellate Court where he remained for two years before he resigned to return to private practice as a principal partner in one of the most influential law firms in the county.

Mercadante and Suozzi's careers illustrate Glen Cove's emergence as a launching pad for the careers of local Italian American politicians. The unique municipality structure and an assured position on the Nassau County Board of Supervisors rendered the mayor's office with a sizeable influence— far in excess of Glen Cove's proportion of the county population. Control of local politics, therefore, assured Italian Americans power in the political affairs of the entire county, an opportunity which they would make the most of from the early 1940s on, and in some cases even earlier. Much of this was through the Democratic Party as in the cases of Nigro, Mercadante, Joseph and Vincent Suozzi, Andrew DiPaola and Angelo J. Martone.

Andrew DiPaola, relative newcomer to Glen Cove, emulated the career of Joseph Suozzi. As mayor, DiPaola exercised energetic leadership in the area of better local housing, calling for a new city charter and the building of a marina and a recreation facility. He also had to contend with emerging racial strife as the city's black population took a more militant stance in demanding an end to discrimination and better housing facilities. DiPaola scored a significant victory when he swept his opponent by a huge 2,000 vote margin.

DiPaola's impressive victory won the attention of Nassau Democrats who nominated him for County Executive in 1970, thereby trying to blunt the Republican appeal to Italian Americans who had chosen Ralph Caso for the office. Once again a local Democrat was chosen the county nominee for the highest county office and once again the Glen Cove Democratic nominee faced an uphill battle. Caso was a seasoned and well-known politician who had served with distinction for many years as Presiding Supervisor of the Town of Hempstead, the largest township in the county. In addition, Caso had behind him the well-oiled efficient Republican machine under Joseph Margiotta. Although DiPaola won many endorsements, he subsequently lost to Caso by a vote of 235,000 to 277,000 (*New York Times*, April 5, 1970). The

Glen Cove Democrat did, however, run and win the mayoralty race for the city for a third term in 1971, a position held until 1972 when he received bipartisan endorsement and was elected State Supreme Court Judge (*Glen Cove Record*, August 3, 1972).

Although Joseph Suozzi had long been active in politics, his brother Vincent did not gravitate toward the same in his youth. Vincent had established a successful accounting practice in Glen Cove when politics began to whet his appetite in the early 1960s. When DiPaola resigned the mayoralty to assume his seat on the State Supreme Court, the Glen Cove Democratic city council named Vincent Suozzi to finish out his term. With strong support from the Italian areas where he campaigned in Italian, he then ran and won the mayoralty three consecutive times, increasing his margin of victory on each occasion. Interpreting the results as a mandate, he proceeded with a multimillion dollar urban renewal program and fostered a bid for charter revision to replace the 50 year old municipal framework—a proposal which had been defeated previously (*Newsday*, November 9, 1977). Under the proposal the old commission form of government whereby council members were elected at large and thereby exercised control over major departments of city operations would now be replaced by a full-time mayor having effective control over all departments. This would leave the six council members with strictly legislative functions. Surprising political observers, Suozzi successfully engineered the charter revision. Thus, it was a stunning shock for him to lose the 1979 race for mayor to relative newcomer Alan Parente (*Newsday*, November 8, 1978).

Parente was the sixth member of the ethnic group to be elected to the office since 1947—a period during which, with the exception of a few years, the ethnic group maintained its grip on city administrations. Parente had come to public attention primarily because of his battle to prevent personnel from the Russian government estate within the city from using city recreation facilities unless it paid its proportionate share of city taxes. The issue took on international proportions with involvement by members of the United States State Department. In 1983 Vincent Suozzi once again won election as mayor of Glen Cove thereby affirming an ongoing predominance of the Suozzis in Glen Cove local politics.

To a lesser extent Republican Italian Americans utilized the city political base for advancement in county positions as in the case of Joseph Stanco who, after his tenure as mayor, was appointed Deputy Superintendent of Building Maintenance for Nassau County. In the 1960s, Pascucci brothers made quite an impact on Glen Cove politics and also came to the attention of county political chieftians. Ernest was elected City Commissioner of Public Works in 1961, assuming a task at which he performed most diligently. At election time the Pascucci brothers, identical twins, showed their innovativeness by hitting on a novel campaign technique—while Ernest was campaigning in one end of town, his twin John made speeches in the other with the electorate unaware that there were two different people, and marveling at Ernest's ability to cover so much ground so quickly. Ernest was re-elected to his post several times and thereby propelled himself into a prime position for the Republican mayoralty nomination —a dream never to be realized. Meanwhile John was making his own mark. A friendly, affable and considerate man, he became chairman of the Glen Cove Republican organization.

PORT WASHINGTON REPUBLICANS

Albert DeMeo stands out as the first Port Washington Italian American to make a major dent in politics. Born in 1898 and a product of local schools, he was the first of his nationality to graduate from Port Washington High School. He received a law degree from Fordham University and won a reputation as a friend of the Italian people. Winning the attention of Republicans, he was appointed Assistant District Attorney for Nassau County in 1928. He remained in that post for ten years during which time he promoted Republican candidates before Nassau County's Italian American electorate.

In the post-war period a number of local Italian-Americans obtained important political posts. One example is Alphonse N. LaPera. By 1950, LaPera was emerging as a major political figure with his election to the Port Washington Police Commission. A Republican, LaPera became a Port Washington resident and community activist, an Assistant District Attorney, and North Hempstead Town councilman. He capped off his career in 1964 as a District Court Judge, subsequently winning re-election with bipartisan support.

Still another Italian American active in Port Washington politics was Joseph Guarino. In the 1980s, a young, articulate lawyer, emerged as a figure within Port Washington's Italian American community. A relative newcomer to the area, he has come to know the vibrancy and potential that exists among ethnic people for an aspiring politician (Interview, Joseph Guarino). He was the youngest appointed town attorney for the Town of North Hempstead. Although originally not ethnically oriented, he soon learned of the rich Italian background of Port Washington and immersed himself deeply into ethnic, civic and political affairs, becoming venerable of the Marino Sons of Italy Lodge and, in 1981, an elected Republican member of the North Hempstead Town Council.

COPIAGUE POLITICS

Italian American involvement in Copiague politics traversed a slow, gradual path. As an unincorporated village, Copiague afforded little opportunity for participation in politics at the level of village municipal government. However, there were other outlets for those with political aspirations—appointive or elective positions within the Town of Babylon government.

The first Copiague Italian Americans to hold elective office in the township were Republicans Charles Barcellona and Joseph Colicchio, who in 1925 and 1931 were elected constables. Designation to these law enforcement offices suggests attempts to keep under submission a growing ethnic minority with people of their own background and culture—a revealing comment on where the host society saw the entry level of the relative newcomers. Robert Curcio was the most important political figure to surface from the ranks of Italian American Copiaguers. Despite his lack of formal higher education, he entertained high aspirations. His appointment as the Secretary of the Suffolk County Republican Committee in 1955, placed the young man in a high post which provided him with the opportunity to exercise leverage for greater political influence. Successful management of G.O.P. campaigns in his area quickly attracted the attention of his colleagues who named him Babylon Town Republican leader in 1964. In 1966, he reached the pinnacle of political goals by being elected to the chairmanship of the Suffolk County Republican organization—the first of his nationality to achieve such an elevated position in the history of the county.

The prestigious position which he had gained was of great moment not only to Robert and his family, but also to Italian Americans and Copiaguers. For years, Americans of Italian descent had complained of being ignored by the Babylon Town Board, a frustration that finally could be surmounted. Thus, they saw Robert Curcio's rise to power as a coming of age of themselves politically. Prior to Curcio, no Copiaguers of whatever nationality had ever achieved such an important political post; his elevation would now usher all Copiaguers into the limelight previously denied them.

The Italian American political leader's rise in Republican circles did not go unchallenged, especially his elevation to county chairman. The pattern of opposition within the party revealed feelings of discomfort with the Marconiville "upstart" and reluctance on the part of older incorporated villages to give up power to the newer unincorporated hamlets.

As 1967 dawned, Robert Curcio was riding high. Backed by the Suffolk County Republican organization he strongly supported Nelson Rockefeller as the next Republican candidate for the presidency.

Curcio was still faced with an opposition within Republican ranks that remained fairly muted so long as he produced winners, but destined to become loud in the event of setbacks. Curcio's 1967 choice of Gilbert Hanse who lost the race for Suffolk County Executive proved his undoing.

WESTBURY POLITICS

Westbury Italians absorbed the prevailing Republican political philosophy, aware that power and patronage were in the hands of that party. Because they sought the attainment of these concrete objectives, members of the ethnic group overwhelmingly enrolled as party members. Such identification held out not only the possibility of a desirable government post for some, but also the promise of favorable consideration for those whose businesses stood to prosper by cooperating with the ruling political element.

Following some abortive efforts, political success was to come to local Italian Americans in the person of Dominick Piscitelli, when in his second effort he was elected Republican Committeeman—a feat which surprised political pundits since he succeeded in defeating a well-entrenched Republican figure. At the same time, a few others who ran for office made impressive showings even though they did not gain election. Republican party loyalty apparently was stronger than ethnic loyalty in the 1939 election for the Town of North Hempstead as an Italian American Democratic candidate elicited no more support among Westbury Italians than did other Democratic candidates.

As the second half of the century unfolded, Dominick Piscitelli continued as the pre-eminent Italian American political figure in Westbury. Active in ethnic organizations and community affairs for years, he was elected mayor of the village in 1974. Piscitelli was an excellent example of an individual spawned by the ethnic community. His career demonstrates that committment and devotion to ethnic roots served to improve the quality of life not only for members of the ethnic group, but also for mainstream society. Significantly, when Piscitelli retired in the early 1980s, he was succeeded by Ernest Strada, the third consecutive Italian American to be elected mayor of Westbury.

OVERVIEW

As the foregoing indicates, the limited political experience which Italians brought with them to the United States proved to be a temporary problem. In the generally more receptive suburban atmosphere where they were able to achieve economic security and become minor businessmen apparently more quickly than did their counterparts in the pressure-laden tenements of the cities, Long Island Italian Americans of the first generation, even with scant formal education and limited financial means, were able to enter the political arena and wield power and influence in surprising numbers. They learned the lessons of participatory democracy in a relatively short time and set the groundwork for their better educated and more financially secure children to follow. Their immigrant roots and ethnic organizations served to make them aware of the political culture of which they now were a part and taught them to forge ethnic political organizations which served as entering wedges into the prevailing political systems. This background enabled them to translate political potential into meaningful power in various suburban villages and municipalities so that by the 1960s they were beginning to contend for major county-wide offices which brought them to the attention of the entire suburban populace, not merely the Little Italies.

With the elevation of Thomas Gulotta and Michael LoGrande to the positions of County Executives of Nassau and Suffolk Counties respectively, early in 1987, it could be asserted that Long Island Italian Americans had indeed arrived politically. For a people who entered the suburbs with limited political experience, their rise constitutes a study in how recent immigrant groups have become acculturated and absorbed into the dynamics of American politics even while retaining a sense of ethnic identity.

CHAPTER SIXTEEN
COMMUNITIES IN CHANGE

Change is a concomitant of American social life affecting the daily experiences of all groups. History has recorded the phenomenon of ethnic succession in urban neighborhoods which has seen older nationality groups supplanted by newer accretions to city populations. What of the suburbs; specifically, what of the Italian enclaves in suburbia? Do they continue to endure as in former eras? Do they still constitute discrete embodiments of subcultures that warrant classification as ethnic entities? Have institutions that served Long Island communities become anachronistic? Have these institutions undergone significant change? Have suburban Italian American communities experienced difficulties with other, newer groups in their midst? In a word, how have suburban Italian Americans dealt with the dynamism of contemporary change? These are some of the questions which will be explored in this chapter.

For more than a century Italian Americans have resided in Long Island. Commencing with small numbers in the 1880s, and constituting only a fraction of the Italian immigrant flow which migrated heavily into the central cities, Italians established enclaves on Long Island by the turn of the century. These enclaves evolved into distinctive ethnic-oriented communities even while they interacted with the host society and gained wider acceptance. However, just as in the central cities, the disappearance of the first immigrant generation, the influx of new racial and ethnic groups and the competition for economic and political power has had its negative effects. At its worst these changes have convulsed Long Island ethnic communities, producing trauma and discord.

TRAUMA OF CHANGING NEIGHBORHOODS: INWOOD

A relatively recent development affecting the Inwood Italian community stands as a monument to governmental blunder when, in the name of progress, it destroyed an old but thriving and vibrant ethnic area. In a flush of euphoria and optimism in 1960, New York State Department of Transportation experts inaugurated plans for the extension of a local road requiring the purchase and destruction of a number of houses in the Italian neighborhood in the path of the road project. Many years of protests proved futile as the work of demolition proceeded. But what followed was a true travesty as the drying up of state funds precluded further operations, leaving a big ditch marked by empty lots and overgrown grass (*Nassau Herald*, January 16, 1964; March 13, 1968; February 1, 1973). Nearly a quarter of a century later the only noticeable improvement was the 1984 opening of a senior citizen complex sponsored by the Rockville Centre Catholic Diocese. The break-up of the neighborhood was a wrenching experience.

Apparently most dispossessed Italian Americans, especially those of middle age or younger, received compensation for their properties and either bought or built new homes in Inwood, and therein lies a relevant truth about the ethnic community—its staying power. Thus, despite the terrible blow to the community, despite instances of internal discord, despite a degree of outmigration, Italian American residents remain. Indeed, a number who have moved out have returned. The devotion of some is so strong that the thought of moving away does not even enter their minds. As of 1980, Italian Americans constituted 40 percent of Inwood's total population. Thus, nearly a century after they began to enter the hamlet, Americans of Italian descent represent the largest single ethnic group in the community. The handful of turn-of-the-century first generation immigrants together with large numbers of second, third and fourth generations remain and thus so does the unique Italian American ambience of Inwood.

Contemporary Inwood presents a paradoxical picture. It is strongly defended by the second generation as an identifiable Italian town, a decent place in which they are content to live. Indeed, former residents wax nostalgically about life in the community, harboring memories of a warm, lively ethnic enclave of a simpler yesteryear. On the other hand there are many others who have disquieting reservations: the movement of old-time residents who, with affluence, exit for more desireable neighborhoods. Thus, compared to its wealthier sister communities in the Five Towns, Inwood continues to evoke images of a lower socioeconomic standard.

INTER-ETHNIC CONTENTION

The most serious recent problem affecting social order was race riots which plagued Inwood and its environs in the early 1970s. Ostensibly white versus black confrontations, they were also Italian American-black struggles. For years many young Italian American Inwood students experienced a sense of inferiority upon entering Lawrence High School where the two large ethnic groups are Jews and blacks. To move from Inwood's elementary schools, which were neighborhood institutions whose faculty had long-time acquaintance with the immediate area and its largely Italian families, to the non-neighborhood junior and/or senior high schools could be a jarring experience. At Lawrence High School, for example, the young Italian American student no longer functioned in the relatively hermetically sealed ethnic world of his childhood. He would now be confronted with people of other cultures, predominantly Jewish, in the Five Towns. Their frustration revolved around a perception that the school atmosphere, while accommodating to Jewish students, proved less congenial to Italian Americans and ironically led to squabbles with blacks—the other poor people in the vicinity. "While resentment of the more affluent members of the community grows, very often a derisiveness between the poorer groups breeds a hatred and a racism that makes working together impossible (*Nassau Herald*, March 5, 1970). Lack of leadership, a generation gap between the youngsters and more recently-arrived Italian immigrant parents, and poor articulation between school authorities and the Italian immigrant element exacerbated alienation in the early 1970s. This was an estrangement expressed through voiced sentiments that Italian Americans were being treated as second class citizens and that the school district provided few role models for them. Whether the changes were in fact valid is perhaps less important than the fact that they were deeply felt perceptions which therefore contributed to malaise in the community.

By 1973 an effort to counter the discord was underway in the school district via the promotion of bilingual education, including the first Italian-English bilingual program funded by the United States Office of Education. A Community Action Program with funding from Nassau County was instituted to foster studies about ethnic group relations between Italian Americans and blacks, even providing summer stipends while studying its ethnic heritages with each other (*Nassau Herald*, September 29, 1974; American Italian Historical Association, *Newsletter*, Summer 1972). Apparently these programs, together with a less volatile atmosphere, helped bring about more community stability.

WESTBURY'S CHANGING SCHOOL POPULATION

Changing ethnic patterns of the 1960s and 1970s which witnessed a rapid growth of blacks in New Cassel, near Westbury, has resulted in a Westbury Public School system which has become 50 percent black. Although the private schools in the area have always had a large enrollment, their numbers have swollen as increasing numbers of non-white minorities entered the public school system. These developments, have, in turn, placed strains on relations between the various ethnic groups locally, raising questions as to the community's ability to cope with the issue of integration. On at least one occasion altercations between black and Italian American students forced the closing of both Westbury junior and senior high schools. As unpleasant as were these incidents, it would be erroneous to conclude that Westbury Italian Americans joined in a mass exodus from the local public schools. Thus, a substantial portion of the public school student population remains Italian American.

FRICTION IN EAST PATCHOGUE AND NORTH BELLPORT

Interracial violence afflicted Patchogue and North Bellport during the 1960s and 1970s as a result of trying to accommodate the growing population of blacks and Hispanics. The result of the discord forced the Bellport High School to close for two extended periods and led to the retirement of the school principal and the appointment of James Gerardi as his replacement. Although contemporary descriptions of the internal turmoil stressed a black versus white confrontation, the reality of the demographic complexion rendered it virtually synonomous with black versus Italian American. Fortunately, succeeding years saw a lessening of racial tensions and informants placed little importance on the situation a decade later.

These examples of friction should not be interpreted as reflecting widespread, universal situations, but rather as unusual extreme scenarios which afflicted some, but not all Long Island Italian enclaves. For most residents of the Italian ethnic neighborhoods it is the changes in community institutions which served them and their forebears which is most notable.

END OF SETTLEMENT HOUSE

The impact of change was to affect community institutions of long-standing such as the settlement house in Glen Cove. The efforts of an Italian American director who worked hard at continuing to offer the facilities for community activities proved unavailing. By 1950 it was clear that interest in the Orchard House was declining and the decaying building was becoming a burden. The hard truth was the Orchard House was bereft of sufficient neighborhood support, thus resulting in a decision to demolish it.

CHANGING TRADITIONAL ITALIAN SOCIETIES AND CUSTOMS

Although the original St.Rocco Mutual Aid Society of Glen Cove, with a few remaining members sharing the balance of the funds, was terminated in the

1960s, it was succeeded by a new St.Rocco Society minus the mutual aid features. It is concerned exclusively with months of planning the feast of St.Rocco to assure continuation of one of the largest events of its kind in contemporary Long Island. Its continued success notwithstanding, the festival has become controversial in recent years because of numerous complaints over the days and hours involved and the congestion and noise accompanying it. What originated as a two-day festival has now become a six-day endurance test for homes which border the church site. The noise factor over an extended period has, in fact, split the community with advocates of the festival on the one hand vociferous in its support because of the successful fund-raising results, while on the other hand opponents argue in favor of curtailment of the festival. Inevitably it has produced a dilemma for many long-time residents, including Mayor Vincent Suozzi, formerly an ardent supporter of the feast (*Newsday*, January 23, 1985).

DECLINE OF ETHNIC PARISHES

Changing demographics and changing times have also impinged on traditional modes of religious worship. Whereas defacto national parishes served many Italian suburban communities in the first half of the twentieth century, the uniqueness of ethnic identity eroded in the second half. While parishes like Our Lady of Good Counsel, Our Lady of the Assumption and Our Lady of Mount Carmel functioned as quasi-ethnic parishes in the earlier period, by the end of the 1960s they no longer were so regarded and indeed were integrated into the traditional geographic parish structure of the Rockville Centre Diocese. The transition of Patchogue's Our Lady of Mount Carmel under Father Raphael Monteleone, the last Italian American pastor of the parish, is a case in point. Father Monteleone, a Calabrian-born veteran priest, was chosen pastor of Our Lady of Mount Carmel in 1953. Although of a much lower profile than his predecessor, Father Monteleone was genuinely interested in the daily activities of his people and succeeded in retaining many parish traditions. However, as the 1960s unfolded it became abundantly clear to him that significant demographic and social changes were making an impact on the area.

To accommodate the needs of the burgeoning mix of nationalities required two significant changes. First was the need for a more comodious church; second, the need to change the very tenor and texture of the parish. Unable to obtain sufficient land on the site of the old church grounds for new buildings, Father Monteleone purchased ten acres of land at a new location more than a mile from the Waverly Avenue "Hill" area where he caused to be constructed a church-auditorium with seating capacity for 1,050, plus room for another 1,000 in the basement. In 1984, a chapel and a religious instruction center were added to make it southern Suffolk's largest and most modern plant, much in keeping with the automobile-oriented suburban society it serves. But the old ethnic flavor is gone. The old Italian worshippers who used to walk to weekday masses in the mornings when the church was located on Waverly Avenue found the new location too distant. The older generation, furthermore, is dying, a phenomenon which led to the end of parish events previously regarded as eternal fixtures.

Father Monteleone retired to Florida at the age of 70; Father Alexander Sledzous, his successor, is of Polish background. None of the current assistant pastors are of Italian ancestry. Accordingly, the altering of the ethnic texture of the parish has occurred. In 1966, Our Lady of Mount Carmel ceased being an Italian national parish, taking its position as a traditional geographic-based parish. The story of transition from ethnic to geographic diocesan parish life also quite accurately portrays the development of St.Joseph the Worker parish in East Patchogue. Thus, while the transplanted religious mentality succored immigrants and their progeny for a few decades, the era was over by the 1960s. Nonetheless, the Italian element in both parishes still predominates. Utilizing the names of requested announced masses as a guide, Father Sledzous estimates that at least half of his congregation is of Italian background.

Another example of changing parishes is Inwood's Our Lady of Good Counsel. After the tenure of Father Agius, the pastors no longer were of Italian nationality. In 1958, for example, Father Galloway became pastor, to be succeeded in 1976 by Father Raymond Davis, the current pastor. Father Galloway's tenure was not without controversy which reached a peak in the fall and winter of 1970. The intra-parish embroglio centered around a decision, rendered in November by the sisters who had been staffing Our Lady of Good Counsel Parochial School to terminate their services—a step which forced the school to close and angered many parishioners. It was not enough to assuage aggrieved parents. Despite much rancor, the decision stayed (*Nassau Herald*, November 12, 1970). The action has some fallout in promoting disillusionment and redirection of religious impulse.

By the middle of the 1960s it seemed that the narrowly Italian phase of Copiague's Our Lady of the Assumption parish life was also gone. The passing away of the first generation of immigrants, the absence of replenishment of new waves of Italian immigrants and the influx of non-Italians presaged a new era. A succession of Italian priests, lasting for almost four decades from 1929, was followed by a non-Italian pastor in 1967 and it has been that way since, although Italian assistant pastors continue to serve the parish. Never an actual national parish in the technical sense, although it performed almost as one for many years, from the mid-1960s it became integrated into the traditional diocesan regional/ geographic system.

The recounting of changing institutions underscores the truism that normal evolutionary processes have impacted Long Island Italian neighborhoods. It can be said that these experiences constitute, in essence, a maturation of the ethnic neighborhoods from discernible, semi-isolated and compartmentalized places to demographic entities which reflect ethnic group accommodation and continue to flourish not only because of the dynamics of the neighborhoods, but also because of continued replenishment from the old country. Westbury offers the best example of the phenomenon of re-invigoration because of a sustained immigration flow from the original town and province sources.

ON-GOING IMMIGRATION

Post World War II migration patterns constituted largely a replay of the phenomena of the late nineteenth and early twentieth centuries. Thus, immigrants continued to come to Westbury from Durazzano prompted by the same motivations of economic betterment and the improvement of family positions.

That there is continued contact between Westbury Italian Americans and Italy is evident in the realization that there are more people from Durazzano living in the Long Island village than there are residents in the Italian parent town. Some recent immigrants of Sicilian background observe that because of the Durazzanesi preference for socializing with their own kind, newcomer Italians do not easily gain entry into the "inner circle" of Italian American life in the community. The manifestation of provincial preference appears to be more enduring in the suburbs than in the large cities. It can be attributed to longevity and endurance of suburban enclaves like that of Westbury, and to a lesser degree of provincial heterogeneity experienced there as compared to big urban centers.

RETAINING ETHNICITY IN SUBURBIA

The Italian Americans of Westbury as a whole are proud of their heritage and identify strongly as Italians. Italian societies continue to flourish with membership from newly-arrived as well as those from the third generation. For example, St.Anthony's Society became the third village Italian organization in 1969, beginning as a women's group but now is co-ed. Its current president is Carmine Daddio, whose family has resided in Westbury for generations. Officially open to all Catholics regardless of ethnicity the overwhelming portion of society members are Italian Americans (Interview, Carmine Daddio).

In so much the same way that they have enriched and enobled city life in America, Italians in Westbury have had the cumulative effect of rendering the community at large more liveable. They play prominent roles in the religious, social, cultural and political lives of the village and indeed the county. Their children seek education on a par with the prevailing customs and now enter professions previously closed to them. They own their share of enterprises within the community and contribute to its well-being.

For Westbury's Italians, customs and traditions have undergone some changes as evidenced by adaptations to dress, styles, schooling, *etc.*, but in many other respects traditions of the old culture persist as in religion, family ties, ongoing ethnic associations, continuing contact with the old country and work patterns. The interesting thing about the work phenomenon among the ethnic group of today is that it is strikingly parallel to that of their parents and grandparents. Thus, to witness workers setting off for a day's work as landscapers either in businesses of their own or for others is to view a modern-day replication of an earlier generation. Of course, time and technology have resulted in some differences as in the mode of transportation, that is using cars or trucks rather than walking or bicycling. But the more striking difference is the realization that many of today's Westburyites who labor in landscaping are self-employed. Not a few of them, moreover, are in positions to hire fellow Italians recently emigrated from Durazzano.

The story of the Italians in Westbury is the story of a poor immigrant people entering a less than hospitable environment to work and improve their economic and social statuses. By laboring hard for their families and their community they have earned the respect of their fellow Westburyites. This is a story, furthermore, of an enterprising people receiving and responding to opportunity, a story of a people who maintain a steadfast adherence to their ethnic heritage and identity—a people which seek to retain contact with its ethnic roots. In this period of renewed fascination in the search for one's background, the Italians of Westbury have enjoyed a unique advantage because they do not have to venture far to strike responsive chords. The sources of their heritage abound in the community and they are available for them to delight in and to savor. They are also available for others to learn not only about the Westbury Italians, but also about the larger community. Much of what pertains in Westbury also pertains in Glen Cove.

LITTLE ITALY ENDURES IN GLEN COVE

Glen Cove in the 1980s remains a microcosm of a large city replete with 40 different nationality groups. The Italian element remains clearly the predominant one numerically as well as in many other respects. Recently-arrived Italian immigrants supplement the earlier comers and their descendants and seemingly thrive by means of the landscaping business. Nominally Catholic, the newcomer Italians present a picture of hardworking people whose aim is to amass quickly the funds necessary to purchase their own home.

Ethnic identity notwithstanding, assimilation has made its inexorable impact—a phenomenon which can be seen in intermarriage patterns in Glen Cove. Although precise statistics are not available, a reading of marriage announcements in the local press over the years leaves the distinct impression that whereas intra-ethnic marriages were the norm for Italian Americans in the 1920s to the World War II period, perceptible change followed the war with a discernible increase in inter-ethnic marriages. According to Father Della Rosa, current pastor of St.Rocco, the more-recently arrived Italian immigrants tend towards intra-ethnic marriage patterns with marriage rites in Italian, whereas the same if not true of the descendants of the earlier generations. As for the Italian American future in Glen Cove, reactions elicited are mixed. Some expect that the children of the recently-arrived will tend to remain community residents, while those of the third and fourth generations are likely to move away, especially after making an initial break by attendance at distant colleges. The Orchard continues to remain heavily Italian although blacks have moved into portions of it seemingly without incident. Ironically, for all their civic service to the community, few centers or buildings have been dedicated to Italian Americans—a reflection of the inability of the ethnic group to unite for this common purpose (*Port Washington News*, June, 1964).

Thus, Glen Cove's enclave endures—testimony to the deep roots planted by the immigrants who settled there in the 1880s and 1890s. People who had a deep respect for the soil, they also possessed an ethnic heritage which they passed on to their children.

While replenishment by third and fourth waves of immigrants were experienced by Westbury and Glen Cove, such was not the case in other suburban Italian enclaves. After the early pioneers, Copiague, for instance, did not witness an influx of northern Italian immigrants as those who came to swell the population in the 1950s and 1960s were predominantly of southern Italian background. All suburban communities have had to contend with the inevitability of change which was bound to alter fundamental characteristics of ethnic group life. Copiague is a case in point.

END OF MARCONIVILLE: BEGINNING OF SUBURBIA

The story of Marconiville, Copiague, is fascinating in many respects: the role of northern Italians in a suburban setting, the evocation of ethnic pride revolving around the fabled name of Marconi, the struggle against an unfriendly and at times hostile social climate, the evolution of a people to positions of social, cultural and political prominence and frequently economic well-being, even while retaining a distinctive ethnic ethos, all form part of the story. Copiague also reflects the impact of the sands of time—the transition from an exclusive ethnic enclave in a suburban hamlet to an increasingly cosmopolitan and variegated society. Although Italian Americans still predominate in what was formerly called Marconiville, they no longer are the only ethnic group in town. A mixture of nationalities is now a more accurate description of the community.

Where Italian names once monopolized, one now sees Hispanic names especially of Puerto Rican derivation, Polish and other nomenclatures throughout the community. While some of the old families continue to reside in the homes built by their parents and grandparents, a number of historic Copiague Italian American families are no longer present, having either passed away or relocated outside or the town. There are other signs of change. No longer called "Marconiville", the town does not denote any exclusively Italian milieu, nor are Italians concentrated in the area north of the railroad tracks as once was the case, since many of them have moved into the southern portions where they had been previously ostracized. Many have moved away altogether, with a sizeable group of older folks relocating in Florida.

However, there is still an Italian predominance in the community, as can be seen by the current membership of the fire department. While it is true that Our Lady of the Assumption parish is no longer strictly Italian—a fact acknowledged by the end to a succession of Italian American pastors—nevertheless, the Italian ethnic group still comprises the largest single nationality in the parish. Then, too, there are the street names which remain a constant evocation of an era when Italian immigrants dreamed of transplanting a way of life to a suburb of New York City. Resistance to American mores was, of course, never an issue, instead what occurred was a gradual assimilation ameliorated by the support of customs familiar to the Italian people. And so thousands of Italians entered more fully into American life through the Marconiville (Copiague) experience. Their descendents, although fewer in number and somewhat changed, continue the journey to the present.

BEING ITALIAN AMIDST SUBURBAN PLURALISM

As it approaches the 1990s, Port Washington remains a vibrant community not dominated by one ethnic group but rather a residential area for a multitude of nationalities and races including representatives from various familiar European cultures and the newer arrivals from the Caribbean and the Far East. Although accurate statistics are elusive the impression is that Americans of Italian descent continue to maintain a significant presence in the town—even though organizations like the Icanusa Society and the Italian Mutual Aid Society are extinct. The local Sons of Italy Lodge thrives as indicated by a three-fold increase in membership in recent years. Italian Americans, furthermore, increasingly participate in a myriad of functions and forms of recreation which are assimilationist in nature and to that extent have passed the earlier stage of acculturation. They seem to be straddling two cultures: those of the first generation maintain a strong sense of their ethnicity, while their progeny have become more assimilated without entirely losing their ethnic interests. For some the pull of assimilation was of such force that it led to a conscious decision to depart from the ethnic community. Thus, although somewhat removed from the immigrant generation, more highly educated than their forebears and more likely to intermingle with people of mixed ethnic backgrounds, most Italian Americans still manifest a genuine recognition and pride in their ethnic past. It remains to be seen whether this interest will persist in the long run; but for the present, a sense of Italianitá continues to be part of Port Washington's social fabric.

ITALIAN IDENTITY IN PATCHOGUE: TODAY AND TOMORROW

It would be useful to assess the staying power of Italian ethnicity after nearly a century in the greater Patchogue area. In this connection several questions arise. How strongly have Italian Americans retained their sense of ethnicity? Have they assimilated into the mainstream? Have they progressed significantly beyong the proletarian stage? Does a meaningful organizational life among the ethnic group still abound? Is there a discernible Italianicity? Answers to all these questions would obviously vary according to individual histories and perspectives.

From the research of scholar Francis Femminella, who studied the Patchogue community of the early 1960s, comes the observation that Italian cultural traditions still influence the community. "The most general conclusion that can be made on the basis of this study is that ethnicity does in fact influence individual behavior, self concepts, value orientations; conscious descriptions of ego ideals are all influenced by ethnicity" (Femminella, 1968). Thus, he asserts the early Italian settlers tended to remain in the original residences in Patchogue, with few returning to Italy as in other locales. For the most part they remained or moved to better residences nearby when economic circumstances permitted.

With Italian Americans currently representing 24.9, 32.5, 28.6 and 20.3 percent of Patchogue village, North Patchogue, East Patchogue and North Bellport, respectively, they constitute the largest of all ethnic groups in these communities (*United States Census*, 1980). That phenomenon notwithstanding, some thoughtful observer residents maintain that beginning in the 1960s, intermarriage and assimilation have led to group dispersion and an erosion of the ethnic identity so it no longer resembles the close-knit neighborhood of yesteryear. The support system for the old traditions have faded and the younger generation is caught up in the currents and influences of the prevailing period.

Italian immigrants to greater Patchogue came for the same reasons they emigrated to other parts of the United States—primarily because they perceived this a land of better economic opportunities—hopes which they would, for the most part, fulfill in the Long Island area through employment possibilities (For impact of economic forces on migration, *See*, di Leonardo). Assimilation and absorption of the predominant American culture has occurred largely without extreme pressures except for the intimidating Ku Klux Klan years of the 1920s. With respect to the importance of Italian heritage, one sees an overall dimunition although it varies from one generation to the next. Femminella, for example, saw the second generation place more emphasis on assimilation that the first. The third generation, which is probably the preponderant one currently, seems to have a greater sense of its heritage than the second "..even those living outside the immigrant residential settlement expressed deep concern for the maintenance of Italian institutions and felt it important that their culture be proud of their Italian ancestry" (Femminella, 1968). Italian organizational activity is reflected in the creation recently of organizations like the Prudenti Sons of Italy Lodge and the Italian American Service Club of Brookhaven. There is even evidence of ethnic pride on the part of some of the leaders of the younger generation.

While evidence of continuing interest in ethnic background is still discernible, there are other indications that Italian organizational life is largely history. Thus, one is confronted with a contradiction. While new ethnic organizations have been created, apparently all the old mutual aid societies are extinct. The ethnic exclusiveness of neighborhoods like "Blood Hill" is gone, although some old-time families still reside there. Perhaps most evident in measuring the decline of ethnicity is the realization that the traditional ethnic parish no longer exists. The transition of Our Lady of Mount Carmel to a geographic diocesan parish meant the virtual end of the heavy Italian dominance replete with Italian Masses, ethnic societies and characteristic feast day celebrations. Italian preponderance may continue to persist numerically in the parish but it no longer reflects an ethnic style. Thus, one is left with a sense that despite the distinctive Italian imprint on greater Patchogue for virtually a century, and despite the awareness that Americans of Italian descent still form a major portion of the population, the singular ethnic style and verve have faded.

This chapter has probed the issue of ethnic persistence and staying power of Long Island's Italian ethnic communities. A review of contemporary history indicates that some Italian enclaves have undergone their share of upheaval and modification which has so altered the demographic landscape as to minimize the Italian background of the areas. Even in the absence of radical, discernible changes, all Long Island Italian neighborhoods have experienced a maturation of characteristics that have rendered older community institutions obsolete. On the other hand the creation and development of new ethnic institutions is also a contemporary phenomenon and thus the case can be made that, although vastly altered, there is a corpus of suburban Italian Americana which survives. It is now time to summarize the import of this phenomenon.

CHAPTER SEVENTEEN
CONCLUSION

Now that several Long Island Italian American communities have been discussed at length the question arises as to whether a study of these suburbs can tell anything significant about other like communities. In many respects Long Island has, from early in the century, earned a reputation as the archetypical American suburbia and accordingly a demographic entity distinct from the urban life of New York City. These suburbs had an early attraction for people who loved being close to the land, people who yearned to raise their families in hospitable physical environments in their own homes. Small groups of Italian Americans, especially in the New York area, were part of this suburban history. They were also part of the growth and expansion of suburbia in the mid-twentieth century and currently form the largest single nationality bloc in proportion to the area's population. Insofar as Long Island served as the prototype for much of the nation which experienced an exodus from the central cities into the outlying areas, then the role of Italian Americans is indeed a relevant one. The way they shaped their lives in the midst of a suburban setting and were in turn influenced by their surroundings helps illuminate an issue of contemporary relevance—the question of whether the suburban experience has proven to be a less harsh, less difficult place to ascend from the bottom to the uppermost rungs of the socioeconomic success ladder.

What unfolded on Long Island may tell us much about what was experienced by new immigrant peoples in other parts of the country whose suburban growth in effect paralleled this area. To aver that this study of Long Island's Italian Americans provides us with valuable insights into the workings of suburban communities or immigrant peoples in the period under review is not to claim that Long Island was representative in any statistical sense. Rather, it is to say that these suburban communities were undergoing a process of transformation that eventually affected all American suburbs to some degree, and it is likely that there were important uniformities in the social consequences of suburbanization.

The purpose of this study, then, was to uncover and narrate the history of Italian Americans on Long Island by concentrating on several selected communities of long standing. Community is used in the sense that it refers to a social group whose members live in close proximity and who share a cultural and historical heritage. On the other hand the unitary view that all of the people studied were impoverished, proud of their heritage and tightly organized would be an exaggeration of the interactions, feelings and perceptions encompassed. This volume deals with the lives of thousands of obscure and some not so obscure people in several communities from the last part of the nineteenth century to the present. An analysis of their social histories serves a number of useful purposes such as that of dispelling certain myths or confirming widely held views about ethnic groups in suburbia. The study should help discern the differences between the dynamics of life in the city ethnic enclaves—the fast-paced, congested and stressful environment—and their more peaceful, relaxed and serene counterparts in suburbia which affirms Oscar Handlin's (1951) observation regarding the less alienating confrontation awaiting immigrants in small towns. It should assist also in tracing and evaluating the process of assimilation in these demographic settings, in the conceptualization of pluralism as a vital entity outside urban neighborhoods, in understanding the dynamics of interaction within ethnic institutions which played a role in making the transition from one culture to another. This study should further explicate how economic forces influenced occupational choices, residential choices, schooling, life-styles, *etc.* It should encourage one to evaluate success on the part of the immigrants, to acknowledge the immigrants contributions to the larger society, and to assess the status of the ethnic group in our times.

One truism that emerges from surveying the totality of the Long Island Italian American experience is the role of choice, that is, the exercise of option regarding settlement outside the congested city neighborhoods. A small but significant minority coming at the height of immigration and in contradistinction to the masses who sought their destinies in the cities, a number of Italian immigrants chose the suburbs. For those who opted for the suburbs, it constituted a conscious effort to satisfy an overwhelming desire to own their own homes, but it also represented an effort to live in residential environments which more closely resembled the lands from which they came, and thus helped to appease a yearning to live in familiar circumstances insofar as they could till the soil—although a few became permanent, full-time farmers. Most Long Island Italians worked the lands to supplement meager incomes and to accommodate that innate desire to maintain connections with the past. In growing vegetables and fruit, in raising chickens, fowl and pigs, they practiced a self-sufficiency which afforded them the comfort of recalling and comparing their present life with that of their youth in the old country.

The overwhelming majority of Italians on Long Island emigrated from small towns and villages, rather than from large Italian cities. They were, for the most part, from southern Italy or Sicily. The chain migration phenomenon which immigration historians have documented pertains here as well; in fact, in many respects it is startling to realize how insular and provincial this migration has been. The relatively closed Italian-Albanian community in Inwood, the equally tight Durazzano settlers in Westbury, and the heavy Calabrian migration to Patchogue and environs were so powerful that decades later other Italian Americans moving into those areas experienced resistance even to the point of exclusion. Coming from small towns in Italy and settling in familiar-sized communities on Long Island enabled them to cushion the shock of resettlement in the new country without having to endure the physical and psychological strains of big city life. The development of small to mid-sized ethnic communities in the Long Island towns also rendered more palatable the transition. The importance of settlement choices in suburbia is attested to by repeated responses elicited from informants as well as an awareness of the staying power that characterizes residential patterns. It is striking to realize how many of the "first families" remained rooted in homes they or their ancestors built early in the century. It is also manifested by continuing immigration from places of origin in Italy, as in Westbury. That so many of their descendants have settled in or near the original enclaves is further affirmation of their positive regard for the settlement choices of their ancestors.

The pre-eminence of economic factors finds validation among Long Island Italian Americans and is reflected in a number of ways. First, in virtually all the communities studied, finding employment in town or nearby played a fairly decisive role. Only in Marconiville did one find Italian Americans of the first generation engaging in extensive travel of an hour or more for employment. In the other locations, work opportunities locally such as nurseries and estates in Westbury, Glen Cove and Inwood, the sand mines in Port Washington and the lace mill in Patchogue proved indispensable in that they offered work opportunities for the semi-skilled laboring classes. They also constituted possibilities for employment for their offspring, especially males. The only Long Island town in which Italian American females of the first generation were employed extensively was Patchogue. In this sense the Micaela diLeonardo (1984) thesis that in evaluating ethnic mobility "...we should consider the encounter between different ethnic economic strategies and the economic structures and the ethnic mix of particular regions of settlement", might seem to pertain. Having said that, however, it would be too strong a statement to invoke materialist preoccupation as the sole determinant of ethnic group life. As Joseph Lopreato (1976) has shown, the causes of emigration were many but,

> Perhaps more important than all these factors, however, was the cruel social and psychological punishment of the peasant by the middle class and its satellites, to the point where to be a peasant, a contadino,

in southern Italy was to be a stupid and despicable earthworm, an image accepted even by the peasant himself (p.3).

Thus, while material circumstances of immigrant settlement choices were significant, they formed part of a larger mosaic of factors which entered the decision (i.e., re-uniting of families, connections with *paesani*, perceived opportunities to enter the *petit bourgeoisie* world, health-related considerations, abandonment of a rigid way of life, the perception of suburbia as intrinsically more desirable than the city. It was not as if they lacked choices regarding the workplace; there were options. "We cannot ignore the role of choice, as applied to determinism, in human actions, immigrants or otherwise", writes Andrew Rolle (1980:182). Donna R. Gabbacia (1984), in her recent study on Sicilian immigration, is close to the mark in analyzing the causes of migration.

> The dissatisfaction of ordinary peasant men and women with their Sicilian social relationships is the background against which migration and life in the United States must be interpreted. Migrants left Italy not to establish familiar social ties elsewhere but to build lives both economically and socially more satisfying than the ones they left behind (p.52).

Furthermore, if we look at the second and third generation who left the cities, we find that here, too, it is inadequate to locate economics as the sole cause for movement. Donald Tricarico, in his 1984 volume *The Italians of Greenwich Village*, confirms as much. "The exodus of Italians to the suburbs was more than the result of favorable material conditions. There was an eagerness to leave the small world of the neighborhood and enter the mainstream of American life..." (p.74).

A second lesson to be gleaned is that to locate in the suburbs required possession of some capital, however small. The fortunate few did indeed have some funds—generally savings accumulated from earnings in the city Little Italies where they lived briefly before relocating. But it would be erroneous to suggest that the first generation of Italian settlers on Long Island were middle class; rather they were in lower class economic circumstances, although not at the very bottom of the economic ladder. As members of the lower middle class, they occupied a position which was potentially revolutionary, that is, they experienced enough success and failure to make them discontent with the *status quo*. Locations were determined by pursuing the chain migration model of seeking out places where relatives and friends were already ensconced. The usual process of home ownership was to purchase land in inexpensive Long Island areas by placing a small down payment and paying off the remainder over a period of time. As financial circumstances and time permitted, they built their own homes with the aid of family members. In many instances permanent settlement was preceded by frequenting places in the summer and gradually finding the where-with-all to make the move.

A third lesson stemming from this study is that suburban Italian Americans, because they were confronted with lesser degrees of discrimination than their counterparts in the large cities, often enjoyed the option of choosing among alternatives. They could opt for rapid assimilation including a negation of their ethnic roots, or they could choose to gain acceptance as Americans of Italian descent, fully conscious of a particular heritage. For the most part they chose the latter, although there was variety. Many perceived themselves as Americans of Italian ancestry pursuing the *via vecchia* (old way) in the new country. For over four generations the family remained the principal socializing institution as well as the major transmitter of its own culture; however, it was not an exclusive family pre-occupation model which characterized these transplanted people—there was a sense of interaction with fellow ethnics, whether kinfolk or paesani, who settled nearby.

Still another important lesson taught by a study of the suburban ethnic experience is that ethnic group life demonstrated considerable utilization and interaction with other institutions beginning with the church. With respect to the Catholic Church to which the overwhelming number of Italian Americans belonged, it is significant to note that no single pattern was followed. In Westbury they were accommodated by the existing Hibernicized parish as they were in Port Washington. In Inwood the Italian immigrants became parishioners of a new Catholic church created primarily but not exclusively for them. On the other hand, in Copiague, Hagerman and Patchogue they helped create Italian national parishes which eventually were transformed into territorial parishes. Only in Glen Cove did Italians originate a parish which continues to function as a national ethnic church.

Italian immigrants and their progeny also interracted with mutual aid societies and fraternal organizations. Indeed the rapid proliferation of voluntary groups was one of the most striking features of social life in the ethnic enclaves of Long Island. The formation, within a short span of years, of dozens of voluntary organizations in response to social needs should give lie to the "amoral familism" thesis propounded by Edward Banfield, which posits the view that because of their dedication to the interests of the nuclear family, southern Italians could not cooperate with others. Clearly one must come to the conclusion that the "amoral familism" label must be abandoned when referring to Italians in America. Likewise the view that stems from that thesis, that Italian Americans were not joiners and refused to collaborate with each other to advance their interests, must also be rejected with respect to Long Island Italians. Thus, sociologist Joseph Lopreato's (1970) assertion that "...cooperative ethnic activity comes hard to Italian Americans", finds much contradiction in the numerous civic, social and political organizations that flourished in Port Washington during the 1930s, for example. This does not mean that these organizations necessarily worked together, although there were significant efforts to unify. One wonders, in fact, that had it not been for the interruption caused by World War II, ethnic group activity might have been more pronounced. When it came to suburban Italians, from the earliest days of their residency in the communities examined one finds strong evidence of a disposition to organize along ethnic lines into voluntary self-help, social, political and religious associations, often maintaining them for decades. One sees, also, an inclination on the part of succeeding generations to join in non-ethnic organizations as well. Participation in civic bodies such as school boards; fire departments; civic, community, fraternal and service clubs; and hospital boards reflect a willingness to assume their share of community responsibilities.

The vaunted reputation Italian Americans had for creating and developing strong, vibrant neighborhoods in cities found verification in suburbia and therefore serves as another lesson of this study. Interestingly, even as many of the urban Italian city neighborhoods have weakened or disappeared, their suburban counterparts have demonstrated remarkable staying power as is evidenced by the Italian communities of Westbury, Glen Cove, Inwood and East Patchogue. Scholars continue to debate the virtues of ethnic group homogeneity and its role as a barrier to assimilation. Stephen Steinberg, in his 1982 volume *The Ethnic Myth*, is extremely critical. "The history of ethnic groups in America is a history of institutional resistance to assimilating forces, and the ethnic revival is only the latest chapter" (p.73). I must take sharp issue with this conclusion, especially with respect to the experience of Long Island's Italian Americans. The history of these ethnic "colonies" is not a history of rigid, inflexible separatism and resistance. Rather, from the outset there were manifestations of interaction and intermingling not only within the ethnic group but with the larger society—in employment, education, marketing and political activity. Although one can cite Italian community after community in which the ethnic group interacted beyond the enclave early in the century, a couple of examples will suffice. The degree of such involvement by Glen Cove's Italians in World War I, a time during which they entered military service in large numbers and were integrated into units outside an ethnic environment, is a case in point. Another instance of this involvement is supplied by the activities of first generation Joseph Cardamone in Patchogue and second generation Dominick Piscitelli in Westbury, both unquestionably products of the Italian hubris, yet both eager to assume active political roles in their communities. Thus, these examples, it could be argued, indicate instances of how individuals from the ethnic community worked to bridge the gaps between cultures and to promote civic and political responsibility among the newcomers.

Still another lesson revealed by this study is that Italian Americans of the first and second generation have helped transform Long Island political life. Within two generations they have moved from the periphery of political activity to a predominant place in current politics, serving in various capacities such as Alphonse D'Amato, United States Senator; Ralph Caso, Nassau County Executive; and numerous members of the New York State Legislature, town supervisors, town board members and village mayors. Italian Americans are extremely conspicuous within the structure of political parties where in recent years they have served as chairmen of the Democratic and Republican parties in Suffolk County and chairmen of the Republican Party in Nassau County. Indeed, in the latter instance Italian Americans have headed the party continuously for almost a quarter of a century. As the largest single nationality bloc on Long Island, the major political parties cannot afford to ignore them.

Another important lesson yielded should serve to dispel myths about the impact of Italian immigrants and organized labor. Coming at a time when the organized labor movement in this country was in its infancy, and working both within organized labor circles and on *ad hoc* bases, these newcomers made important contributions toward the improvement of the lot of working people on Long Island. Their leadership role proved indispensable in improving working conditions in the nurseries of Westbury, the sand mines of Port Washington, the garment factories of Copiague and the Long Island Railroad, all prior to World War I. Accordingly, these examples should render mistaken the notion that adumbrates Italian immigrants as inimical to organized labor. Clearly a revision of this traditional reading of labor history at the turn of the century is required.

Comprehensive examination of the communities under study in this volume suggests that criminal activity was not a natural sequence of the existence of Italian enclaves. Of the several Long Island Italian-American neighborhoods which were flourishing in the pre-World War I era—the period when crime in the form of the Mafia or the Black Hand (*La Mano Nera*) was the preoccupation of urban Italian colonies, there was, with the exception of Inwood, no such focus. Inwood presented a singular case wherein public concern over organized criminal activity among the Italian element approached hysteria. Why this was so requires further scrutiny. Perhaps its proximity to New York City offers an explanation, although this is speculation. The conclusion one draws is that, given the excessive and protracted fixation with Italian crime in large cities such as New York and Chicago, its near absence in the suburbs constitutes a remarkable contrast. With the unique exception of Inwood, the bottom line conclusion is that organized crime did not play a major role insofar as Long Island Italians were concerned.

Closely connected with the crime issue is the evolution of law enforcement in Long Island Italian neighborhoods. Specifically, the early and extensive use of indigenous ethnic community people to enforce laws locally is worthy of comment. It was more than mere coincidence which found Vincent Zavatt, Dominick Posillico, John Stephani and Charles Barcellona elevated to deputy sheriffs or town constable. What is evident is the degree of prescience on the part of local politicians, virtually all Republicans, in selecting leaders within the ethnic community to their first public posts. Indeed, these would be the first public positions that members of the ethnic group achieved. By this calculated move, the political power brokers extended recognition to individuals of standing within the ethnic community and by association sowed the seeds of partisan political incubation within the group.

The 1980 United States Census, by addressing itself to questions regarding ethnic background, provides extremely useful data on issues of self-identity and self-perceptions. The data yields information that about 12 million persons claimed Italian ancestry in the United States, or approximately 5.4 percent of the total population. For Italian Americans on Long Island this data is especially significant in that it reveals that almost one quarter (24.56) of the residents of the two counties identify themselves as of Italian ancestry—the largest of all ethnic groups in the region. This is to be compared to New York City figures which show 1,132,861 or sixteen percent of the city's total population are Italian Americans. On Long Island, Italian Americans represent at least 40 percent of the total population in six individual towns or hamlets (Franklin Square, 42.5%; Deer Park, 41.6%; Elmont, 41.0%; Shirley, 40.1%; North Lindenhurst, 40.1%; Inwood, 40.0%). With respect to the selected communities under study in this volume, the 1980 Italian population is as follows: Inwood, 40.0%; Copiague, 38.0%; North Patchogue, 32.5%; Glen Cove, 31.2%; Westbury, 29.7%; East Patchogue, 28.6%; Port Washington, 24.9%; Patchogue Village, 24.9% and North Bellport, 20.1%. These statistics confirm a continuing attachment to the Long Island communities which first attracted Italian immigrants approximately a century ago.

Given the large number of Americans of Italian descent, one can conclude that they do not reflect a monolithic, clone-like people all of whom manifest identical characteristics, interests and outlooks as is repeated so frequently in literature as to become stereotypes. We are reminded of this by Andrew Rolle (1980), whose penetrating psychological history, *The Italian Americans, Troubled Roots*, says that, "In their search for selfhood the immigrants assumed no single identity. Each worked out an accommodation in unique ways, realigning the personality to fit new realities. The idea that we historians can homogenize the ethnics into one national experience has become ridiculous" (p.180). While the first and second generation were heavily represented in the laboring, unskilled and semi-skilled classes, for example, the third and fourth generations span the occupational ladder and are represented in every economic sphere. Although precise data on the following is wanting, the impression gleaned from years of research and observation is that they attend and complete educational goals on a level with the Long Island population at large, have significant representation in the various professions of law, medicine, education, dentistry, *etc.*, and are involved in business activities as entrepreneurs in numbers approximating their percentage of the population. Their representation among the Catholic clergy of Rockville Centre is probably below their proportion of the Catholic population of the diocese. However, increased percentages of Italian names seem to have appeared in recent years among the younger clergy. Overt discrimination of the type practiced in the early part of the century and as exemplified in the real estate broadside excluding Italians from purchasing Woodside, Long Island property is fortunately a thing of the past.

The question of success is an intriguing one. American mythology and folklore have always emphasized the Horatio Alger theme of this country as a place of unquestioned opportunity leading toward upward mobility, a land wherein people of impoverished background could rise to the uppermost rungs of the social and economic ladder; a nation where opportunity abounded and hard toil paid handsome dividends. It would be the height of naivete to generalize that Long Island Italian Americans have "made it" and that the heady dream of American success has in fact been realized—obviously such an assertion would be exaggeration and misrepresentation. Yet in a number of respects these sons and daughters from Italy can be said to have improved their collective statuses over the past few generations. As Richard Alba (1985) has written, "Given the socioeconomic advances of the Italians, it was only natural that they should participate in the suburban pilgrimage" (p.88). There are two definitions of success, Thernstrom (1975) reminds us. One revolves around the commonly held view that success is measured as mobility out of the status of manual laborer and into positions of supervision such as foremen, clerks, managers, professionals or business-owners. The second definition of success has as its criterion property ownership, which obviously presupposes the ability to save money with which to negotiate this type of ownership. Arguably these models of success may not be accepted as sufficiently inclusive, thereby overlooking large areas of action, thought and feeling. Be that as it may, within the parameters of Thernstrom's definitions, Long Island Italian Americans enjoy modest success.

By any measure these unskilled or semi-skilled manual laborers who formed the vast majority of Italian newcomers to the area stood at the bottom of the social ladder; but it was not to be a permanent underclass status and in the course of a relatively short period a degree of mobility was discernible in improved occupational and home-ownership categories.

Other researchers use the term social mobility rather than success. Richard Alba (1985), for instance, chooses to single out two indicators of social position—education and occupation—to measure mobility. Using descendants from the British Isles for comparison, he concludes that in certain categories such as all members of an ethnic group who have attended college, Italians are behind British Americans. Likewise they trail British Americans when it comes to representation on the upper end of the occupational spectrum. However, differences in the lower end are not so great so that even if Italians are more represented in blue-collar jobs, presently there are virtually no Italians in the ranks of unskilled, which in itself reflects a significant change from a few decades ago. Further, when one considers the more recent generations, much of the disparity between British Americans and Italian Americans disappears. "The third and fourth generations, those born after World War II and those of mixed background, have either caught up or are about to do so" (Alba, 1985:130).

The Italian-descended population of Long Island is, then, a variegated people, a many-dimensioned populace who offer a wide variety of ethnic behavioral patterns. There are those who have retained much of their Italian culture including strong family attachment based on blood kinship; their married children live in close proximity, the Italian language is spoken in the home, there is a love for working the land, a high priority is accorded to home ownership, there is support for old ethnic organizations such as the now resurgent Sons of Italy lodges or for new ethnic-based organizations such as the Italian American Service Club of Brookhaven. This group of Italian Americans, furthermore, tends to identify unhesitatingly as of Italian background, and travels to Italy extensively either to visit family or absorb the culture of their ancestors. Having said that, one also notices Long Island Italian Americans living life-styles, enjoying family incomes, aspiring to professions, attending schools, joining civic organizations, becoming involved in politics, and entering the entrepreneural world in patterns not too dissimilar from the prevailing culture. They are, to a considerable extent, assimilated, but not altogether. Even when studying the complacent 1950s when ethnicity seemed to have receded, scholars have found that it nonetheless continued as a persistent theme in the suburbs. Richard Polenberg (1980) in *One Nation Divisible*, found that just as class distinctions persisted, "so too, did distinctions based on ethnicity" (p.144). When one can point to a rebound of ethnic organizations, to an increase in the numbers studying Italian in schools, to large attendance at feast-day practices, then one concludes that despite apparent assimilation, the ethnic past is not wholly blotted out; it endures, altered in shape and format from the ethnic style of yesteryear, but nevertheless distinct enough for participants to acknowledge that they are of Italian background and that others in society identify them as such. It is as if the words of anthropologist Milton Gordon were designed for them.

> My essential thesis here is that the sense of ethnicity has proved to be hardy. As though with a wily cunning of its own, as though there were some essential element in man's nature that demanded it—something that compelled him to merge his lonely individual identity in some ancestral group of fellows smaller by far than the whole human race, smaller often than the nation—the sense of ethnic belonging has survived. It has survived in various forms and with various names, but it has not perished, and twentieth-century man is closer to his stone-age ancestors than he knows (1964:245).

There is a need to be reminded that inter-group relations revolve around a number of social forces among which ethnicity has played and continues to play an important part. It functions as a basis for social life of people not only in urban centers but also in the nation's suburbs. The history of Long Island Italian Americans provides a strong argument for the incorporation of the ethnic dimension in any understanding of the past history of a group as well as in assessing the social record of an area. It is hoped that this history will help develop a better appreciation for the dynamics of ethnic group life in suburbia.

PHOTO ESSAY

Long Island railroad employed Italian immigrant workers extensively to extend its operations. 1904. (Suffolk County Historical Society).

Young Italian boys such as the one shown in this photograph were employed by the Long Island Railroad as water boys. 1905. (Nassau County Museum and Reference Library).

228 FROM STEERAGE TO SUBURBS

3. Italian immigrant workers for the Hicks Nursery were called upon to beautify Westbury estates by transplanting enormous trees. c. 1924.
(Hicks Nursery)

	Marcus Daddio.	Hrs. per wk.	Storms.	Absent while men
1905.	Sept.	54-68-63-64	No outside work.	same grade worked outside.
	Oct.	66-57-53-54	1 rain	
	Nov.	65-63-61-61-50	1 rain	
	Dec.	59-64-44-40	1 rain	1 absent
1906.	Jan.	52-56-40-61	1 storm	1 absent
	Feb.	43-50-57-31	2 storm	2 "
	Mar.	60-40-35-49	2 storm	2 "
	Apr.	63-45-63-57		
	May	65-60-54-63		2 "
	June	47-67-60-55-62	1 storm	
	July	52-53-43-63		3 "
	Aug.	54-63-63		
	12 mo.	2721 hrs	@ 15 = $408	
	Storms, 9 da. @1 50		13 50	
	Absent days, 11 day		16 50	
			$438 00 Year.	

Wages of Italian workers at the Hicks Nursery, Westbury, 1906.
(Hicks Family)

FROM STEERAGE TO SUBURBS   229

Italian workers on the sand pits of Port Washington. c. 1960.

Italian American children in support of their parents who were on strike in Port Washington. 1937.

The Romeo Construction Company of Patchogue was responsible for building numerous roads in Suffolk County. c. 1920.

Deer Park, Long Island real estate advertisement appeared in Il Progresso Italo Americano, 1927, highlighting an "Italian" community. Sales promotion enticed many city residents to rid congested areas for spacious surroundings.

FROM STEERAGE TO SUBURBS 233

MARCONIVILLE, L. I.

Ameno villaggio Italiano vicino al mare.
Economia—Salute—Lavoro—Acqua—Gas—Luce elettrica—
Scuola—Carro elettrico—Stazione sulla proprietà

Case e Lotti a condizioni vantaggiose. Rivolgersi al
Presidente della

SOVEREIGN REALTY COMPANY,

GIOVANNI CAMPAGNOLI, 45 W. 34th Street, New York.

Marconiville real estate advertisement extolling the virtues of buying land in Marconiville. c. 1914

The entire Italian community of Marconiville came out to greet world famous inventor Guglielmo Marconi in 1917. The northern section of Copiague was for years known as Marconiville.

W. G. PLATT,
OAKLAND VIEW,
WOODHAVEN, L. I., N. Y.

Enclosed please find Map of my property located adjoining Ozone Park Heights. The Map explains its proximity to the city and its Trolley, Elevated and Long Island Railroad advantages.

TERMS OF SALE:

The terms of sale are 20 per cent. cash; 5 per cent. of original amount of purchase money monthly until paid, or 5 per cent. discount for all cash.

We allow 5 per cent. brokerage, if the Broker comes with the party and makes the sale, or 2½ if you send the purchaser and we make the sale.

In connection with the above property we have for sale some very desirable Railroad front lots, suitable for manufacturing purposes; there being a switch on the property.

HOTEL OR STORE PROPERTY.

Also a place that can be used as a Store or Hotel, located on Broadway, between City of Brooklyn and Jamaica, about one-quarter of a mile from two railroad stations. The building contains two stores on first floor and 7 living rooms on the second floor, with Hall attached 50x60. There is a building loan mortgage of $2,400. Will sell for $5,000, price asked, or bid requested.

COTTAGES FOR SALE.

We have also for sale cottage on Welcome Place, first house from corner of Rockaway Road. It contains 7 rooms, reception hall, vestibule, coat room, attached closet, pantry, bath room, hot air furnace in cellar, etc. Price, $3,500.

Also cottage on Welcome Place, third house from corner of Rockaway Road, containing 7 rooms, reception hall and bath, furnace in cellar. Price, $3,000.

Both houses have all improvements. $500 cash, remainder on installments, if desired. Brokerage, $100 on either of the above houses.

Further information supplied on application.

WELCOME G. PLATT,
Oakland View,
Italians Excluded.   Post Office Address, Woodhaven, N. Y.

DeBEVOISE MAP COLLECTION

Italians were not universally accepted on Long Island as this 1916 real estate broadside indicates. (Queensborough Public Library)

Pioneer Italian settler of North Bellport Antonio Fuoco built a home which housed a general store, family rooms and meeting rooms. Constructed in 1907, this extant home served as an unofficial community center and is still inhabited by family members.

Some Italian immigrants became successful entreprenuers and built impressive edifices. The Port Washington home of sand mine operator James Marino was built by Italian labor. It was demolished in the 1970's to make room for a supermarket parking lot.
(Nassau County Museum and Reference Library).

Italian family poses for a photograph c. 1890 in Roslyn, Long Island, where many immigrants worked in road building. (Nassau County Museum and Reference Library).

Vincent Zavatt, Inwood Italian pioneer, takes his family for an outing at nearby beach resort. 1910.

The Zaino family of Westbury enjoy a family anniversary. c. 1935.

FROM STEERAGE TO SUBURBS 241

MRS. CARMELA RUSSO
North Bellport, L. I.
Telephone 7-M Bellport

LICENSED MIDWIFE
20 Years Experience   Prompt Service

LA SIGNORA CARMELA RUSSO
Levatrice Apatentata Italiana
North Bellport, L. I.

(Above) The mid-wife was indispensable to Italian American LongIsland families in the pre World War II period as this 1916 advertisement demonstrates.

RELIGION

Religion was a major institution for Italian Americans. Many areas in Long Island started catholic parishes, reflecting a religious ethnic heritage. Marconiville's Our Lady of the Assumption is a case in point.

242   FROM STEERAGE TO SUBURBS

A minority of Long Island Italian Americans became protestants and created their own churches which clearly reflected their ethnic background.

Immigrant Carmen Bianco was the organizer of the feast of St. Liberata which was celebrated for decades by Patchogue's Italian Americans.

WORLD WAR I.
1917—1918
THEIR ADOPTED COUNTRY
FOUND THEM READY

AFFUSA, GIACOMO.
AGRESTI, MICHELE.
BARCELLONA, CARLO.
BALZOLA, GIOVANNI.
BALL, FRANK.
BERNAGOZZI, GIUSEPPE.
BOGNI, ANGELO.
BOSELLI, LUIGI.
CAMPAGNOLI, HUGO.-FIRST LIEUT.
CARUSO, PASQUALE.
FAGONE, VITO.-DOTT. MEDICO.
FATTORUSO, VINCENZO.
FOGLIA, NICOLA.
GIORGINI, NATALE.
MAZZA, ANTONIO.
ORLANDO, SILVIO.
PARODI, BENIAMINO.
SPARACINO, FILIPPO.
SEGALE, ANTONIO.
TASSINARI, CESARE.
TRONGIOLITO, FRANCESCO.

REDEDICATED MAY 19, 1963
REDEDICATED JULY 4, 1973

World War I monument memorializing contributions of Italians of Marconiville (Copiague).

Immigrant Fiorentino Nuzzolo, Inwood barber, belatedly received an award for heroism as a United States soldier during World War I. An Italian American newspaper boasted about the deed with banner headlines.

Celebration of St. Rocco's feast is an on-going festival in Glen Cove's Little Italy.

Italian American Civic League of Inwood dedicating a Veteran's organization building. c. 1925.

Italian American social organizations held many functions in Glen Cove's orchard house. In this photograph the Circolo Generale Graziani celebrates. 1937.

> **New Italian Society.**
> P. O. Box 275, Bellport, L. I.
>
> **HENRY SICCARDI.**
> On Oct. 4th, 1891, there was formed an Italian Society of the name of Concordia Society, Benevolent and Political, of Bellport.
> This Society has an Employment office on Post Ave., near Atlantic Ave., one block from the old station, where all the American people and others can obtain Masons, Carpenters, Farm Hands, Common Laborers, etc. No charge for furnishing the help.
>
> **ADMINISTRATION.**
> HENRY SICCARDI, President.
> ANTONIO NARDO, 1st Vice Pres.
> PETER CRESCENZA, 2d Vice Pres.
> FRANK RUSSO, Sec. of Correspondence.
> GAETANO LAPENTA, Sec. of Finance.
> HUGANNET ANTAINE, Treasurer.
> ANTONIO RUSSO, ROCCO GIOIO and GUISEPPE MORRONE, Trustees.

Perhaps the oldest Long Island Italian American organization was formed in 1891. This newspaper announcement indicates its pre-occupation with supplying laborers for local needs.

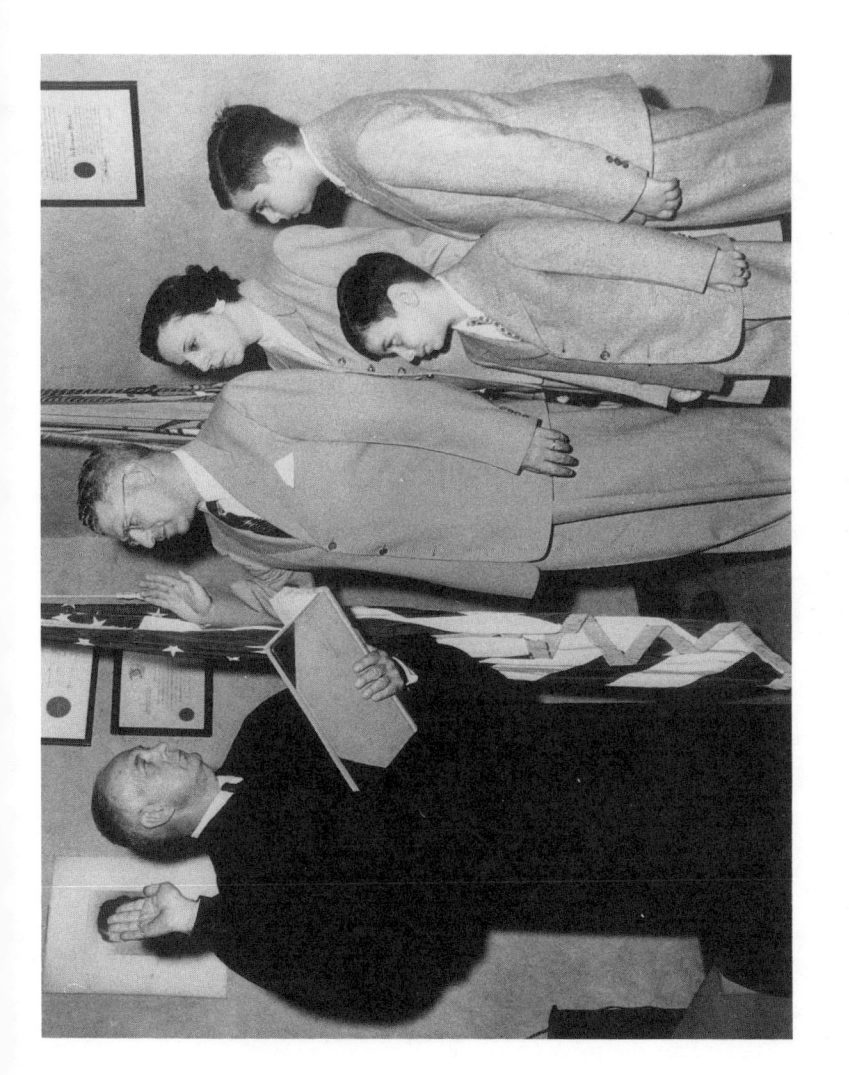

Frank Gulotta, the first Italian American elected to a countywide post, being sworn in as Nassau County District Attorney in 1945. His son Thomas in foreground, is currently Nassau County executive.

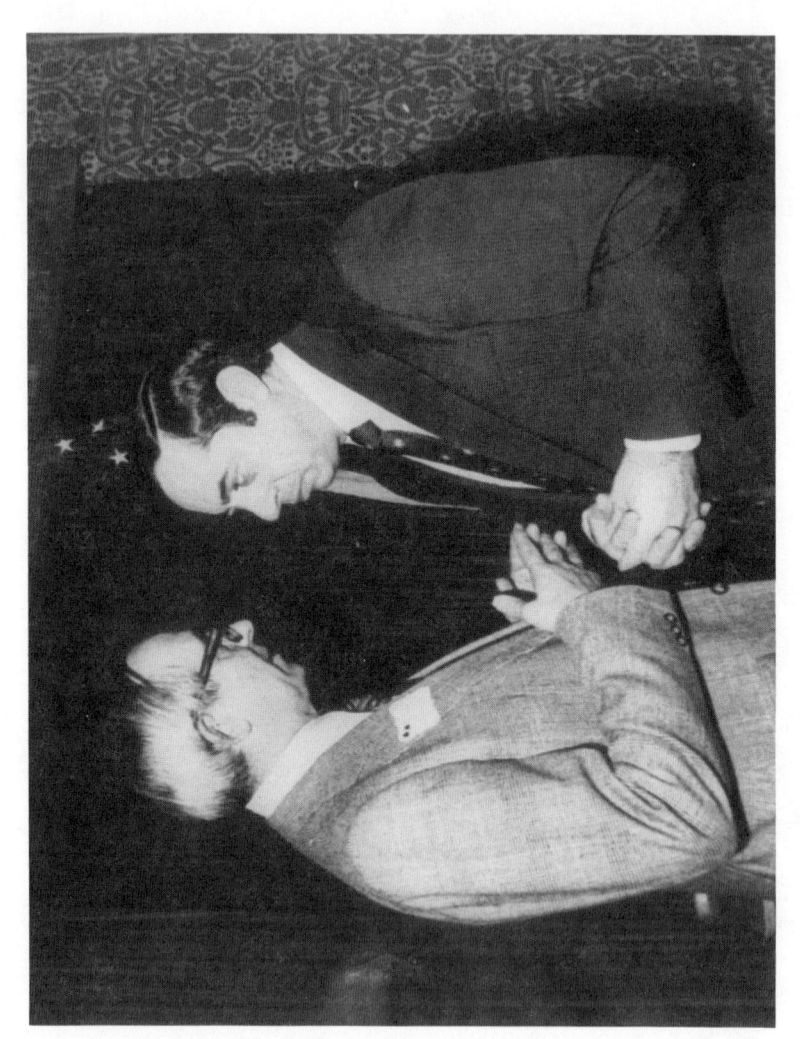

New York Governor Cuomo, resident of the Queens portion of Long Island, confers with Mayor Vincent Suozzi of Glen Cove.

Appendix I

LARGEST CONCENTRATIONS OF ITALIAN AMERICANS IN NASSAU AND SUFFOLK COUNTIES BASED ON 1980 CENSUS PC 80-1C p.34 New York, Table 60.

Place	Total Persons	Single Italian Ancestry	Multiple Italian Ancestry	Total Italian Ancestry	Percent
Franklin Square	29,051	9,598	2,685	12,284	42.5
Deer Park	30,394	9,009	3,666	12,674	41.6
Elmont	27,592	9,332	2,149	11,481	41.0
Shirley	18,072	4,508	2,744	7,252	40.1
North Lindenhurst	11,511	3,141	1,486	4,627	40.1
Inwood	08,228	2,797	0,564	3,361	40.1
Selden	17,259	3,972	2,692	6,664	38.6
North Babylon	19,019	4,679	2,592	7,271	38.2
Copiague	20,132	5,298	2,394	7,692	38.0
Valley Stream	35,769	10,359	3,175	13,534	37.8
Rocky Point	07,012	1,781	0,856	2,637	37.6
West Babylon	41,699	10,937	4,656	15,593	37.4
North Massapequa	21,385	5,626	2,393	8,019	37.4
Lindenhurst	26,919	6,601	3,388	9,989	37.1
Island Park	4,847	1,092	705	1,797	37.0
Bayville Village	7,014	1,724	769	2,493	35.5
North Valley Stream	14,530	3,881	1,231	5,112	35.1
Lynbrook Village	20,424	5,185	1,870	7,055	34.5
South Farmingdale	16,437	3,711	1,952	5,663	34.4

LARGEST CONCENTRATIONS OF ITALIAN AMERICANS IN NASSAU AND SUFFOLK COUNTIES
BASED ON 1980 CENSUS PC 80-1C p.34 New York, Table 60.

Holbrook	24,382	4,986	8,370	34.3
Hauppauge	20,960	4,753	7,170	34.2
Farmingville	13,398	2,546	4,491	33.5
Plainedge	6,626	2,301	3,221	33.4
Fort Salonga	9,550	1,207	3,142	32.9
Bethpage	16,801	3,847	5,523	32.8
Manorhaven Village	5,384	1,259	1,758	32.6
Lake Ronkonkoma	38,336	7,194	12,464	32.5
North Patchogue	7,126	1,263	2,323	32.5
West Bayshore	5,113	772	1,664	32.5
North New Hyde Park	15,114	3,737	4,880	32.2
Mastic	10,413	1,960	3,322	31.9
West Hempstead	18,536	4,169	5,858	31.6
Centereach	30,136	5,497	9,426	31.2
Glen Cove	24,618	5,845	7,683	31.2
North Bellmore	20,630	4,612	6,383	30.9
Bohemia	9,308	1,694	2,878	30.9
Nesconset	10,706	2,088	3,294	30.7
Commack	34,719	7,325	10,612	30.5
New Hyde Park Vill	9,801	2,112	2,971	30.3
Islip Terrace	5,588	985	1,690	30.2
Mount Sinai	6,591	1,021	1,988	30.1

LARGEST CONCENTRATIONS OF ITALIAN AMERICANS IN NASSAU AND SUFFOLK COUNTIES
BASED ON 1980 CENSUS PC 80-1C p.34 New York, Table 60.

Malverne Village	9,262	1,865	901	2,766	29.8
Westbury	13,871	3,237	887	4,124	29.7
Lake Grove	9,692	1,710	1,138	2,848	29.4
Mastic Beach	8,318	1,452	997	2,449	29.4
Albertson	5,561	1,031	602	1,633	29.3
Middle Island	5,703	880	766	1,646	28.8
Floral Park Vill	16,794	3,523	1,299	4,822	28.7
Massapequa	24,454	4,853	2,168	7,021	28.7
East Patchogue	18,139	3,281	1,911	5,192	28.6
Mitler Place	7,877	1,201	1,021	2,222	28.2
Massapequa Park	19,779	3,864	1,686	5,550	28.0
Oyster Bay	6,497	1,061	764	1,825	28.0
South Huntington	14,854	2,586	1,534	4,130	27.8
Smithtown	30,906	6,083	3,478	8,561	27.7
Seaford	16,117	2,751	1,692	4,443	27.5
St. James	12,122	1,963	1,365	2,328	27.4
Medford	20,418	2,904	2,696	5,600	27.4
Kings Park	16,131	2,550	1,843	4,393	27.2
East Islip	13,852	2,300	1,470	3,770	27.2
Sound Beach	8,071	1,487	2,680	2,167	26.8
Garden City Park	7,712	1,536	531	2,067	26.8
North Bayshore	35,020	5,712	3,642	9,354	26.7
North Merrick	12,848	2,171	1,238	3,409	26.5
Dix Hills	26,693	4,985	2,040	7,025	26.3

LARGEST CONCENTRATIONS OF ITALIAN AMERICANS IN NASSAU AND SUFFOLK COUNTIES BASED ON 1980 CENSUS PC 80-1C p.34 New York, Table 60.

Port Jefferson	17,009	2,438	2,026	4,464	26.2
Oakdale	8,090	1,323	786	2,190	26.0
Levittown	57,045	8,581	6,214	14,795	25.9
East Meadow	39,317	6,700	3,354	10,054	25.5
Williston Park	8,216	1,256	831	2,087	25.4
Islip	13,438	2,104	1,311	3,415	24.5
East Farmingdale	5,522	968	419	1,387	25.1
Coram	24,752	3,610	2,592	6,202	25.0
Port Washington	14,521	2,080	930	3,010	24.9
Patchogue Village	11,291	1,668	1,149	2,817	24.9
Hewlett	6,986	1,236	461	1,697	24.6
East Northport	20,187	2,936	2,037	4,973	24.6
Hicksville	43,245	7,641	3,964	11,605	24.5
Mineola	20,757	3,524	1,512	5,036	24.2
Ridge	8,977	1,285	896	2,181	24.2
Wantagh	19,817	3,056	1,657	4,713	23.7
West Islip	24,533	6,287	647	6,934	23.4
Brentwood	44,321	6,409	3,975	10,384	23.4
South Westbury	9,732	1,414	866	2,280	23.4
Syosset	9,818	1,704	581	2,285	23.2
Huntington Station	28,769	3,925	2,745	6,670	23.1
Babylon Village	12,388	1,527	1,282	2,809	22.6
East Rockaway	10,917	1,717	735	2,451	22.4
Bellmore	18,106	2,710	1,351	4,061	22.4

LARGEST CONCENTRATIONS OF ITALIAN AMERICANS IN NASSAU AND SUFFOLK COUNTIES BASED ON 1980 CENSUS PC 80-1C p.34 New York, Table 60.

North Wantagh	12,677	1,702	2,803	22.1
Melville	8,139	1,143	1,790	21.9
West Sayville	8,185	891	1,774	21.6
Sayville	12,013	1,274	2,592	21.5
Oceanside	33,639	4,912	7,141	21.2
Plainview	28,037	4,531	5,938	21.1
Old Bethpage	6,254	951	1,325	21.1
Bayport	9,282	861	1,927	20.7
North Bellport	7,432	978	1,510	20.3
Baldwin	31,630	3,793	6,409	20.2
Centermoriches	5,703	624	1,155	20.2
Munsey Park Vill	2,806	413	565	20.1
Greenlawn	13,869	1,629	2,635	18.9
Manhasset	8,485	1,055	1,579	18.6
Huntington	21,752	2,256	3,987	18.3
West Amityville	6,623	811	1,201	18.1
Montauk	2,828	338	514	18.0
Cold Spring Harbor	5,336	468	960	17.9
Muttontown Village	2,725	316	468	17.1
Lloyd Harbor Vill	3,405	386	578	16.9
Bayshore	10,784	1,013	1,832	16.9
Centerport	6,576	513	1,092	16.6
Merrick	24,478	2,731	3,997	16.3
Brightwaters	3,286	230	529	16.0
Cedarhurst	6,162	712	988	16.0

LARGEST CONCENTRATIONS OF ITALIAN AMERICANS IN NASSAU AND SUFFOLK COUNTIES BASED ON 1980 CENSUS PC 80-1C p.34 New York, Table 60.

Woodbury	7,048	745	520	1,265	15.9
Central Islip	19,734	1,789	1,314	3,103	15.7
Northport Village	7,651	540			
Amityville Vill	9,076	822	513	1,335	14.7
Bellport Village	2,809	205	208	413	14.7
Garden City Vill	29,927	2,709	1,644	4,353	14.5
Port Jefferson Village	6,699	578	363	941	14.0
Roslyn Heights	6,546	619	301	920	14.0
Long Beach City	34,073	3,186	1,568	4,754	13.9
Stonybrook	16,155	1,103	1,140	2,243	13.8
Old Westbury	3,297	353	95	448	13.6
Seacliff Village	5,364	380	252	632	11.7
Carle Place	5,470	130	453	583	10.6
Freeport Village	38,272	2,534	1,485	4,019	10.5
S. Valley Stream	5,462	345	142	487	8.9
Mattituck	3,923	172	101	273	6.9
Wyandanch	13,215	279	582	861	6.5
Hempstead Vill	40,404	1,582	1,008	2,590	6.4
Woodmere	17,205	868	249	1,117	6.4
Cutchogue	2,772	29	144	173	6.2
Monsey	12,380	509	249	758	6.1
East Hills	7,160	150	83	233	3.2
North Amityville	13,140	415	176	591	3.1

Appendix II

The Scalamandre Story

The saga of Italian immigrants rising from positions of relative poverty to positions of economic success and social esteem deserves to be recorded and reviewed when studying Long Island history, for in truth it confirms the belief that honest, hard-working people responded to opportunities this land offered. These stories also demonstrate that the newcomers gave to their adopted land as much as they received.

Clearly one of the little-known yet most important of these stories is that of the Scalamandre family of Freeport which currently functions as one of the largest and most successful construction businesses on Long Island. The Scalamandre story began in the town of Scaliti, province of Calabria where Peter Scalamandre was born in the late 1800s. Desirous of improving his fortune, he had journeyed to America twice before deciding to make it his permanent home. While on a visit to Italy during World War I, he was called into service and served as a soldier for a few years. Peter went back to the United States until 1930, when he returned to Scaliti to marry Bettina Pagnota.

Peter was attracted to Freeport because of the emergence of a small but cohesive enclave of Calabrians with whom he felt comfortable and with whom he could identify. Because so many of his compatriots were in similar occupations, it was not surprising to learn that he joined with them as a laborer in construction work. Determined to go further, he learned the masonry craft, becoming so proficient and so confident that after a few years he embarked into the entrepreneurial field for himself by serving as a subcontractor for larger builders in the Freeport area. A modest operation employing four or five workers mostly from his home town in Italy, Peter undertook small jobs such as building brick steps, sidewalks, foundations, chimneys and patios.

Bettina and Peter had three children, Fred, Joseph and Rosemary, who were born and raised in Freeport, attended local schools and absorbed their parents' culture even while imbibing in the mainstream culture of their Long Island environment. As teenagers, both sons became acquainted with their father's construction operation, with Joseph making it his full-time occupation as soon as he finished high school while Fred joined the company after a stint in the Army. Because his father's illness kept him from personally supervising work, as a young man Joseph learned to run the small business. When Fred joined the business in the early 1950s, the Scalamandre firm reached a critical turning point regarding its future. Realizing that specialization in either concrete construction or masonry work was the key was to obtain major job contracts, the issue was decided by the toss of a coin which accordingly led Joseph and Fred to concentrate on concrete construction. The brothers also acceded to unionization of the firm which assured them labor peace and they immediately won contracts for larger jobs beginning with the foundation for a huge shopping center in Freeport.

The over thirty years tenure as concrete specialists has seen the Scalamandre firm establish an enviable record in recent Long Island construction history. In the 1970s, the firm designed and built the Jamaica Savings Bank in Lynbrook, an award-winning job which was cited for design and aesthetics by the construction industry. In the early 1980s, the Scalamandre brothers undertook one of the largest curb construction jobs ever in the area, and perhaps the state, when they obtained the contract to replace all the curbs in Levittown—one of the most extensive developments on Long Island. Energized by progressive management, the firm proceeded in the daunting task by purchasing the first slip-form machine in the county which facilitated a highly efficient work pattern. Not finding local concrete mixing companies able to satisfy the special needs of this machine, the Scalamandres decided to build their own concrete mixing company, an undertaking which has since grown to two such plants and twenty-five trucks to haul the product.

The Scalamandre success story is truly remarkable. As children of a family with limited means, Fred and Joseph recalled their inferior social/ economic positions as youngsters which precluded their use of a number of facilities in Freeport. Even had they had the means, there were doubts whether they would have been welcome in the exclusive yacht club or the private beach which graced the shore. They likewise rankled at the prejudice which emanated from the precincts of an influential local fraternal association which was said to have accommodated the notorious Ku Klux Klan in its heyday. It was a source of considerable satisfaction for the Scalamandres when, by the 1980s, they had purchased all the facilities and sites which they have since transformed into the Salty Bay Yacht Club, condominiums and a shopping center. The days of discrimination and the demeaning of Italian Americans in Freeport seemed to have at last come to an end. Having experienced discrimination, the Scalamandres were sensitive to the plight of others who were in less fortunate positions, translating their concern into action. Thus they consider it one of their most important accomplishments to have played a significant role in forming the first minority company on Long Island designed to undertake work on major road jobs.

A vision of growth and development of opportunities has marked the progress of the Scalamandre brothers. Thus, from a base of concrete work, they branched out to general construction and road building. These activities in turn led to the creation of their own concrete supply, asphalt plants and mining companies to supply their material needs in the foregoing companies. As one of the largest firms of its kind in the county it employs 500 people at peak of activity, a record few competitors can match.

Success in the business world, however, has not isolated them from involvement in civic, social, religious and ethnic activities—indeed they have been duly honored for involvement and participation. The Freeport Chamber of Commerce has singled them out for Man of the Year awards as has the local Sons of Italy Lodge and the Nassau County Columbian Association. Perhaps most important of all is the deep sense of pride they take in their ethnic and religious roots. For Fred and Joseph this pride means a revival of the St.Rocco Society which sponsors fund-raising activities in behalf of the Holy Innocents Roman Catholic Church. It means also their deep commitment to assist Italian American students via the Dante Society which provides scholarship aid. They have not forgotten from whence they came and they have an appreciation for what their parents and the earlier generation had to endure. They have an abiding love of Italianitá

Surely the Scalamandre story is a saga of how Italian immigrants and their children have utilized their heritage to contribute to the betterment of life on Long Island.

BIBLIOGRAPHY

ARTICLES

American Italian Historical Association (AIHA)
1972   *Newsletter.* Summer.

Capobianco, A.
1985   "Pratt Estate of Years Gone By Was a City Within a City", *Long Island Heritage*, April, p.9.

Carucci, J.M.
1981   "The Sand Pits of Port Washington", *Long Island Heritage*, October.

Cavaioli, F.
1983   "The Long Island Chariot of Fire", *Long Island Forum*, 41(1):8-13. January.

_____
1979   "The Ku Klux Klan on Long Island", *Long Island Forum*, 42(5):100-106. May.

Copiague Public School District Newsletter
1973   2(3):September; *Il Lavoro*, July 14, 1917.

Cowell, D.D.
1986   "Funerals, Family and Forefathers: Italian-American Funeral Practices". In *The Italian Americans Through the Generations*. Edited by R. Caporale. Staten Island, NY: American Italian Historical Association. Pp. 237-252.

Femminella, F.X. and J. Quadagno
1976   "The Italian American Family". In *Ethnic Families in America*. Edited by C.H. Mindel and R.W. Habenstein. New York: Elsevier. Pp. 61-68.

Juliani, R.
1978   "The Settlement House and the Italian Family". In *The Italian Immigrant Women in North America*. Edited by B.B. Caroli, R.F. Harney and L.F. Tomasi. Staten Island, NY: American Italian Historical Association. Pp. 103-123.

LaGumina, S.J.
1985   "Long Island's Italians and the Labor Movement", *Long Island Forum*. 43(1):4-11 and 43(2):31-38. January and February.

_____
1982   "American Education and Italian Immigrant Response". In *American Education and the European Immigrant: 1840-1940*. Edited by R.J. Weiss. Urbana, IL: University of Illinois Press, Pp. 61-77.

_____
1979   "Sabelli, Italian American Aviation Pioneer", *La Parola Del Popolo*. Pp. 49-64. May-June.

_____
1977   "American Political Process and the Italian Participation in New York State". In *Perspectives in Italian Immigration and Ethnicity*. Edited by S. Tomasi. Staten Island, NY: Center for Migration Studies. Pp. 85-100.

1970   "The New Deal, The Immigrants and Congressman Vito Marcantonio", *International Migration Review*. Pp. 57-74. Spring.

Long Island University Magazine
1970   "Sylvester Cangaro, Head Gardener", p. 36.

Mathias, E., E.L. Mathias
1983   "Sardinian Born and Bread", *Natural History*. 92(1):54-62. January.

McLaughlin, V.Y.
1974   "A Flexible Tradition: South Italian Immigrants Confront a New Work Experience", *Journal of Social History*. 7(4):429-445. Summer.

Milstein, S.
1984   "The Crusader Who Lost His Way", *The American Lawyer*. April.

The National Law Journal
1984   *The American Lawyer*, April.

Newsday
1981   "Old Marconiville Still Lives", May 13.

Plimpton, G.
1984   "The Grucci's Trial by Tragedy", *Newsday Magazine*. Pp. 8-24. July 1.

Scarpaci, J.
1975   "Immigrants in the New South: Italians in Louisiana's Sugar Parishes, 1880-1910", *Labor History*. 16(2):165-183. Spring.

Vecoli, R.J.
1972   "European Americans. From Immigrants to Ethnics", *International Migration Review*. 6(4):403-434.

1969   "Prelates and Peasants: Italian Immigrants and the Catholic Church", *Journal of Social History*. 2:217-268. Spring.

Williams, G.L.
1983   "Sand Mining in Port Washington: Its Impact on the Community", *Long Island Forum*. Pp. 32-38. February.

Zolotow, M.
1947   Opera's Funny Man", *Saturday Evening Post*. 220:30-31. November 29.

BOOKS

Alba, R.
1985   *Italian Americans: Into the Twilight of Ethnicity*. Englewood Cliffs, NJ: Prentice-Hall.

Allen, F.L.
1931   *Only Yesterday*. New York: Harper and Brothers.

Bailey, P.
1949   *A History of Two Great Counties, Nassau and Suffolk*, Vol. III. New York: Lewis Historical Publishing Company.

Banfield, E.
1958   *The Moral Basis of a Backwards Society*. New York: Free Press.

Bell, D.
1967   *The End of Ideology*. New York: Collier.

Bellot, A.
1918   *A History of the Rockaways.* Far Rockaway, New York.

Bookbinder, B.
1983   *Long Island: People and Places, Past and Present.* New York: Abrams.

Crispino, J.
1980   *The Assimilation of Ethnic Groups: The Italian Case.* Staten Island, NY: Center for Migration Studies.

Davis, A.L.
1967   *Spearheads for Reform.* New York: Oxford.

diLeonardo, M.
1984   *The Varieties of Ethnic Experiences.* Ithaca, NY: Cornell University Press.

Dibbins, E., S. Purcy and C. Rubbles
1980   *A Backward Glance.* Amityville, NY: Amityville Historical Society.

Dobriner, W.C.
1963   *Class in Suburbia.* Englewood Cliffs, NJ: Prentice-Hall.

Eide, M.
1971   *Copiague, Your Town and Mine.* Copiague Board of Education.

Gabaccia, D.R.
1984   *From Sicily to Elizabeth Street.* Albany, NY: New York State University Press.

Gallo, P.
1975   *Ethnic Alienation.* Rutherford, NJ: Fairleigh Dickinson University Press.

Gambino, R.
1977   *Vendetta.* Garden City, NJ: Doubleday.

Giovanetti, A.
1979   *The Italians in America.* New York: Manor Books.

Gordon, M.
1964   *Assimilation in American Life.* New York: Oxford University Press.

The Full Gospel Christian Church
1982.

Handlin, O.
1951   *The Uprooted.* New York: Grosset and Dunlap.

Hansen, M.L.
1961   *The Atlantic Migration.* New York: Harper and Brothers.

Higham, J.
1971   *Strangers in the Land, Patterns of American Nativism, 1860-1925.* New York: Atheneum.

Iorizzo, L. and S. Mondello
1971   *The Italian Americans.* New York: Twayne Publishers.

Jones, M.A.
1961   *American Immigration.* Chicago, IL: University of Chicago Press.

Kaplan, S.
1977   *The Dream Deferred: People, Politics and Planning in Suburbia.* New York: Seabury Press.

LaGumina, S.J.
1979   *The Immigrants Speak, Italian-Americans Tell Their Story.* Staten Island, NY: Center for Migration Studies.

LaGumina, S.J., Ed.
1973 WOP, A Documentary History of Anti-Italian Discrimination in the United States. San Francisco: Straight Arrow Press.

Lopreato, J.
1970 Italian Americans. New York: Random House.

Long Island, The Sunrise Homeland
1924 The Long Island Railroad, n.a.

Musmanno, M.
1965 The Story of the Italians in America. Garden City, NY: Doubleday.

Pitkin, T.M.
1977 The Black Hand, A Chapter in Ethnic Crime. Totowa, NJ: Littlefield, Adams and Company.

Polenberg, R.
1980 One Nation Divisible. New York: Penguin Books.

Rolle, A.
1980 Italian-American, Troubled Roots. New York: The Free Press.

Segre, C.G.
1987 Italo Balbo: A Fascist Life. Los Angeles: University of California Press.

Sellers, M.
1977 To Seek America, A History of Ethnic Life in the United States. Englewood, NJ: Jerome S. Ozer.

Seyfriend, V.A.
1966 The Long Island Railroad, A Comprehensive History, the Age of Expansion, 1833-1880. Garden City, New York.

Smits, E.J.
1974 Nassau Suburbia U.S.A. The First Seventy Years 1899 to 1974. Syosset, NY: Friends of the Nassau County Museum.

Steinberg, S.
1981 The Ethnic Myth: Race, Ethnicity and Class in America. New York: Atheneum.

Stevens, S.
1981 Angela Pruess, Party Plan Sales. Richmond, VA: Skipworth Press.

Thompson, B.F.
1962 History of Long Island, 3rd Edition, Vol. II. Port Washington, NY: Ira J. Friedman.

Thernstrom, S.
1975 Poverty and Progress: Social Mobility in a Nineteenth Century City. New York: Antheneum.

Tomasi, S.
1975 Piety and Power, The Role of Italian Parishes in the New York Metropolitan Area. Staten Island, NY: Center for Migration Studies.

Tricarico, D.
1984 The Italians of Greenwich Village. Staten Island, NY: Center for Migration Studies.

Whyte, A.J.
1965 The Evolution of Modern Italy. New York: W.W. Norton and Company.

Whyte, W.F.
1943 Street Corner Society. New York: The Free Press.

Williams, P.
1938 Southern Italian Folkways in Europe and America. New Haven: Yale University Press.

Wysong, C.
1939 A History of Port Washington. Port Washington: American Legion.

Zinn, H.
1958 *LaGuardia in Congress.* New York: W.W. Norton and Company, Inc.

NEWSPAPERS

Amityville Record
Brooklyn Times-Union
Corriere D'America
Far Rockaway Journal
Glen Cove Echo
Glen Cove Guardian
Glen Cove Record-Advance
Hempstead Sentinel
Il Crociato
Il Lavoro
Il Progresso Italo-Americano
Long Island Enterprise
Long Island Press
Long Island Catholic
Nassau Herlad
Nassau Star-Review
Nassau Daily Review
Newsday
New York Daily News
New York Times
North Shore Daily Journal
Oyster Bay Guardian
Patchogue Advance
Patchogue Argus
Port Washington News
Port Washington Post
Port Washington Times
Queens County Review
Rockaway News
Roslyn News
Sea Cliff News
South Side Observer
South Side Record
Southside Signal

South Shore Record

Suffolk Eagle

Westbury Times

PAPERS, REPORTS, PROCEEDINGS, ETC.

The Argus Business and Residential Directory of 1904. Patchogue, 1904.

Atlas of the Ocean Shore of Suffolk County, Long Island, Westernly Section, Amityville to Eastport Inclusive. E. Belcher Hyde, New York, 1915, plate 17.

Department of Elections, Nassau County Enrollment. New York, December 31, 1930. Chapter, City of Glen Cove.

Directory of Patchogue, Long Island, New York, November 1, 1926. Patchogue Chamber of Commerce.

Golden Jubilee Journal of Our Lady of the Assumption, R.C. Church. Copiague, 1977.

Map and Listing of Copiague, undate and untitled publication of Copiague Chamber of Commerce.

Map of Section The Brinckerhoff Manor, Copiague, Long Island, Suffolk County, 1906.

Mormino, G., 1978, "A House on the Hill: Mobility Patterns in an Italian Neighborhood". Paper presented at the 1978 Annual Conference of the American Italian Historical Association.

Nassau Land Record, p. 18 of text.

Neighborhood Association of Westbury Long Island, 1916-17, undated and no publisher. In Westbury Folder, Nassau County Museum.

New York State Census, Brookhaven Township, 1915.

New York State Manuscript Census, 1915.

New York State Manuscript Census, 1925.

Patchogue Business and Residential Directory, 1904. Patchogue, 1904, Pp. 9-11.

Polk's Glen Cove Directory, 1923-24.

Societa M.S. Dell' Assunta Registro Processi Verbali, September 1, 1940. Statuo E. Regalamente Della Societa Maria SS. ma Dell' Assunta Di Westbury L.I. Incorporata il 27 Luglio 1920.

St.Brigid's 1856-1956, 100th Anniversary, Westbury, 1956.

St.Rocco Parish, Souvenir Journal of St.Rocco's Parish, 1937.

Statuo Della Durrazano Societa, Italo-Americano di Mutuo Soccorso, Westbury, N.Y.

Fifteenth Census of the United States, 1940. Population Vol. II. Characteristics of the Population, Part V. p. 110. Census of the Population, 1950. Vol. VI. Characteristics of the Population, Part 22. New York. p. 136. United States Census, Characteristics of Housing Units and Population by Block, 1970. Table 2.

W.P.A., The Story of the Five Towns. Writers Project, American Guide Series.

United States Census 70., The Nassau-Suffolk Regional Planning Board, Vol. 8, Nativity.

UNPUBLISHED WORKS

Alfieri, Antoinette, Letter to the author.

Aviano, E., "An Interview With a Senior Citizen, June 2, 1984". In possession of Joanne Gerrato.

Angelo Cocchiola Papers, in possession of Catherine Cocchiola.

Baptism Record of Our Lady of Good Counsel, Inwood. New York, 1910.

Baptism Register (SS. Perpetua and Felicitas) Our Lady of Mount Carmel, Patchogue; St. Joseph, Hagerman, and St. Sylvester, Medford.

Barbuti, Raymond J. Scrapbook, Quicky Lake, New York.

Carucci, M., "The Sand Pits of Port Washington", unpublished paper.

Computer run of city rankings of Italian population from 1980 Census undertaken by F.G. Bohme, Chief, Census History Staff, in correspondence with the author, January 4, 1984.

Confirmation Register Our Lady of Mount Carmel. Patchogue, New York.

Diary of Antonio Cesare. Staten Island, NY: Center for Migration Studies.

Femminella, F.X., "Ethnicity and Ego Identity", Doctoral Dissertation. New York University, 1968.

Giardina, C., *Collected Writings,* Vol. 6, "History of My Life as I Remember". Port Washington Public Library, Reference Division.

Glen Cove Folder, Nassau County Museum and Reference Library.

Hicks Labor Record. In possession of Hicks Family.

Marriage Register, Our Lady of Mount Carmel, Patchogue; St.Joseph, Hagerman; St.Sylvester, Medford.

Matrimoniorum Registrum, Our Lady of Good Counsel. November 20, 1910 to July 23, 1945.

Misierewicz, L., "The Story of Glen Cove". In *Glen Cove Folder,* Nassau County Museum and Reference Library.

Minutes of Societa di Mutuo Succorso. In possession of Catherine Cochiola.

Nassau County Voting Behavior in 1968. S.B. Dember, Undergraduate Dissertation, Princeton University, 1969.

Nassau Land Records, Liber 238.

Nuzzolo, Ferdinand. Scrapbook, Inwood, New York.

New York State Manuscript Census, Nassau County, 1915, 1925.

New York State Manuscript Census, Suffolk County, 1915, 1925.

"Particles of the Past: Sandmining on Long Island, 1870s-1980s". Port Washington Public Library Exhibit, May 1983.

Port Washington Folder, Nassau County Museum and Reference Library.

Shenton, J. Speech, "Sands of Port". Program Port Washington Public Library, January 31, 1982.

Soveriegn Realty Company in 1906. *See, Suffolk County Deeds,* Liber 600, p. 448 and Liber 690, p. 281, 1906.

Suffolk County Records Date of Incorporation, Liber 22.

United States Census Street Schedules, Nassau County, 1880, 1900, 1910.

United States Census Street Schedules, Suffolk County, 1880, 1900, 1910.

Vacca, A., *History of Copiague,* 1948, unpublished.

Vigotty Records, in possession of June Vigotty and Allen Vigotty, Lake George, New York.

Westbury Folder, Queensborough Public Library.

Westbury Folder, Nassau County Museum and Reference Library.

Wohl, R.A., "Reflection on the Airplane in Italian Culture, 1910-1940". Presentation on occasion of conference "Reappraisals in Modern Italian History", Columbia University, September 30, 1983.

INTERVIEWS

Abbondandolo, Lawrence, Glen Cove, February 23, 1983.

Abbatiello, Joseph, Westbury, January 11, 1979

Barbuti, Raymond, J., Quichy Lake, November 10, 1983.

Barry, Ronald, Fr., Massapequa, September 20, 1982.

Bassi, Santo, Port Washington, May 9, 1983.

Buffalino, Carmen, Westbury, April 10, 1979.

Capobianco, Carmine and Louis, January 17, 1983.

Carta, Antonio Maria, Port Washington, May 8, 1983.

Cavallaro, Mrs., Westbury, March 2, 1979.

Ciardullo, Frank, Westbury, January 11, 1979.

Ciminera, Josephine, Port Washington, June 6, 1983.

Cocchiola, Antoinette and Catherine, Glen Cove, February 28, 1983.

Constantino, Rocco, Copiague, September 7, 1980.

Contino, Marie, Patchogue, April 9, 1985.

Curcio, Daniel, Massapequa, October 4, 1980.

Curcio, Robert, Copiague, January 16, 1984.

Daddio, Carmine, Westbury, January 11, 1979.

DeJanna, Helen, Port Washington, June 20, 1983.

De Laura, Anthony, Monsignor, Valley Stream, March 23, 1982.

Della Rosa, Fr., Glen Cove, January 11, 1983.

Dell Vecchio, Francis, Fr., Brooklyn, March 31, 1976.

DeMeo, Jennie, Port Washington, June 22, 1983.

Emory, Mrs. John, December 8, 1978.

Felice, Pat, Patchogue, April 9, 1985.

Fromma, Maria Givanna, Port Washington, June 22, 1983.

Fuoco, Elizabeth, Louis and Stephen, Patchogue, December 13, 1984.

Galasieski, Virginia, Bethpage, January 15, 1984.

Pontiero, Marge, Patchogue, March 7, 1985.

Posillico, Al, March 10, 1979.

Posillico, Dominic, Farmingdale, December 4, 1981.

Posillico, Fred and Joseph, Westbury, March 9, 1979.

Razzano, Anthony and Josephine, Westbury, March 9, 1979.

Renaldo, Mary L., Glen Cove, January 17, 1983.

Renzullo, Catherine, Greenport, June 17, 1983.

Romeo, Albert, Arthur, Ernest and Rose, Patchogue, March 7, 1985.

Rudolph, Mary Ann, Copiague, November 6, 1981.

Salerno, Lucy, Port Washington, May 3, 1983.

Saxton, William, Amityville, May 11, 1982.

Selesky, Evelyn Cisario, Copiague, January 15, 1984.

Sica, Rose, Bethpage, January 15, 1984.

Sledzous, Alexander, Fr., Patchogue, July 26, 1985.

Starace, Carl, Babylon, December 15, 1982.

Stephani, Catherine and Charles, Patchogue, December 14, 1984.

Stephani, Joseph, December 14, 1984.

Suozzi, Joseph, Mineola, March 17, 1983.

Suozzi, Vincent, Glen Cove, January 25, 1983.

Tommassone, Ralph, Patchogue, April 9, 1985.

Tranquili, Tito, Copiague, July 1, 1980.

Vacca, Angelo, Copiague, June 5, 1984.

Vigliotti, Crescenzo, Blue Point, January 8, 1984.

Vigotty, Alan and June, Massapequa, December 17, 1983.

Wickey, Ina, Westbury, January 26, 1979.

Yannacone, Fortunata, Victor, Patchogue, October 2, 1984.

Zavatt, Joseph, C., Garden City, July 15, 1984.

INDEX

Abbatiello, G., 152, 168, 169
Abbatiello, J., 267
Abbondondolo family, 156
   Abbondandolo, L., 81, 267
   Abbondondolo, M., 117
   Abbondondolo, N., 81
Adjustment, 81
Aggeola, F., 12
Agius, Fr., 132, 206
Alba, R., 222, 223, 261
Albano-Italians, 16-17, 91, 131, 216
Alfano, P., 146
Alfieri, A., 265
Alienation, 90
"All for a Woman's Honor, Joseph Fucci Shoots James Renzulo and Salvatore Russo of Inwood for Defending a Woman's Name", 60
Allen, F.L., 261
Allied Powers, 99
American Civil War, 14
"American Education and Italian Immigrant Response", 260
American Education and the European Immigrant, 1840-1940, 260
American Federation of Labor, 49, 50
American Holy Name Society, 133
American Immigration, 39n., 262
American Italian Historical Association (AIHA), 260, 265
   Newletter, 203, 260
American Lace Manufacturing Company, 54
American Lace Operators, 54
American Lawyer, The, 261
American Legion, 24n., 109
   American Legion, Port Washington, 263
"American Political Process and the Italian Participation in New York State", 260
American Red Cross, 178
"American Relief for Italy", 160, 169
Amfithreatrof, E., 41
Amityville Historical Society, 262
Amityville Record, 20, 21, 24n., 35, 37, 38, 43, 68, 69, 70, 71, 72, 77, 78, 126, 128, 129, 160, 172, 264
Anel, T., 100
Angela Pruess, Party Plan Sales, 263
Angelo Cocchiola Papers, 265
Anniello, C., 26
"Another Italian Holdup", 60
Arcese, Msgr., 123
Andreoti, G., 170
Argus Business and Residential Directory of 1904, The, 265
Assimilation in American Life, 262
Assimilation of Ethnic Groups, The: The Italian Case, 262
Atlantic Bridge Authority, 187
Atlantic Migration, The, 39n., 262
Atlas of the Ocean Shore of Suffolk County, Long Island, Westernly Section Amityville to Eastport Inclusive, 265
Auburn University, 191
Austria, 159
   Austria-Hungary, 99
Aviano, E., 265
Aviano, M., 119
Axis Powers, 153, 160

B
Babylon Town Board, 68, 77, 79
Baccaloni, S., 125
Backward Glance, A, 262
Bacon, R.L., 142
Bailey family, 20
   Bailey, A., 20
   Bailey, P., 261
Balbo, I., 166-168
Balbo, Msgr., 125
Banfield, E., 218, 261
Baptism Record of Our Lady of Good Counsel, Inwood, New York, 1910, 133, 266
Baptist Church, 109
"Barber of Seville", 125

Barbuti family, 112
　Barbuti, R.J., 112, 267
　Barbuti, R.J., Scrapbook, 266
　Barbuti, T.V., 112
Barcellona family, 36
　Barcellona, C., 198, 221
Barry family, 128
　Barry, R., 128, 267
Bassi, S., 47, 267
Bell, D., 261
Bellot, A., 130, 131, 262
Bellport Columbus Sick and Benevolent Association, 91
Bellport High School, 204
Bellport School Board, 73
Benicase, A., 54, 174
Bernagazzi family, 23, 35, 38, 69
　Bernagazzi, W., 72, 171
Bertucci, P., 173
Bethpage Golf Course and Polo Grounds, 21
Bianchi, J.W., 119, 185
Bianco, C., 136, 242
Bilingualism, 145-148, 203
Black Americans, 42, 145, 202, 203, 204, 209, 221
Black Hand, 56-57, 58, 220
Black Hand, A Chapter in Ethnic Crime, The, 263
"Black Hand At Work", 59
Blessed Virgin Sodality, 104
Board of Mangers of the Five Towns YMCA, 178
Bohme, F.G., 266
Bolletino della Sera, 35
Bookbinder, B., 262
Boston, Massachusetts, 38
Botta, D., 20-21
Branucci, Vice Consul, 155
Brennan, T., 130, 160
Brinckerhoff Manor, 23
　Map of Section The Brinckerhoff Manor, Copiague Long Island, Suffolk County, 39n.
British Navy, 156
Brookhaven Town Board, 183
Brooklyn Times-Union, 264
Brooklyn Water Works, 22
Brotherhood of St. Cono, 91
Brothers of Columbus, 91
Bruno, J.F., 127
Buffa, D., 139
Buffalino, C., 267

Buffalino, J., 40
Buffalino, R., 100
Bugala, A., 158
Burns, Mayor, 102, 189

C

Caboto, 36, 77
Calabria, J., 178
Calderone, F., 118
Calderone, S., 118
Calella, J., 139
Calvelli, Jr., E., 175
Calvelli, Sr., E., 175
Camillo, T.J., 173-174
Caminera, J. DiLeo, 48
Campagnoli, H., 37
Campagnoli, J., 22, 23, 34, 35, 36-39, 39n., 68, 69, 78, 103, 126, 127, 129,
Campagnoli, Jean, 160
Campagnoli, L., 171
Canamare, J., 178
Cancer Society, 178
Cangaro, S., 29-30
Canivan, Msgr., 12, 122
Cannizaro, J., 132
Capobianco family, 29, 130, 156, 157
　Capobianco, A., 157, 260
　Capobianco, C., 28, 80, 267
　Capobianco, E., 123, 127
　Capobianco, F., 28, 151
　Capobianco, L., 67, 102, 267
　Capobianco, V., 28, 96, 151
Capobianco, Fr.124
Caporale, R., 260
Capozzi, C., 16
Carbonelli, P.P., 155
Cardamone, J., 120, 136, 184, 185, 219
Carnegie Library, 118
Caroli, B.B., 260
Carta, A.M., 267
Carucci, M., 266
Caruso family, 157
Caso, R., 195, 220
Castle, 130
Catapano, G., 26
Catholic Committee for Relief Abroad, 170
Catholic Youth Organization, 129
Catroppa, 130
Cavalieri, F., 118, 260
Cavallaro, 267

Cavelli, D., 16
Census of the Population, 1950. Vol. VI. Characteristics of the Characteristics of the Population, Part V, 265
Center for Migration Studies, 260, 262, 263, 266
Cerullo, R., 102
Cesare, A., 76
Class in Suburbia, 262
Cocchiola, A., 39n., 84, 92, 117, 122, 123, 188, 267
Cocchiola, C., 27, 28, 39n., 265, 266, 267
Cocchiola, G., 117
Cocchiola, S., 117
Cohen, A., 195
Cold War, 169
Colicchio, J., 198
Colin Pants Factory, 44
Collected Writings, Vol. 6, 266
Colombo, C., 36
Colonial Park, 1
Colonial Sand and Gravel Company, 49
Columbia University, 175, 266
Communism, 154, 168, 169, 170
Community Action, 203
Community Chest, 178
Concordia Society, 95
Confirmation Register of Our Lady of Mount Carmel, Patchogue, 266
Constantino, R., 267
Contino, M., 136, 267

Contino, R., 181
Copiague Board of Education, 172, 262
Copiague Chamber of Commerce, 182, 265
Copiague Civic Association, 97, 172
Copiague Fire Department, 72
Copiague Lions Club, 77, 78, 79
Copiague Public School District Newsletter, 260
Copiague Railroad Station, 103
Copiague School Board, 171
Copiague Town Board, 77
Copiague. Your Town and Mine, 24n., 262
Coppola, F., 41
Corriere D'America, 105, 112, 155, 264
Corsi, E., 193
Costanza, 59
Cotillo, S., 69
Cottone, S., 136
Court Vittoria, 96
Cowell, D.D., 260
Crescent Sand and Gravel Company, 11
Crime, 54, 56-65, 66
Crispino, J., 262
Il Crociato 123, 264
Cronin, J., 135
Cross, Rev., 67
"Crusader Who Lost His Way, The", 261
Cunningham, 130
Cuomo, M., 250
Curcio family, 160
    Curcio, A., 72, 77
    Curcio, Mrs. A., 160
    Curcio, D., 71, 267
    Curcio, R., 198, 267
C.W. Post College, 29

D

D'Agostino, A., 16, 130
D'Amato, A., 220
D'Annunzio, G., 106
D'Elia, 130, 180
Daddio, A., 40
Daddio, C., 207, 267
Daddio, J., 42
Daddio, M., 42
Damita, J., 11
Dante, 36
Davi, R., 139
Davis, A.L., 262
Davis, R., 206
DeFalco, D., 177
DeFeo, Guy, 111

DeJanna, H., 267
DeJanna, H.S., 47, 48, 49, 138
del Monte, R., 194
DeLaura, A., 125, 129, 137, 267
Deliza, B., 14
DeMarco, J., 127
DeMaria, L., 44
DeMeo, A., 49-50, 111, 147, 154, 164, 175, 197
DeMeo, J., 12, 138, 267
DeMeo, M., 46
DeSantis, A., 182
Del Vecchio, F., 127
Dell Vecchio, Fr., 267
Dell'Assunta Hall, 115
Dell'Assunta Society, 73, 74, 75, 93, 151, 158
Dell, Jr., J., 165
Della Pietra, J., 136
Della Rosa, Fr., 125, 209, 267
Della, J., 136
Democratic Party, 185, 186, 187, 188-189, 190, 192, 194, 195, 196, 220
Department of Elections, Nassau County Enrollment, 265
Desmond, 130
DiLiberte,Fr., 125
DiCroce, 130
DiGiovanni, G., 151
DiGiuseppe, 43
DiLeo family, 156
   DiLeo, C., 81
diLeonardo, M., 212, 216, 262
DiMita, G., 28
DiMita, J., 28
DiPaola, A., 195, 196
DiPietrantonio, 151
DiSibio, P., 186-187
Diary of Antonio Cesare, 266
Dibbins, E., 262
Dioguardi, P.S., 117
Diranna, S., 12
Directory of Patchogue, Long Island, New York, 120, 265
Discrimination, 1, 57, 65, 66, 67, 163, 172, 173
Dobriner, W.C., 262
Dodge family, 10
"Don Pasquale",125
Doughty, W.G., 185, 186
Dowling, 130
The Dream Deferrd People; Politics and Planning in Suburbia New York, 1977, 24n., 262
Durazzano Society, 74, 137, 151, 152
Dwyer, Judge, 75

E
E. Bailey and Sons, 51
East Patchogue School Board, 171
Eide, E., 24n., 262
"Emigrant, The", 115
Emory, J., Mrs., 8, 267
End of Ideology, The, 261
England (English), 12, 70, 154, 223
English Language Education, 70
Epaminonde, A., 164, 165
Episcopal Church, 115
Esposito, A., 128
Ethiopia, 153, 154
Ethnic Alienation, 262
Ethnic Families in America, 260
Ethnic Myth, The, 219
Ethnic Myth: Race, Ethnicity and Class in America, The, 263
"Ethnicity and Ego Identity", 266
Europe, 99, 210
Caribbean, 210
"European Americans. From Immigrants to Ethnics", 261
Evolution of Modern Italy, The, 263

F
Fabrizio, N., 14
Famigletti, A., 84
Far East, 210
Far Rockaway Auxiliary of the Peninsula General Hospital, 179
Far Rockaway Journal, 59, 112, 264
Farfariello, 96
Farina, N., 173
Farrell, H.F., 130
Fasano family, 157
   Fasano, A., 157
   Fasano, P., 12
Fascism, 153, 155-156
Feast of the Assumption, 23
Felice family, 31, 32
   Felice, A., 185
   Felice, F., 31
   Felice, M., 174
   Felice, P., 19, 34, 97, 118-119, 120, 267
Femminella, F.X., 32, 211, 212, 260, 266
Ferlazzo family, 119
Fiala, J., 119
Fidelity Party, 180
Fifteenth Census of the United States, 1940 Population, Vol. II. Characteristics of the Popu-

lation, Part V. p.110. Census of the Population, 1950. Vol. VI. Characteristics of the Population Part 22, 265
"Figlia d'a Modonna, A", 115
Fiore, F., 61
Fiorentino, D., 123, 125
First Souvenir Journal of St,. Rocco's Parish, 124, 188
Five Towns Child Care Center, 179
Five Towns Planning and Zoning Committee, 179
"Flexible Tradition: South Italian Immigrants Confront a New York Experience, A", 261
Florida, 206, 210
Foerster, R., 58
Follini, R., 119
Ford Auto Agency, 119
Fordham Law School, 190
Fordham University, 175
Foresters of America, Court Vesuvius No. 408, 95, 96
Fox Movie, 118
France (French), 14, 105, 154
 Argonne Forest, 105
Frappoala's Bakery, 48
Fraumeni, J., 181
Freschi, J., 104
Friends of the Nassau County Museum, 263
From Sicily to Elizabeth Street, 262
Fromma, M.G., 267
Frommja, M., 49-50
Frugone, F., 104
Full Gospel Christian Church, 262
"Funerals, Family and Forefathers: Italian-American Funeral Practices", 260
Fuoco family, 32, 90, 119, 185
 Fuoco, A., 33, 119, 120, 136, 184, 185, 236
 Fuoco, E., 33, 90, 119, 267
 Fuoco, L., Jr., 119, 120, 185, 267
 Fuoco, S., 267
Fusco family, 29
 Fusco, J., 127

G
Gabaccia, D.R., 217, 262
Gabarino, D., 119
Galasieski, V., 102, 103, 267
Gallitelli, R., 132
Gallo, A., 16
Gallo, L., 119
Gallo, P., 262
Gallo, R., 119
Galloway, Fr., 206
Galuzzi, I., 23
Galuzzi, M., 72
Gambino, R., 262
Garafola family, 32
Garibaldi, 36, 77
Garibaldi Lodge, Order of the Sons of Italy, 97
Gazola family, 32
Gennovario, J., 22
Genova, D., 160, 169
Gentile, C., 63
Gerardi, J., 204-205
Germany (Germans), 11, 42, 80, 99, 146, 154, 157, 159
Gerrato, J., 265
Giardina, C., 266
Ginocchio J., 33-34
Ginocchio's Corner, 34
Giordano, F., 101-102
Giorgini family, 23, 38
 Giorgini, I., 23, 35, 36
 Giorgini, R., 37, 72, 126, 171-172, 181
Giorgio, F., 167
Giornale d'Italia, 35
Giovanetti, A., 98, 262
"Giovanezza", 155
Gitto, G., 12
Glen Cove Advance, 161
Glen Cove Echo, 83, 85, 87, 92, 96, 101, 102, 151, 155, 170, 264
Glen Cove Guardian, 156, 157, 264
Glen Cove High School, 191
Glen Cove Loggia, 94
Glen Cove Neighborhood House, 85
Glen Cove Pentecostal Church, 139
Glen Cove Record, 12, 80, 117, 118, 139, 141, 142, 150, 151, 156, 169, 170, 188, 189, 190, 191, 193, 194, 195, 196
Glen Cove Record-Advance, 116, 190, 264
Glen Cove Zoning Board, 193
Glen Cove's Neighborhood House, 85
Golden Jubilee Journal of Our Lady of the Assumption, R.C. Church, Copiague, 265
Goodwin-Gallagher Sand and Gravel Company, 46
Gordon, M., 223, 262
Gorgolione, J., 139
Gorgone, A., 36, 43
Grace family, 29
Great Depression, 28, 36, 123, 127, 141-152, 166
Grella, R., 117, 124

Grucci Fireworks, 182-183
Grucci family, 32
 Grucci, J., 183
 Grucci, Sr., F., 182-183
"Grucci's Trial by Tragedy, The", 261
Guarino, Joseph, 197
Guidera, Mrs. T., 182
Guido, D., 139
Guiment, L., 122
Gulotta, F., Nassau County District Attorney, 178, 249
Gulotta, T., 200
Gumo, J.T., 178

H
Habenstein, R.W., 260
Hagerman Band, 134
Hagerman Firehouse, 133
Hagerman Hall, 133, 134
Handlin, O., 50, 215, 262
Hanse, G., 198
Hansen, M.L., 39n., 262
Harney, R.F., 260
Harvard Law School, 194
Healy, 130
Hempstead Sentinal, 40, 264
Hempstead Town Deputy Highway Commissioner, 187
Hempstead Town Highway Department, 186
Henry's Factory, 143
"Heroism of An Italian in War, Obscured for 16 Years, Today Shines in N.Y., The", 105
Hesah Home, 48
Hicks Labor Record, 26, 41, 42, 266
Hicks Nursery, 228
Hicks Nursey Company, 40-43
Hicks, 228
Hicks, E., 8
Higham, J., 116, 262
Hispanics, 204
History of Copiague, 266
History of Long Island, 263
"History of My Life as I Remember", 266
History of Port Washington, A, 24n., 263
History of Two Great Counties, Nassau and Suffolk, The, 261
History of the Rockaways, A, 262
Hitler, A., 153
Holy Name Society, 138
Holy Name Society of Our Lady of Good Counsel, 178

Holy Name Society of St. Peter Alcantara Church, 164
Holy Rollers, 139
Home Defense Corps, 103-104
"House on the Hill: Mobility Patterns in an Italian Neighborhood, The", 265
Hyde, C., 147
Hyde, E.B., 265

I
Iacini, S., 128-129, 132
Iannarone, C., 178
Iannuci, R., 42
Ianucci family, 68
Ianucci, A., 75, 158
Ianucci, H., 99
Ianucci, J., 168
Icanusa Society, 179, 180, 211
Il Circolo, 148
Imbese, D., 179
Immigrants Speak, Italian-Americans Tell Their Story, The, 262
"Immigrants in the New South: Italians in Louisiana's Sugar Parishes, 1880-1910", 261
Immigration Law, 58, 70
Immigration Restriction League, 112
Impellitteri, V., 193
India (Indians), 168
Ingoglia, B., 181
International Migration Review, 261
Interparish Monthly, 104
"Interview With a Senior Citizen, June 2, 1984, An", 265
Inwood Businessmen's Association, 178
Inwood Fire District Board, 187
Inwood Homeowners Civic Association, 178
Iorizzo, L., 262
Ireland (Irish), 11, 49, 67, 80, 122, 126, 130, 134, 137, 138, 218
Irwin, J.F., 127
Isaac Hicks and Sons, 8
Istitto, 12
Italian Affiliated Church of God of the Christian Assemblyin North America, 140
Italian Americans, 262, 263
Italian American Civic Association, 152
Italian American Civic League, 246
Italian American Civic Club, Local No. 3, 97
"Italian American Family, The", 260
Italian American Federation of Republican Clubs, 74

Italian American Republican Club, 152, 164, 165, 186
Italian American Service Club of Brookhaven, 212, 223
Italian American Social club of Manorhaven, 179
Italian Americans Into the Twilight of Ethnicity, 3, 261
Italian Americans Through the Generations, The, 260
Italian Americans. Troubled Roots, The, 221, 263
"Italian Battlefront, The", 106
Italian Bersiglieri, 101
"Italian Bulletin", 162
Italian Central Committee, 165
Italian Civic Center of Inwood, 149
Italian Concordia Society, Benevolent and Political of Bellport, 94-95
Italian Education Society of Inwood, 154
Italian Evening Bulletin, 104
Italian Holy Name Society, 133
Italian Immigrant Women in North America, The, 260
Italian Mutual Aid Society, 138, 147, 152, 164, 179, 211
Italians of Greenwich Village, The, 217, 263
Italian Pentecostal Church of Copiague, 139
Italian Political Club of Port Washington, 96-97
Italian Political Club of Glen Cove, 102, 188, 189
Italian Red Cross, 153-154
Italian Republican Club, 178
Italian Republican Club of Glen Cove, 189
"Italian Review", 162, 164
Italian School, 155
"Italian Shooting Fray", 60
Italian Welfare Club of Glen Cove, 96
Italian American Service Club of Brookhaven, 212
Italian Children's Relief Society, 160
Italian Navy, 156
Italianitá, 22
Italians in America, The, 262
Italians of Greenwich Village, The, 263
Italo Balbo: A Fascist Life, 263
Italo-Ethiopian War, 154, 155
Italy, 16, 99, 100, 153, 154-155, 156, 159, 211
   Abruzzi, 129
   Avellino, 11, 26, 28, 106
   Bari, 138
   Benevento, 12
   Calabria, 16, 32, 33, 92, 205, 216

Coreggio, 168
Cosenza, 33, 186
Durazzano, 6-7, 8, 25-26, 30, 93, 99, 168, 207, 208, 216
Fiume, 106
Florence, 34
Frugento, 29
Genoa, 20
Messina, 16, 18
Naples, 6, 7, 12, 26, 28, 117, 128, 159
Nola, 6, 7, 8, 26, 93
Nusco, 28
Paduli, 12, 29
Piacenza, 14
Ponte Corvo, 169, 170
Potenza, 12, 194
Puglia, 16
Romagna, 23
Rome, 117
Salerno, 157
Sardinia (Sardinians), 144, 180
Saviano, 6, 7, 8, 26, 93
Sicily, 12, 16, 17, 18, 61, 118, 136, 215, 207, 217
   Pioppo, 139
Sturno, 29, 92, 122
Terranova di Sibari, 32
Torella dei Lombardi, 26, 48, 102
Trieste, 11, 47, 106, 117
Tufo Avellino, 104
Venice, 117
Izzo family, 117, 124
Izzo, C., 21
Izzo, P., 117
Izzo, P., 124

J

J. Franklin Bell American Legion Post, 178
James Marino Lodge, 160
Jamestown Exposition, 40
Japan (Japanese), 153
Jenkins, J.J., 154
Jenkins, J., 146, 147
Johnson, B., 39n.
Jolly Gang Club, 112
Jones, M.A., 39n., 262
Jonotta, R., 117
Journal of Social History, 261
Judaism (Jews), 72, 137, 202, 203
Julian, B., 15
Juliani, R., 260
Juliano, F., 152

K

Kamelia, 72
Kaplan, S., 24n., 179, 262
Kelly family, 16
Knights of Columbus, 67, 72, 73, 126
Knights of Mount Carmel, 160
Korea (Koreans), 179
Ku Klux Klan, 72-73, 178, 109, 212
"Ku Klux Klan on Long Island, The", 260

L

LaGuardia in Congress, 264
LaGuardia, F., 189
LaGumina, M., 139
LaGumina, S., 56, 95, 142, 260, 262, 263
LaPera, A.N., 197
LaPorte, 160
LaSalle Military Academy, 119
Labor History, 261
Ladies' Republican Victory Club, 188
Lado, P., 156
Lagnese family, 109
Lamberti, R., 26, 27, 48, 137
Larriga, D., 46
Laviano, J., 185
Lavoro, Il, 260, 264
Lawrence High School, 146, 173, 174, 202, 203
Lazzarino, J., 41
Leonardo, J.V., 182
Leone, F., 181
"Life of St. Anthony, The", 115
Limongelli family, 189
   Limongelli, A.M.M., 68
   Limongelli, J., 29
   Limongelli, R., 189
Limongelli's Democratic Club, 189
Lincoln Lodge, Order of the Sons of Italy, 94
Lions Club, 78, 178
Little Italies, 1, 9, 14, 18, 23, 31, 34, 35, 38-39, 60, 64, 80, 81, 87, 92, 98, 153, 156, 176, 184-185, 208-209
LoGrande, M., 200
Lombardo, S., 61
Long Island
   Amityville, 19, 20, 35, 36, 70, 127, 129, 268
   Babylon, 18, 198, 268
   Bellport, 12, 18, 19, 33, 64, 91, 95, 106, 119, 134, 135, 182, 185
   Belmont, 35
   Bethpage, 20, 21, 267, 268
   Blue Point, 135, 268
   Boomertown, 19, 133
   Branch, The, 13, 111
   Breezy Hill (*See also*, Nanny Goat Hill), 7
   Brookhaven, 18, 185
   Camp Upton, 105, 106
   Cedarhurst, 13, 14, 96, 105, 173
   Colonial Springs, 1
   Copiague, 1, 3, 9, 19-24, 24n., 34, 35, 36, 38, 43, 44, 68-70, 71-72, 73, 77, 78, 80, 111, 123, 125, 126, 127, 128, 129, 137, 171, 172, 181, 197-198, 206, 209, 218, 220, 221, 234, 243, 267, 268
   Crow's Hill, 15, 148
   Deer Park, 1, 221, 232
   East Patchogue (*See also*, Hagerman), 17, 18, 23, 31-33, 50, 80, 95, 106, 119-120, 133, 134, 155, 158, 171, 185, 204, 206, 211, 219, 221, 218
   East Port, 137
   Elmont, 221
   Far Rockaway, 61, 96, 130, 167, 175
   Farmingdale, 20, 21, 23, 126
   Five Towns, 13, 145, 149, 166, 173, 185, 202
   Franklin Square, 221
   Garden City, 48, 268
   Glen Cove, 3, 9, 12-13, 19, 23, 28-29, 44, 56, 67, 80, 81-87, 92, 94, 101, 102, 109, 115-116, 117-118, 121-122, 127, 139, 141, 142, 149, 151, 155, 156, 157, 160, 169, 170, 187-197, 189, 192, 193, 194, 195, 196, 208, 209, 216, 218, 219, 221, 245, 247, 250, 265, 267, 268
   Greenport, 267
   Greenvale, 170
   Hagerman (*See also*, East Patchogue), 18, 23, 50, 80, 95, 106, 119, 133, 134, 218
   Hempstead, 13, 74, 118, 195
   Hempstead Plains, 8
   Hewlett, 13, 14
   Inwood, 9, 10, 13-17, 19, 58, 60, 61, 62, 63, 64, 65, 80, 91, 95-96, 103-105, 111, 112, 113, 125, 130, 131, 144, 145, 146, 149, 153, 154, 160, 173, 174, 185-187, 218, 219, 201-203, 206, 216, 221, 239, 244, 246, 266
   Lawrence, 13, 14, 17, 63, 96, 146
   Lindenhurst, 19, 20, 129
   Locust Valley, 24n., 29
   Manorhaven, 138, 167, 180-181
   Marconiville, 1, 3, 19-24, 34-39, 43, 68, 69, 71-72, 77, 78, 79, 80, 103, 109, 126, 127, 161, 171, 172, 181, 198, 209, 210, 216, 233, 234, 243
   Massepequa, 20, 22, 128, 267, 268
   Mineola, 74, 268
   Montauk, 18, 118

Montauk Point, 118, 141
Nanny Goat Hill (*See also*, Breezy Hill), 7
Nassau County, 3, 15, 17, 23, 27, 58, 62, 63, 84, 94, 109, 112, 130, 137, 142, 158, 163, 166, 175, 185, 186, 187, 190, 191, 192, 193, 196, 197, 200, 203, 249
New Cassel, 7, 26, 76, 203
North Bellport, 23, 31, 50, 80, 119, 135, 158, 185, 204, 211, 221, 236
North Hempstead, 74, 197, 199
North Lawrence, 148
North Lindenhurst, 221
North Patchogue, 211, 221
Oakdale, 119
Orchard, The, 80-81, 83, 84, 85, 101, 102, 116, 117, 143, 188, 189, 190, 191, 193, 195, 024, 209
Oyster Bay, 12, 23, 86, 92, 122, 123, 143, 170, 188, 190
Patchogue, 3, 9, 17-19, 31, 32, 33, 34, 50, 51, 72, 73, 80, 90, 91, 94, 95, 97, 106, 118-120, 125, 133, 134, 140, 143, 155, 158, 160, 174, 182, 184-185, 204, 205, 211, 212, 216, 218, 219, 221, 231, 242, 265, 267, 268
Patchogue Village, 221
Port Washington, 3, 9-12, 13, 19, 24n., 26, 27, 28, 47, 48, 49, 50, 80, 99, 102, 109, 111, 137-138, 144, 151, 152, 154, 157, 160, 162, 164, 165, 166, 167, 168, 170, 175, 179, 180, 197, 216, 218, 219, 220, 221, 229, 230, 237, 267
Rockaway, 16-17, 60, 130, 166
Rockville Centre, 137, 175, 222
Roslyn, 11, 168, 170, 238
Shirley, 221
South Huntington, 19
Suffolk County, 3, 17, 18, 19, 20, 23, 34, 94, 97, 136-137, 163, 185, 198, 231, 163, 200, 206, 220, 231
Valley Stream, 267
Wallage (*See also*, Westbury), 6
West Patchogue, 135, 158
Westbury (*See also*, Wallage), 3, 6, 7, 8, 9, 19, 22, 23, 24n., 25, 26, 30, 40, 42, 43, 74, 76, 80, 83, 87-89, 93, 99, 100, 108, 109, 113, 114, 115, 126, 137-138, 149, 151, 158, 159, 160, 169, 170, 182, 198, 199, 203-204, 207, 208, 209, 216, 218, 219, 220, 221, 228, 240, 267, 268
Woodmere, 13, 14
Wyandanch, 1
Yaphank, 72, 106, 183
Long Island Catholic, 264, 134
"Long Island Chariot of Fire, The", 260

Long Island Enterprise, 21, 22, 23, 24n., 264
Long Island Forum, 260, 261
Long Island Garden Landscapers Association, 179
Long Island Heritage, 260
Long Island Lighting Company, 69
Long Island People and Places, Past and Present, 262
Long Island Press, 264
Long Island Railroad, 10, 13, 18, 20, 28, 43, 51, 80, 109, 111, 220, 226, 227, 263
Long Island Railroad, A Comprehensive History, the Age of Expansion, 1833-1880, 263
Long Island Record, 20
Long Island Univesity, 29
Long Island University Magazine, 29, 261
"Long Island's Italians and the Labor Movement", 260
Long Island. The Sunrise Homeland, 111, 263
Lopreato, J., 2, 216, 218, 263
Lord's Trade School, Mrs., 148
Lordi, J.S., 176
Lorenz, J., 31, 46
Lost Battalion of the 77th Division, 102
Lotito family, 32
   Lotito, F., 54
   Lotito, L., 32, 33
Louisianna, 42
   New Orleans, 118
Lunati family, 120

M

Maccarone, P., 101, 116, 151
Macolino, I.W., 14
Mafia, 57, 63, 220
Mahon, J.J., 104, 130
Mailer family, 31
Malta, 132
Malvella, S., 139
Mama Leone's Restaurant, 181
Mamorale, N.L., 67-68
"Man without a Face, The", 115
Manfredo, 151
Manno, A., 136
Manorville Bible Protestant Church, 140
Map and Listing of Copiague, 182, 265
Marafioti family, 117
   Marafioti, R., 156
   Marafioti, S., 156
Marchisio, J., 169

Marconi Community League, 69
Marconi Community League Clubhouse, 35
Marconi, G., 34-35, 36, 38, 69, 77, 234
Margiotta, 132
Margiotta, J., 195
Mariani, Fr., 138
Marinello, "Papa", 181
Marino family, 27-28
　Marino, A., 11, 27-49
　Marino, J., 11, 26, 237
　Marino, John, 181
　Marino, Joseph, 12, 28
Marion, M.G., 165
Marriage Register, Our Lady of Mount Carmel, Patchogue; St. Joseph, Hagerman Patchogue; St. Joseph, Hagerman and Saint Sylvester, Medford, 266
Martilotta, F., 15
Martin, J.W., 170
Martone, A.J., 117, 192, 193, 195
Mary Immaculate Church, 133, 134, 135
Mason, Mayor, 190, 191
Masons, 73
Mastalio, R., 156
Mathias, E.L., 261
Matrimoniorum Registrum, Our Lady of Good Counsel, November 20, 1910 to July 23, 1945, 266
Mayo, M., 40, 41
Mazza, M., 149
Mazza, N., 133
Mazza, R., 133
Mazzini family, 77
　Mazzini, G., 36
Mazzotti family, 32
　Mazzotti, R., 32, 33
McAlpin Estate, 40
McCahill, 57
McDonnell, 132
McLaughlin, V.Y., 42, 261
Meadowbrook Hospital, 175
Medford, 95
Medici, Professor, 147
Mercadante, L., 191-192, 193, 195
Mercy Hospital, 175
Merendino, C., 178, 179
Messina Earthquake of 1908, 18
Metropolitan Opera House, 38, 125
Michelangelo, 123
Migliacco, E., 96
Milano, A., 73
Milstein, S., 261

Mindel, C.H., 260
Minutes of Societa di Mutuo Succorso, 266
Misierewicz, L., 266
Moies, R.L., 78
Molloy, T., Bishop, 122, 123, 124, 127, 135
Mondello, S., 262
Monteforte, J., 24, 74, 115
Monteleone, R., 136, 205
Montemarano, T., 178
Moral Basis of a Backwards Society, The, 261
Morelli, C., 178
Morgan family, 6, 29
Morino, G. 26
Mormino, G., 265
Morris, 130
Mundelein, Bishop, 130-131
"Murderer Makes His Escape", 60
Murro, C., 181
Musmanno, M., 263
Musso family, 120
Mussolini, B., 153, 154, 155
Muzante, 151

N

Naples, T., 40
Nassau Board of Supervisors, 187
Nassau County Museum and Reference Library, 227, 237, 238, 265, 266
Nassau County Police Force, 157
Nassau County Voting Behavior in 1968, 266
Nassau Daily Review, 187, 264
Nassau Herald, 112, 148, 154, 160, 173, 174, 177, 178, 179, 202, 203, 206, 264
Nassau Industrial School, 148, 149
Nassau Land Records, 14, 266
Nassau Review Star, 24n., 264
Nassau Suburbia U.S.A. The First Seventy Years 1899 to 1974, 4, 263
Nassau Suffolk Reginal Planning Board, Vol. 8, 265
Nassau County Medical Society, 175
Nassau-Suffolk Diner-Restaurant Owners Association, 181
Natale, T., 46
National Law Journal, The, 261
National Origins Quota Act of 1924, 70
Natural History, 261
Neary, E., 158
Neighborhood Settlement House, 96
Neighborhood Association of Westbury, Long Island, 1916-17, 265

New Deal, 49
"New Deal, The, The Immigrants and Congressman Vito Marcantonio", 261
New Jersey, 19
  Morristown, 40-41
New Mutual Aid congregation, 91
New Orchard House, 116
New York, 10, 11, 13, 14, 17, 18, 22, 23, 29, 31, 35, 44, 62, 80, 81, 84, 104, 105, 118, 121, 128, 129, 143, 154, 176, 179, 180, 181, 185-188, 210, 214, 220-221
  Buffalo, 32, 42
  Bronx, 35
  Brooklyn, 14, 19, 22, 28, 31, 36, 43, 96, 122, 123, 126, 127, 129, 130, 132, 135, 161, 267
    Bushwick, 36
  Central Park, 21
  East Harlem, 35, 194
  Lake George, 266
  Queens, 12, 45, 250
    Long Island City, 135
New York City Board of Aldermen, 189
New York Daily News, 264
New York Herald Tribune, 24n., 66
New York State Census, 1915, 33
New York State Census, Brookhaven Township, 1915, 265
New York State Department of Transportation, 201
New York State Legislature, 69
New York State Manuscript Census, 84, 109, 111
New York State Manuscript Census, 1915, 87, 265
New York State Manuscript Census, 1925, 265
New York State Manuscript Census, Nassau County, 1915, 1925, 266
New York State Manuscript Census, Suffolk County, 1915, 1925, 266
New York State Supreme Court, 75
New York Times, 56, 183, 195, 264
New York University, 38, 175
Newsday Magazine, 39n., 57, 140, 183, 186, 191, 196, 205, 261, 264
Nigro, 156
Nigro, G., 94, 190, 192, 193, 195
North Shore Daily Journal, 264
North Shore Italian American Society, 49
North Shore Italian American Civic Association, 165, 166
Norton, Senator, 44
Nuzzolese, G., 181

Nuzzolo, F., 104, 105, 132, 244
Nuzzolo, F., Scrapbook, 266
Nuzzolo, Fudie, 104-105

O
O'Brien Sand and Gravel company, 48
O'Rourke, 130
O'Shea, J., 24n.
Oakdale, 119
Odd Fellows Club, 178
"Off Again On Again Finnegan", 96
"Old Marconiville Still Lives", 261
Oliveri family, 177
Omerta, 61
One Nation Divisible, 223, 263
Only Yesterday, 261
"Opera's Funny Man", 261
Operation Democracy, 170
Orchard House, 94, 100, 115, 117, 122, 161, 194, 204
Orchard, S.J., 192
Order of the Sons of Italy, 93-94, 109, 133, 152, 160, 164, 223
  John M. Marino Lodge, 147, 175, 179, 180,
  Lodge 1016, 169-170
  Prudenti Lodge, 212
Orlando, A., 160
Our Lady of Fatima Church, 138
Our Lady of Good Counsel Church, 92, 104, 130, 205
  Our Lady of Good Counsel Chapel, 130
  Our Lady of Good Counsel Church, Inwood, 206
  Our Lady of Good Counsel Parochial School, 206
Our Lady of Mount Carmel Church, 136, 205, 212
  Our Lady of Mount Carmel Church, Patchogue, 205-206
Our Lady of the Assumption Church 37, 123, 126-129, 137, 205, 206, 210
  Our Lady of the Assumption Church, Marconiville, 241
  Our Lady of the Assumption Society, 126
Our Lady of the Island, 137
Our Lady of the Snows, 135
"Our Westbury Heritage", 24n.
Oyster Bay Guardian, 12, 24n., 45, 57, 85, 86, 92, 264
Oyster Bay Town Board, 86

P

Pacelli, E., 122
Pacetta, T., 179
Padrone System, 9, 11-12, 13, 22, 41
Pagano, M., 132
Pagliaulo family, 127
Palermo, A., 119
Palmer, S., 64
Palminteri, A.R., 181
Pan American Airways, 167
Panama Canal, 144
Pancia, M., 178
Panciatichi, F., 155
Parascandola, H., 127, 136
Parente, A., 196
Parola Del Popolo, La, 260
"Particles of the Past: Sandmining on Long Island, 1870s-1980s", 266
Pascarella, 26
Pascucci family, 156, 196
  Pascucci, E., 196
  Pascucci, J., 117
  Pascucci, J., 197
  Pascucci, L., 159
  Pascucci, Mary, 189
  Pascucci, M., 123-124, 127
Pascuzzo, R., 51
Patchogue Advance, 18, 31, 32, 50, 51, 54, 64, 72, 73, 91, 94, 95, 97, 106, 118, 119, 120, 134, 135, 136, 140, 155, 161, 171, 174, 182, 183, 264
Patchogue Argus, 72, 94, 171, 174, 264
Patchogue Business and Residential Directory, 1904, 265
Patchogue Chamber of Commerce, 120, 265
Patchogue Home Guard, 106
Patchogue Italian Band, 95
Patchogue News, 64, 72
Patchogue School Board, 174
Patchogue Village Board, 185
Patchogue-Plymouth Lace Mill Band, 95
Patuso, M., 60
Pavone, L., 138
Pearl Harbor, 156, 157
Peasants No More, 2
Pecora, F., 193
Peerless Factory, 118
Peninsula Golf Club, 112-113
Pennsylvania, 22, 29, 144
Pentecostalism, 139
Percivalli, 155
Perotti, 168

Perspectives in Italian Immigration and Ethnicity, 260
Petito, P., 154
Petroccia, M.A., 190-191
Pfc. John J. Oliveri Veterans of Foreign Wars Post, 177-178
Phipps family, 6
Piety and Power, The Role of Italian Parishes in the New York Metropolitan Area, 263
Pio Nono X, 36, 77
Piscitelli family, 73, 74, 75, 219
  Piscitelli, A., 42
  Piscitelli, Aniello, 7, 41, 100
  Piscitelli, D., 25, 26, 73, 76-77, 152, 199, 219
  Piscitelli, N., 25, 152
Pitkin, 58, 61, 263
Pitrone, Fr., 138
Plimpton, G., 261
Plymouth-Patchogue Lace Mills, 54
Poland (Poles), 11, 22, 28, 42, 44, 46, 48, 122, 137, 206, 210
Polenberg, R., 223, 263
Police Boys' Club of Inwood, 178
Polizzi, F., 101
Polk's Glen Cove Directory, 1923-24, 265
Pollizzi, C., 119
Ponte, G., 178
Pontiero, M., 267
Pope, Generoso, 49, 180
Porcella family, 157
Port Washington Board of Education, 175
Port Washington Businessman's Association, 181
Port Washington Chamber of Commerce, 181
Port Washington Gildo Restaurant, 181
Port Washington High School, 175, 197
Port Washington Ice and Coal Service, 181
Port Washington News, 10, 11, 12, 27, 28, 46, 47, 67, 99, 100, 101, 109, 111, 138, 146, 147, 148, 152, 157, 162, 163, 164, 165, 166, 168, 175, 176, 179, 180, 209, 264
Port Washington Police Commission, 197
Port Washington Post, 24n., 167, 264
Port Washington Public Library, Reference Division, 266
Port Washington School Board, 146
Port Washington Times, 154, 155, 264
Port Washington High School, 175, 197
Port Washington National Federtion of Small Businessmen, 181
Posillico, A., 267
Posillico, C., 30-31, 39n.

Posillico, D., 21, 221
Posillico, F., 267
Posillico, Fred, 30, 39n.
Posillico, Joseph, 6, 21, 30, 39n., 267
Post, M., 29
Poverty and Progress: Social Mobility in a Nineteenth Century City, 263
Pratt family, 29
"Pratt Estate of Years Gone By Was a City Within a City", 260
Pratt Institute, 123
Pratt Kenilworth estate, 101
Prejudice, 65, 66-79
"Prelates and Peasants: Italian Immigrants and the Catholic Church", 261
Prime, W.A., 29
Privatera, S., 127
Privati, L.M., 117
Il Progresso Italo Americano, 34, 35, 49, 180, 232, 264
Prohibition, 149
Protestantism, 139-140, 186
Provenzano family, 130, 173
Provenzano, B., 14, 16
Provenzano, P., 173
Provenzano, V., 149
Prudent family, 32
Prudent, M., 95, 184, 185
Public School 4, 104
Puccini, G., 125
Puerto Rico (Puerto Ricans), 210
Pumilia, 149
Purcy, S., 262

Q
Quadagno, J., 260
Quaker, 24n.
Quakers, 6
Quality Fish Market, 181
Queens County Review, 6, 264
Queensborough Public Library, 235, 266
Quichy Lake, 266, 267

R
Razzano family, 100
Razzano, Anthony, 7, 100, 169, 267
Razzano, J., 267
Razzano, James, 6, 7
Razzano, Tet Zaino, 100
"Reappraisals in Modern Italian History", 266

Red Cross, 101, 103, 104
"Reflection on the Airplane in Italian Culture, 1910-1940", 266
Remigration, 12
Renaldo, M.L., 81, 267
Renaldo, Mary, 83, 143, 189
Renzullo, C., 267
Republican Party, 59, 97, 184, 185-187, 188, 189, 192, 193, 194, 195, 197, 198, 199, 220
"Residents Make Town Say Uncle", 78
Ressa, A.A., 175
Rhode Island, 40
Rizzo, D., 14
Roberto, P., 127
Robinson, J.J., 134
Rockaway News, 15, 17, 59, 60, 61, 62, 63, 92, 96, 103, 104, 112, 130, 132, 133, 146, 166, 167, 264
Rockville Centre Catholic Diocese, 202, 205
Roe, A., 31-32
Roe, J., 32
Rolle, A., 21, 217, 263
Roman Catholic Church, 72, 73, 121, 126-127, 139-140, 151, 208-209, 218
Romano, A., 182
Romeo Construction Company, 231
Romeo, A., 267
Romeo, Albert, 159, 267
Romeo, E., 267
Romeo, Eugene, 174
Romeo, F., 33, 34, 119
Romeo, M., 174
Romeo, R.M., 32, 51, 267
Roosevelt, F. 154, 156
Roosevelt, T., 86, 188
Rosa, R., 115
Rose, J., 178
Roselli, Mrs., 160
Roslyn News, 11, 264
Ross, J., 41
Royal Italian Flying Squadron, 167
Rubbles, C., 262
Rudolph, M., 267
Rudolph, M.M., 37
Russia (Russians), 44, 196
Russo, C., 119
Ruvo Del Monte, 194

S
"Sabelli, Italian American Aviation Pioneer", 260

Sabia, G., 127
Sacco family, 106
Sacco's Hall, 154
St. Anthony's Society, 207
St. Brigid's Church, 74, 137
St. Brigid's Hall, 115, 160
St. Brigid's Parochial School, 114
St. Brigid's Rosary Society, 182
Saint Brigid's, 1856-1956, 100th Anniversary, Westbury, 265
St. Cono Society Band, 104, 133
St. Dominic's Catholic church, 12, 92, 122, 123
St. Francis DeSales Church, 133, 134
St. Francis Hospital, 175
SS. Felicitas and Perpetua Church, 134-137
St. George Athletic Association, 112
St. Hyacinth Church, 122
St. Joseph Church, 135
St. Joseph's Hospital, 175
St. Joseph Mission Chapel, 133-134
St. Joseph's Mission Church, 134
St. Joseph the Worker Parish, 133, 206
St. Liberata, Feast of, 242
St. Louis, Missouri, 42
St. Marino Society, 92, 122
St. Martin's Catholic Church, 27, 126-127
St. Mary Star of the Sea Church, 130
St. Patrick's Church, 44, 67, 80, 92, 122
St. Patrick's Elementary School, 191
St. Paul's Episcopal Church, 140
St. Peter Alcantara Church, 157
St. Peter's Church, 138
St. Rocco Anniversary Booklet, 123
St. Rocco's Church, 120-125, 156, 161
St. Rocco's Day, 23
St. Rocco's, Feast of, 245
St. Rocco Mutual Aid Society of Glen cove, 204
St. Rocco's Parish, 209
Saint Rocco Parish, Souvenir Journal of St.Rocco's Parish, 1937, 265
St. Rocco Society, 92-93
St. Rosalie Parish, 135
St. Rose of Lima Parish, 128
St. Vincent De Paul Society, 125
Salerno family, 157
 Salerno, C., 46, 48
 Salerno, L., 267
Salmoni, L., 130
Salvation Army, 178
Salvatore, L., 158
"Sand Mining in Port Washington: Its Impact on the Community", 261

"Sand Pits of Port Washington, The", 266
Sandomenico, C., 106
Santopolo, M., 174
Saponare, F., 133-134, 136
Saporito, Fr., 138
"Sardinian Born and Bread", 261
Saturday Evening Post, 261
Savoia Marchetti Company, 167
Saxton, W., 268
Scandanavia (Scandinavians), 11, 46
Scarpaci, J., 42, 261
Scarpia family, 120
Schettino, Jr., J., 146
Schettino, J., 15
Schiano, J., 136
Scotland (Scots), 51
Scutari, F., 174
Sea Cliff News, 66, 67, 116, 264
Sea Cliff, 125
Seek America, A History of Ethnic Life in the United States, To, 263
Segale, C., 24n.
Segre, C.G., 263
Selesky, E.C., 268
Sellers, M., 263
Serrabella, A., 158
"Settlement House and the Italian Family, The", 260
Seyfriend, V.A., 263
Shanely, 130
Shenton, 46
Shenton, J., Speech "Sands of Port", 266
Shillito, E., 132
"Shot Down by Italian on Mott Avenue",60
Siano, B., 115
Sica, N., 102, 103
Sica, R., 268
Simonetti, P., 26
Simpson, G., 116
Sistine Chapel, 123
Slachta, I., 131
"Slashed with a Razor",60
Sledzaus, A., 136, 206, 268
Smit, E., 4, 167
Smith, J. R., 171
Smits, E.J., 21, 263
Snow, Chief, 46
Societa M.S. Dell'Assunta Registro Processi Verbali, 1940, 265
Societa di San Cono, 91
Solamita, P.A., 180
Somma, T., 41

Sommese, N., 26
South Shore Record, 265
South Side Observer, 58, 264
South Side Record, 21, 264
South Side Signal, 21
Southern Italian Folkways in Europe and America, 263
Sovereign Realty Company, 22, 23, 24n., 39n.
Sovereign Realty Company, 1906, 266
Spain (Spanish), 14
Spania, T., 178
Spearheads for Reform, 262
Spina, J., 14
Spina, P., 132
Spina, S., 14
Sprague, 186
Sprague, F., 59
"Stabbed During Quarrel", 60
Stanco family, 29
　Stanco, A., 28
　Stanco, Aniello, 102
　Stanco, J.A., 193, 194, 196
　Stanco, M., 124
Stango's Restaurant, 117
Stango, C., 117
Stango, F., 117
"Star Spangled Banner", 155
Starace, A., 20
Starace, C., 268
Starace, G., 20
State Department of Education, 172
State University of New York Research Foundation, 3
Statuo Della Durrazano Societa, Italo-Ameicano di Mutuo Soccorso, 265
Statuo E. Regalamente Dell Societa Maria SS. ma Dell'Assunta Di Westbury, Long Island, Incorporata il 27 Luglio 1920, 265
Steam Electrical and Mechanical Engineers, 49
Steinberg, S., 263
Steinberg, Stephen, 219
Stella Albanese Society, 16, 91
Stella, A., 84
Stephani family, 31, 32
　Stephani, C., 268
　Stephani, Catherine, 31, 51
　Stephani, G., 18
　Stephani, J., 268
　Stephani, James, 34
　Stephani, J.N., 21, 119, 184, 221
　Stephani, Joseph, 19, 171
　Stephani, R., 18
Stevens, S., 263
"Story of Glen Cove, The", 266
Story of the Italians in America, The, 263
Strada, E., 199
Strangers in the Land. Patterns of American Nativism, 1860-1925, 262
Street Corner Society, 263
Suburbanization, 3
Suffolk County Deeds, 24n.
Suffolk County Eagle, 265
Suffolk County Historical Society, 226
Suffolk County Legislature, 183, 185
Suffolk County Records, Date of Incorporation, 24n., 266
Suffolk County Republican Committee, 198
Sullivan, 119
Sullivan, Fr., 137
Sulzer, Governor, 62
Summa, J., 182
Suozzi, J., 191, 192, 194-195, 196
Suozzi, V., 195, 196, 205, 250, 268
"Sylvester Cangaro, Head Gardener", 261

T
Tabona family, 132
Tassinari, 23
Tassinari, S., 172
Tavermina, 43
Thernstrom, S., 222, 263
Third District Regular Democratic Club, 188
Thompson, B.F., 263
Tomasi, L.F., 260
Tomasi, S., 98, 260, 122, 263
Tomassone, R., 51, 136, 143, 183, 268
Tortora, Cyrus, 136
Tranquili, Tito, 34, 268
"La Traviata", 25
Tricarico, 217, 263
Trombetta, D., 154
Trotta, F., 182
Trotta, M., 151
Tufaro, F., 75
Tufaro, Fred, 26
Tufts Medical School, 175
Turkey, 100

U
Unification of Italy, 83
Unions, 44, 45, 47, 49, 54

Union of Operating Engineers, 49
Union of Steam Electrical Mechanical Engineers, 49
United Italian Society of Port Washington, 179
United Service Organization, 160
United States, 157, 244
United States Army, 159, 175, 183
United States Census, 130
United States Census 70, 265
United States Census, 1980, 212, 221
United States Census of 1900, 14, 15, 18, 20, 82
United States Census, Characteristics of Housing Units and Population by Block, 1970, 265
United States Census, Street Schedules, Nassau County, 266
United States Census, Street Schedules, Suffolk County, 266
United States Census Tracts, 12
United States Coast Guard, 156
United States Department of State, 196
United States Navy, 14, 183
United States Office of Education, 203
University of Bologna, 22
University of Georgia Law School, 191
Uprooted, The, 262

V
Vacca, A., 69, 127, 266, 268
Vanderbilt II, William K., 21
Varieties of Ethnic Enterprises, The, 262
Vatican, 122
Vecoli, R.J., 261
Vendetta, 262
Verdi, G., 36
Verrazano, 36
Vespucci, A., 36, 77
Veterans Memorial park, 103
Vezzani, A., 168
Vichiotti, C., Commissioner, 136, 155, 268
Vigotty Records, 266
Vigotty, A., 266, 268
Vigotty, J., 14, 268
Vigotty, M., 14
Vigliota, C., 136
Villa Nova House, 179
Village Welfare Society, 162
Villani, J., 99
Villano, Joseph, 119
Virginia, 40, 103
Hampton, 40
Norfolk, 40
Vivona, A.A., 172
Voice of America, 169
Volstead Act, 63

W
WOP, A Documentary History of Anti-Italian Discrimination in the United States, 263
War Bond Drives, 158
Weiss, R.J., 260
Weli, F., 26
West Point, 156
West Sayville Reformed Church, 72
West, M.G., 30
Westbury American Legion, 74
Westbury Horticulture Society, 30
Westbury Times, 7, 24n., 74, 75, 76, 115, 159, 168, 182, 265
Westbury's Neighborhood House, 115
Westpoint Academy, 156
Westville, 14
Whitney family, 6
Whitney, H.P., 6
Whyte, A.J., 263
Whyte, W.F., 263
Wickey, I., 113, 268
Willett, W., 16
Williams, G.L., 11, 261
Williams, P., 263
Wilson, W., 189
Winthrop family, 6
Wohl, R.A., 266
Women in Migration, 84
Women's Auxiliary of the Dell' Assunta Society, 152
Wood, Sherrif, 44
Woolworth family, 29
W.P.A. The Story of the Five Towns, 13, 14, 265
World War I, 26, 34, 38, 40, 58, 72, 82, 91, 98, 99-107, 115, 119, 134, 149, 156, 157, 162, 168, 175, 185, 188, 189, 219, 220, 243, 244
World War II, 1, 74, 138, 143, 149, 153, 156, 157, 158, 162, 168, 171, 172, 174, 177, 180-181, 183, 191, 207, 209, 219
World's Fair at Chicago, 167
Wysong, C., 24n., 263

Y
Yannacone, F., 73, 268

Yannacone, Sr., V., 174, 268
Yans-McLaughlin, V., 90
Yanuchi, J., 42
Yorio family, 157
Your Westbury, 24n.
Yugoslavia, 159

Z

Zaino family, 109
Zaino, 240
Zanuzzi, F., 174
Zavatt, J.C., 149, 178, 186, 268
Zavatt, V., 16, 58, 96, 105, 149, 186, 221, 239
Zinn, H., 264
Zolotow, M., 125, 261
Zucca, A., 104
Zuccala, G., 162-168

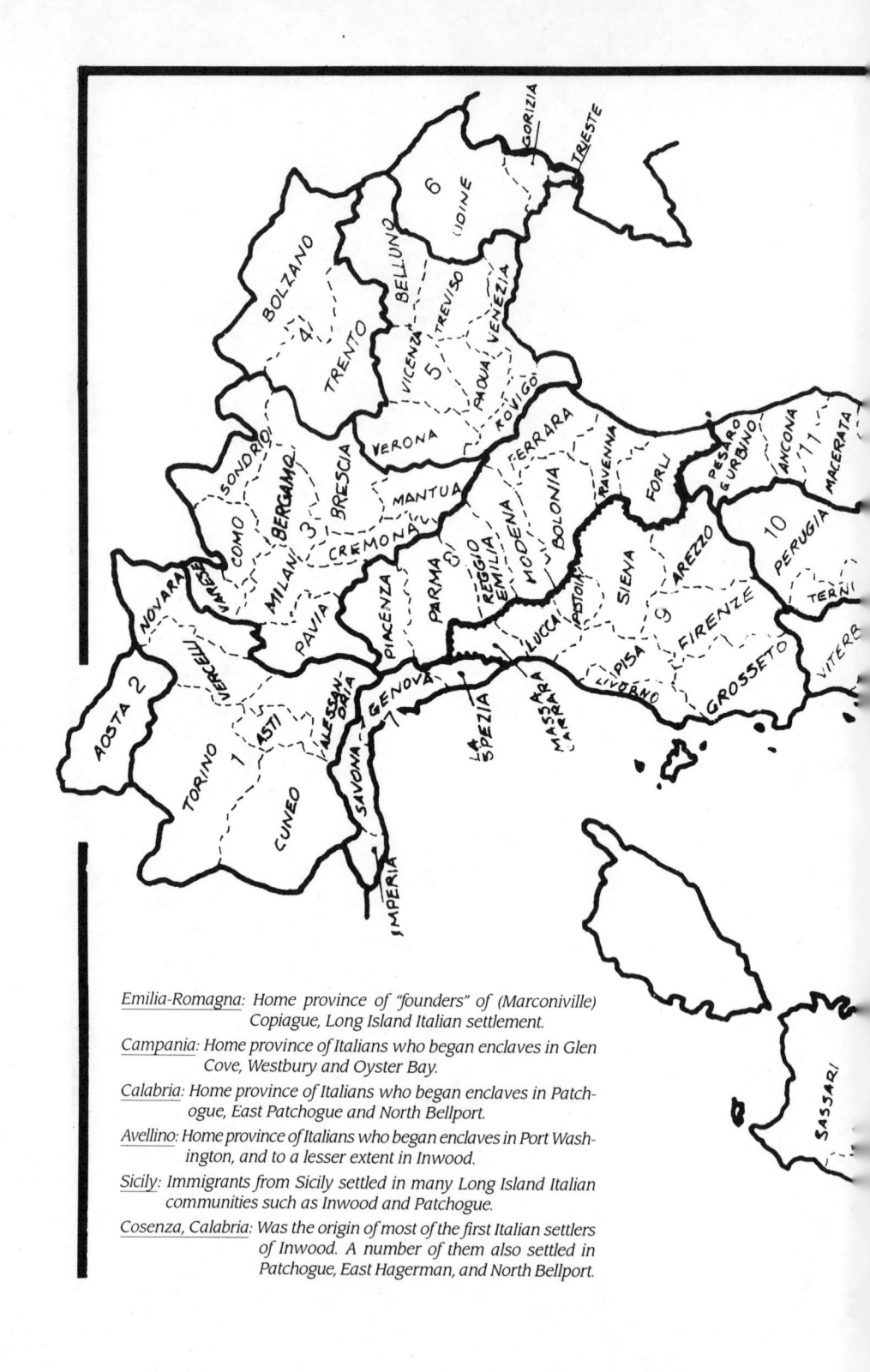

Emilia-Romagna: Home province of "founders" of (Marconiville) Copiague, Long Island Italian settlement.

Campania: Home province of Italians who began enclaves in Glen Cove, Westbury and Oyster Bay.

Calabria: Home province of Italians who began enclaves in Patchogue, East Patchogue and North Bellport.

Avellino: Home province of Italians who began enclaves in Port Washington, and to a lesser extent in Inwood.

Sicily: Immigrants from Sicily settled in many Long Island Italian communities such as Inwood and Patchogue.

Cosenza, Calabria: Was the origin of most of the first Italian settlers of Inwood. A number of them also settled in Patchogue, East Hagerman, and North Bellport.